743-8901

Title page of The Great Bible (1539) authorized by King Henry VIII, illustrating the close relationship between church and commonwealth.

THE GODLY KINGDOM OF TUDOR ENGLAND

Great Books of the English Reformation

by

John E. Booty, editor
David Siegenthaler
John N. Wall, Jr.

Morehouse-Barlow Company, Inc.
Wilton, Connecticut

Portions of Ch. 2 are printed by permission of the *Anglican Theological Review* and Scholars' Facsimiles and Reprints and of Ch. 3 by permission of the *Anglican Theological Review* and The Folger Shakespeare Library. Illustration from Erasmus' *Paraphrases* and *The First Book of Homilies* are reproduced by permission of The Houghton Library, Harvard University; those from the 1552 Prayer Book by permission of the Library of the Episcopal Divinity School; and that from *The Primer,* 1545, by courtesy of The Diocese Library and Archives, Diocese of Massachusetts. The illustration from *A Devout Treatyse* is reproduced by permission of The Folger Shakespeare Library.

Copyright © 1981 John E. Booty

All rights reserved. No part of this publication may be reproduced, stored in a retrieval system, or transmitted in any form or by any means, electronic, mechanical, photocopying, recording, or otherwise, without the prior permission of the copyright owner.

Morehouse-Barlow Co., Inc.
78 Danbury Road
Wilton, Connecticut 06897

ISBN 0-8192-1287-3

Library of Congress Card Catalog Number 81-80626

Printed in the United States of America

Dedicated with gratitude

to the memory of

Robert M. Gilday

CONTENTS

Preface   *ix*

I   Introduction: The Basic Theme   1
     John E. Booty, Episcopal Divinity School

II   Godly and Fruitful Lessons: The English   47
Bible, Erasmus' Paraphrases, and
the Book of Homilies
     John N. Wall, Jr., North Carolina State University in Raleigh

III   Communion and Commonweal: 139
The Book of Common Prayer
     John E. Booty

IV   Religious Education for Citizenship: 219
Primer and Catechism
     David Siegenthaler, Episcopal Divinity School

Afterword   251
     John E. Booty

List of Illustrations   264

Index   265

Preface

This book is a study of the English Reformation by means of an investigation of the "Great Books" it produced, books which come closer to embodying that reformation than any thing, individual, or group. The books owe much to Thomas Cranmer and yet none of them bears his name for they were all published as "official" books, books of a people, books peculiarly English and yet identified with the basic documents of Christianity, linking the sixteenth century to the first. The English Bible, the *Paraphrases* of the New Testament, the Homilies, the *Book of Common Prayer,* the *Primer,* and the Catechisms, are all undeniably important, easily accessible to the student, providing a vital means by which to look at the English Reformation and to assess its meaning and influence.

In making such claims for the "Great Books" this study also asserts the contemporary relevance of them. The English Reformation involved social, political, and economic reform. Late medieval reformist trends, Christian humanism with its strong moral impact on individuals and society, and Reformation faith issuing in such fruits of faith as changed people and institutions —all are present in the English Reformation. And all are present in the "Great Books." Too often the "Great Books" have been treated in such a manner that their social, political, and economic importance has been obscured or ignored. This book proposes to correct such error and to investigate the books both as reflecting the social, political, and economic concerns of the time and as instruments designed in part at least to deal practically with those concerns.

The *Annales* school of post-World War II France, and in particular the work of Lucien Febvre and Henri-Jean Martin, has demonstrated the importance of printing and of the advent of the printed book occurring at the very time when the Reformation was in process of formation.[1] Indeed, it can now be argued with assurance that printing was essential to the spread of the Reformation and that one thing which differentiates the Reformation of the sixteenth century in Europe from other similar periods of reform is the advent and widespread distribution of the printed book. To ignore this fact and the "Great Books" which are the subject of this study is clearly wrong: to emphasize the fact and the books is surely justified.

The authors of this book are well qualified to make their appointed contributions. John Wall wrote his doctoral dissertation on the *Book of Homilies* (1547) and has written an introduction to a facsimile edition of Erasmus' *Paraphrases* (1548).[2] In both instances his concern has been with the books in their social and literary contexts and especially with the impact of Christian humanism on the development of the Christian commonwealth. John Booty has edited the Elizabethan Prayer Book and is writing the commentary for Richard Hooker's great defense of the Prayer Book in Book V of the *Lawes of Ecclesiastical Polity* (1597).[3] He has for years ruminated on the themes which are considered in this book and explored the same in classes taught on the English Reformation. David Siegenthaler, a church historian, as is John Booty, is expert in medieval studies with a particular interest in spirituality. He has worked on Henry VIII's *Primer* (1545) and on related documents concerned with spiritual formation in the reigns of the early Tudors.[4]

The authors are diverse as to their scholarly interests, devoted as they are in varying degrees to the study of political history, church history, theology, liturgy, the medieval church and society, religious literature of the English Rensaissance, the Elizabethan Settlement of Religion, Puritanism, Richard Hooker, and much more. Their chapters differ in various ways. Most importantly, they differ in the ways they assess the relative importance of Christian humanism, Reformation theology, and the continuing influence of medieval thought and customs. Wall most strongly emphasizes the influence of humanism on the English Reformation. Booty emphasizes the influence of the Reformation as effected by Christian humanism. Siegenthaler is more dispassionately descriptive, as befits the church historian whose foundations are laid in the Middle Ages. These differences are noteworthy and must be kept in mind by the dispassionate—and passionate—reader. But the authors are all concerned with the serious study of "The Godly Kingdom of Tudor England" through an investigation of the "Great Books of the English Reformation" and their effects.

Finally, we are grateful to all who have supported us in our labors, our students, our colleagues, and those in administration over us. We dedicate this book to Bob Gilday who showed serious interest in our work at an early stage of our endeavour and nursed us along until his untimely death. He was a skilled editor and a good and sensitive friend.

> Anima ejus, et animæ omnium fidelium
> defunctorum per Dei misericordiam
> requiescant in pace. Amen

John E. Booty

NOTES

Preface

[1] Lucien Febvre, Henri-Jean Martin, *The Coming of the Book: The Impact of Printing, 1450-1800*, trans. by David Gerard, Foundations of History Library (London: NLB, 1976), esp. Ch.8.

[2] See Wall's "Vision of a Christian Commonwealth in the *Book of Homilies* of 1547" (Ph.D. thesis, Harvard University, 1973); his introduction to *The First Tome or Volume of the Paraphrase of Erasmus upon the Newe Testamente* (1548), A Facsimile Reproduction (New York: Scholar's Facsimiles and Reprints, 1975); and "The 'Book of Homilies' of 1547 and the Continuity of English Humanism in the Sixteenth Century," *Anglican Theological Review* 58(1976), pp. 75-87.

[3] See Booty's edition of *The Book of Common Prayer 1559: The Elizabethan Prayer Book* (Charlottesville, Va.: The University of Virginia Press, for the Folger Shakespeare Library, 1976); and "Church and Commonwealth in the Reign of Edward VI," *Anglican Theological Review*, Supplementary Series 7 (1976), pp. 67-79.

[4] Siegenthaler introduced *The Primer Set Furth by the Kinges Maiestie & His Clergie (1545)*, A Facsimile Reproduction (New York: Scholar's Facsimiles and Reprints, 1974); he did the select bibliography for the 1559 Prayer Book, cited above; and see his "Zodiac and Prayer Book," *The Journal of Theological Studies*, New Series 26(2) (1975), pp. 427-434.

Part One

INTRODUCTION

The Basic Theme

John E. Booty

—I—

INTRODUCTION
The Basic Theme

John E. Booty

The Importance of the Revolution in Printing

This book presents a view of the English Reformation that is not altogether customary. It emphasizes the importance of the revolution in printing during the fifteenth and sixteenth centuries and argues that certain great books, sometimes neglected by historians, sometimes merely mentioned in passing, were instrumental in the development of the reform movement in England.

To begin at the beginning, no serious student will deny the historical importance of the advent of mechanical printing (*ars artificialiter scribendi*) in the mid-fifteenth century. The process of making a page of print from separate pieces (*Stücke*), or moveable type, was perfected by Johann Gensfleisch, known as Gutenburg, of Mainz, somewhere around 1439, by Procopius Waldvogel of Prague in the 1440s, and by others. The invention was one of those amazing events, involving many people, sometimes working separately and sometimes in contact with one another, which seem destined to occur and to have immense influence on culture.[1]

The astounding growth of the printing trade from 1450 to 1500 is indicated by the realization that in that half century some 10,000 to 15,000 different books were printed in 30,000 to 35,000 different editions. Allowing no more than 500 copies per printing, we are led to believe that some 20 million individual volumes were printed at a time when the industry was still striving for maturity and the population of those countries where printing was done numbered somewhat fewer than 100 million persons, only a small percentage of whom could read the books produced. Furthermore, the largest percentage of books printed were religious. More than 100 Latin Bibles and numerous translations into German, Italian, and other languages were printed before 1500, indicating something of the demand for Scripture before the Reformation. Theological works, including the *Sententiae* of Peter Lombard and the treatises of Thomas Aquinas, Duns Scotus, and William of Ockham, were not as much in demand as were the more popular books of devotion. Such devotional books accounted for about one-sixth of the total production and included works such as *The Imitation of Christ*.[2]

Religious books continued to be printed in large number after 1500, but before 1517 they represented an increasingly smaller percentage of the total. The works of Desiderius Erasmus and Lefevre d'Étaples were in considerable demand, but religious books did not seem to attract as large a percentage of literate persons as they evidently did in the fifteenth century. Then came the Reformation. John Foxe devoted a section of his *Actes and Monumentes* (The Book of Martyrs) to "The Invention and Benefit of Printing." Of the fruit and profit of printing, the martyrologist wrote:

> hereby tongues are known, knowledge groweth, judgment increaseth, books are dispersed, the Scripture is seen, the doctors be read, stories be opened, times compared, truth discerned, falsehood detected... through the light of printing the world beginneth now to have eyes to see, and heads to judge... By this printing, as by the gift of tongues, and as by the singular organ of the Holy Ghost, the doctrine of the gospel soundeth to all nations and

countries under heaven; and what God revealeth to one man, is dispersed to many, and what is known in one nation, is opened to all.[3]

The influence of the typographical revolution as a causative factor involved in the beginning of the revolution called the Reformation has often been disputed. Most often "preaching the Word" is emphasized while the dissemination of the printed word is virtually ignored. Yet even granting the importance of the preached Word over the printed word in the Reformation, the great influence of printing and of books cannot be denied. At Strasbourg, for instance, the presses were active long before Luther, producing a Bible in German, humanist works of various kinds destined to prepare the way for the reformers, and other books stimulating learning and critical judgement. Elizabeth Eisenstein points out that at the time when the presses of Strasbourg were so active, with printing shops becoming "gathering places for erudite laymen" and "serving as focal points for opinion-forming groups":

> new concepts of German history and national character were shaped and publicized; the civic and religious duties of Christian laymen were reevaluated; programs for a new system of public education were set forth. The latter in particular was urgently promoted. For 'without education,' as Wimpfeling noted, 'the people could not read the Holy Scripture or the laws of the city.'[4]

It is also true, however, that with the advent of the Reformation, there was a marked increase in the publication of religious books, indicating an increased demand.

As Lucien Febvre writes, the decline of religious books in relation to other kinds of books "changed abruptly in 1517 in Germany, a little later and more gradually elsewhere. Religious issues swiftly became questions of the foremost importance and unleashed the strongest passions. For the first time in history there developed a propaganda campaign conducted through the medium of the press. The capacity of the press to serve the interests of those who wished to influence thought and mould public opinion was revealed."[5] The rapidity with which Martin Luther's ideas spread must be attributed at least in part to the printing press and the book trade. The Theses of 1517, translated into German and printed as flysheets, were found all over Germany within fifteen days. The pamphlets of 1520, including the manifesto *To the Christian Nobility of the German Nation*, which went through thirteen editions in two years, were printed and distributed throughout Europe within weeks of their initial publication. Shortly after Luther was excommunicated, and his books condemned to be burnt in 1520, there was a book burning at Cambridge, England, in front of the west door of Great St. Mary's, two shillings being granted "for drink and other expenses about the burning of the works of Martin Luther." This was followed by a similar ceremonial burning in London, at the preaching station outside of St. Paul's Cathedral, called Paul's Cross, with John Fisher, bishop of Rochester, preaching.[6] But it was all to little avail. Luther's tracts continued to be printed and circulated.

Authorities opposed to the "heresy" of Luther were quick to discern the power of the printed book as an instrument for effecting change. All over Europe magistrates sought to control the book trade and to use it for their own political and religious purposes. Vernacular Bibles, church orders and other books for the conduct of public worship, and catechisms and primers for the education of the people were soon pouring from the presses, influencing language and customs, politics and social policies, as well as religious beliefs and piety. In addition, in emphasizing word over image, the reformers were encouraging the development of reading skills among an ever growing segment of the people and thus placing increasing emphasis on printing and the book trade.

In England, in 1477, William Caxton published the first book printed according to the new methods there, *The Dictes or Sayengis of the Philosophres*, a folio volume of 156 pages. Dominated by skilled aliens, printing developed steadily in England. An Act of Parliament in 1534 sought to protect the rights of English printers and signaled the beginning of the government's efforts to control the trade. At the same time the government sought to prevent the spread of Lutheran ideas and in 1546 issued a proclamation which forbade "the reading of all works by Reformers such as Bale, Becon, Barnes, Coverdale, Frith, Joye, Tracy, Turner, and Tyndale." As H. S. Bennett goes on to say: "The coming to the throne of Edward VI did nothing to check the ardour of those wishing to control the activities of the printing press."[7] In 1538 a proclamation ordered that nothing could be printed until it had been approved by the Privy Council or its agents, and thus books began to appear inscribed: "*Cum privilegio regali ad imprimendum solum.*" Such a proclamation did not prevent the printing of books without license, but as time passed it became increasingly more difficult and dangerous to do so.

Recognizing the power of books as instruments for influencing the minds of citizens and the policies of the nation, the English government not only sought to control the printing presses but also strove to use printing to buttress its authority and extend its influence. Among the books brought forth by the government or published at the direction of governmental officials, clerical or lay, there were the books which are the subject of this study. The "Great Bible" is not simply another edition of the Holy Scriptures. Its very appearance in English, with the explicit approval of king and Parliament, signified an historical event of great importance to the populace at large. Furthermore, it was printed in order that it might be set up and read in every parish church, from London to the most obscure villages in the north and the west. The specific ways in which words were translated were often indicative of partisan convictions. Cranmer's Preface of 1540 was not without political and social importance. So it was with all of the books we shall consider. They were all instruments for theological and institutional reform *and* vehicles for the dissemination of the government's policies and intentions. This should not seem surprising when one realizes that there was no separation of church and state in sixteenth-century England comparable to that existing in the United States and elsewhere in the world at present. The chief officers of the church were also officers of the Crown. This is a subject often considered in the following pages. It is sufficient here to emphasize the fact that books were powerful agents for change in the sixteenth century and that the English Bible, the *Paraphrases* of Erasmus, the Homilies, the *Book of Common Prayer,* and the *Primer* and Catechisms were not only literary agents for change but official social documents contributing toward the formation of modern Britain.[8]

The English Reformation: the story of great books

The English Reformation was intricately involved with the writing and printing of books, especially the great books which were official publications of the Church of England. Before proceeding to a detailed examination of those books it may be helpful to review the Reformation in terms of its official books. The initial events associated with the Reformation Parliament from 1529 to 1536 involved the withdrawal of England's allegiance to the Church in Rome and the declaration of Henry VIII as Supreme Head of the Church of England.[1] In 1536 the lesser monasteries were dissolved and in 1539 the larger ones were seized by the government, the first step in a grand scheme intended to absorb the church's considerable wealth into the depleted royal treasury.[2] The twin pillars of the medieval church, the papacy and monasticism, were thus brought down that the English state might rise, its authority unchallenged by any foreign powers.

To achieve what was seen even then to be radical change, governmental propaganda to the contrary notwithstanding, the king came to rely on the support of English Protestants such as Thomas Cromwell, his vicegerent, and Thomas Cranmer, his Archbishop of Canterbury—persons who had reason to rejoice in the change. In return for their support, Henry made certain concessions, allowing publication of the Bible in English, countenancing Cranmer's liturgical experiments, and taking an interest in the publication of books intended to edify the people and thus direct them toward that truth which the Crown espoused. Such books included a revised Primer, the Bishop's Book, and the King's Book. In addition, Henry promoted the drafting of articles of religion, defining true and acceptable doctrine, especially when such seemed necessary while negotiating with the German princes of the Schmalkaldic League. In such ways King Henry fostered the Reformation in England, not as a reformer but as a conscientious head of state.

Henry did not particularly like Protestants and expressed his anger against those, such as John Lambert and John Frith, whose doctrine—especially Eucharistic doctrine—seemed to be blatantly heretical. The fact that he committed the education of his son and heir, Edward, to Protestant humanists such as Sir John Cheke and William Grindal was probably due to the influence of his last queen, Catherine Parr, and should not be construed to be an indication of secret Protestant convictions or of his political astuteness.

If the chief end of King Henry's reign was the establishment of royal supremacy, the major concern of those in power during the reign of Edward VI was for the achievement of religious uniformity. Under Henry, England was decreed to be an "empire" (24 Henry VIII, c. 12), that is, an independent autonomous nation state owing allegiance to no foreign powers. Under Edward VI this status was further defined by religious publications which, while preserving continuity with the universal church, were distinctly English and thus patriotic. The English Bible, whose use had been severely restricted since the 1540s, was once more openly acknowledged as authoritative and made available to all people. At the very outset of the Edwardian reign, the royal injunction of 1538 commanding use of the English Bible was revived and it was ordered that within three months "one book of the whole Bible of the largest volume in English" should be installed in every parish church in the land.

The Bible was provided with a companion volume intended to assist those in need with an interpretation of its essential meaning. This was a translation of Erasmus' *Paraphrases of the New Testament*, a publication in which Queen Catherine Parr played an important role. By royal command, the *Paraphrases* were to stand in the churches beside the English Bible. To provide a further means for understanding the Word of God in Scripture, and to help prevent heresy and schism, the first *Book of Homilies*, begun in Henry's reign, was published on Edward's accession to the throne. Thus in every parish church one could expect to find the English Bible and Erasmus' *Paraphrases*. Parishioners could also expect to hear the Word preached through the reading of the homilies.

The first homily, "A Fruitful Exhortation to the Reading and Knowledge of Holy Scripture," begins forcefully:

> Unto a Christian man there can be nothing either more necessary or profitable than the knowledge of holy Scripture; forasmuch as in it is contained God's true word, setting forth his glory and also man's duty. And there is no truth or doctrine necessary for our justification and everlasting salvation, but that is or may be drawn out of that fountain and well of truth.[3]

The Scriptures are the rock on which all else is to stand. The *Paraphrases* and the homilies affirm this, guarding as they seek to do the scriptural truth against error and promoting the unity of the nation based upon pure and undefiled Christian belief. All three—Bible, *Paraphrases*, and homilies—were published by authority and were thus official. Taken together they expressed an understanding of the Christian faith which is identified in subsequent essays as humanist, perhaps Protestant, at least Christian humanist, melding into one the theological understandings of Luther, Erasmus, and the reform-minded ecclesiastics, theologians, religious, and mystics of the late Middle Ages.

By 1549 the *Book of Common Prayer* was completed and was published, providing a liturgy for use in the church where Bible, *Paraphrases*, and homilies were already in use. This book of worship, of which Thomas Cranmer was the chief author and editor, was also official. It was authorized, and justified, by an Act of Uniformity which ordered its use in all churches and prescribed penalties for those not using it. The book provided ample evidence of its composer's concern to maintain continuity with the past. Vestments and ceremonies such as were retained were those familiar to worshippers in the late Middle Ages. The prayer of consecration in "The Supper of the Lord and the Holy Communion, Commonly Called the Mass," was an inspired revision of the venerable Roman *Canon Missæ*. In other respects the book was overtly humanist and Protestant. It was Protestant in its rejection of much so-called popish ceremony and in its strong emphasis on the Word of God, alongside the dominical sacraments of Baptism and the Lord's Supper. It was humanist in its use and development of the vernacular language of England, in its fidelity to ancient sources, in its encouragement of the use of right reason, and in its reliance on the distinction between things necessary to salvation and things indifferent. A decorous, stately book, the first *Book of Common Prayer* provided an aesthetically impressive and yet evangelical and reasonable common worship of God.

A new edition of the Prayer Book appeared in 1552, making more explicit the book's emphasis on the Word of God. At the same time, and partly as a consequence, the book intensified the view of the Lord's Supper as a Holy Communion. To some people since the sixteenth century it has appeared that the 1552 book represents a decline from the excellence of the 1549 book. Such a decline, it has been argued, was the result of Cranmer's yielding to the pressures of foreign reformers in residence in England and of the claims of resident prelates that the Prayer Book Eucharist could be interpreted in line with the doctrine of transubstantiation. But it is also possible to view the further reform of the liturgy as a stage toward a more biblical and people-oriented common worship, following the example of the early church. The second *Book of Common Prayer* was in many ways a fit companion to the English Bible, with the *Paraphrases* and the homilies. Thus the Bible was in daily use in the context of a scripturally ordered Prayer Book, with prescribed homilies regularly preached.

Furthermore, during the reign of King Edward VI the religious education of the church was carried forward in *Primer* and in catechisms. *The Primer set forth by the King's Majesty and his Clergy, to be taught, learned, and read: and none other to be used* throughout all his dominions (1545) was maintained as a basic educational instrument and to it were added catechisms such as that of Justus Jonas, which Cranmer translated, and most importantly the Prayer Book Catechism. This latter "catechism for children" which was to be learned by every child before confirmation by the bishop, was concentrated on the Apostles' Creed, the Ten Commandments, and the Lord's Prayer. These three concerned more than preparation for confirmation, however. They were to be prominently displayed in every parish church in the conviction that they provided the basis for the Christian life: true doctrine, a moral code, and the model prayer. Richard Hooker, writing at the end of the sixteenth century, put it this way:

> With religion it fareth as with other sciences. The first delivery of the elements thereof must...be framed according to the weak and slender capacity of young believers: unto which manner of teaching principles in Christianity, the Apostle in the sixth to the Hebrews is himself understood to allude. For this cause therefore, as the Decalogue of Moses declareth summarily those things which we ought to do; the prayer of our Lord whatsoever we should request or desire: so either by the Apostles, or at the leastwise out of their writings we have the substance of Christian belief compendiously drawn into few and short articles, to the end that the weakness of no man's wit might either hinder *altogether* the knowledge, or excuse the utter ignorance of needful things.[4]

Finally, in 1553 there were published by authority Forty-Two Articles of Religion. The product of Convocation, these articles were most definitely Protestant, or reformed, steering a narrow course between Roman Catholicism on the right and the radical reformers on the left. Articles on Justification, Works of Supererogation, the Sacraments and Purgatory were opposed to Roman teaching. Articles on the Holy Trinity, the Church, and the Civil Magistrates were opposed to much of the teaching on the left-wing of the Reformation, including that of the Socinians, the Family of Love, and the like. Such articles were intended to exclude dangerous persons rather than to define acceptable doctrine and yet for many they provided the rule of faith by which to

Introduction 13

measure orthodoxy in an age when truth was plain and absolute and error utterly destructive. Subscription to the articles was required of all the clergy of England.[5]

King Edward's reign was short-lived, lasting from 1547 to 1553 when the frail boy died. Religious uniformity such as Cranmer and others desired had no sooner been achieved and promulgated than it was all negated. Queen Mary, daughter of Henry VIII and his first queen, Catherine of Aragon, came to the throne a staunch defender of the "old religion." Papal allegiance was restored, an attempt was made to reinstitute monasticism, and the English Bible, with the *Paraphrases* and the homilies, and the *Book of Common Prayer,* with its catechism, were all swept away. The English Reformation, so it seemed, had flourished but for a brief time before it was brought to a sudden and inglorious end. It had not had a chance to win its way among its opponents or inspire the indifferent. Many of the reformers fled to the continent, there to wait, planning for a new day and another opportunity. Many, such as Thomas Cranmer, were seized, imprisoned, tried, and executed—burned at the stake, condemned as heretics and traitors. The queen, however, who came to the throne on a wave of popular acclaim, became progressively more and more unpopular. Her marriage to Philip of Spain, the consequent exercise of Spanish influence in England, the loss of England's last foothold on the continent at Calais, and the burning of numerous English commoners at Smithfield and elsewhere helped to turn the sentiments of the people against her. Furthermore, although at one time she thought herself to be pregnant, Mary failed to provide England with a male heir. By the Fall of 1558 she was dead.

Elizabeth I, daughter of Henry VIII and Anne Boleyn, came to the throne hailed as England's Deborah and was soon regarded as the embodiment of the nation, England's Eliza. During her long reign, lasting from 1558 to her death in 1603, the English Reformation was revived and a religious settlement agreed to which was to last and to be regarded as customary by succeeding generations. Elizabeth's first aim was to secure her place on the throne. This required recognition of the legality of her father's will and the illegality of her half-sister's legislation denying her right of succession. Next, she sought to assert her supremacy over the English Church. A bill to revive royal supremacy was thus introduced in Parliament in 1559. She seemingly intended to stop there, at least for the time being, putting off decisions concerning religious uniformity, including the publication of a new Prayer Book, until a later session of Parliament. Such a gradual course seemed reasonable at the time, but by the end of the Parliament the Elizabethan Supremacy Act (I Eliz. I, c.1) was accompanied by a full-scale Uniformity Act (I Eliz. I, c.2). The gradualist policy had been jettisoned. This was due to the recalcitrance of the Marian bishops, the zeal of the Marian exiles, and the end of the war with France. Her bishops meeting in convocation could not be counted on to support their queen. The Marian exiles, upon whom she was forced to rely for support in Parliament, were clamoring for a thorough-going revival of the Reformation in England, including a more reformed Prayer Book. With the war with France concluded and Philip of Spain seemingly complacent, the threats confronting her from abroad had dwindled to manageable proportions. As a consequence, in a very short space of time much that had been enacted during the reigns of Henry VIII and Edward VI, and nullified under Mary, was restored. The English Reformation was resurrected and given new life.

As a consequence, the English Bible was restored to the people. At first this was the Great Bible, that which had been authorized during the reign of Henry VIII. This was soon to be displaced by the Geneva Bible (1560) in popular usage. The work of Marian exiles, most likely William Whittingham, probably Miles Coverdale and John Knox, this translation was highly regarded by the Puritans, whose sentiments were expressed in the dedicatory epistle, addressed to the queen:

> The Lord of lords and King of kings who hath ever defended his, strengthen, comfort and preserve Your Majesty, that you may be able to build up the ruins of God's house to his glory, the discharge of your conscience, and to the comfort of all them that love the coming of Christ Jesus our Lord.[6]

Eliz.

Introduction

This was followed in 1568 by the so-called "Bishops' Bible," a work of considerable scholarship, reserved in its commentary and palid by comparison with the Geneva Bible. Nevertheless, the Bishops' Bible was official, a worthy predecessor to the more famous King James Version (1611).

Alongside the English Bible the *Paraphrases* of Erasmus and the first *Book of Homilies* were restored. A second *Book of Homilies* was added in 1563, the work of John Jewel, bishop of Salisbury and famed apologist of the English Church, assisted by others. This second book contains homilies on prayer, sacraments, rebellion, and difficult places in Scripture. The homily "Of the Place and Time of Prayer" strikes the keynote, beginning with a warning against hypocrisy, and with Matthew 22:12-13, on the punishment of the man without a wedding garment:

> To the intent ye may avoid the like danger at God's hand, come to the church on the holyday, and come in your holyday garment; that is to say, come with a cheerful and godly mind; come to seek God's glory, and to be thankful unto him; come to be at one with thy neighbour, and to enter in friendship and charity with him. Consider that all thy doings stink before the face of God, if thou be not in charity with thy neighbour. Come with an heart sifted and cleansed from worldly and carnal affections and desires. Shake off all vain thoughts which may hinder thee from God's true service. The bird, when she will flee, shaketh her wings: shake and prepare thyself to flee higher than all the birds of the air; that, after thy duty done in this earthly temple and church, thou mayest flee up, and be received into the glorious temple of God in heaven, through Christ our Lord.[7]

The 1552 *Book of Common Prayer* was restored as conservatively amended. The changes demonstrated, among other things, that while the queen appreciated the support of the nascent Puritans, she would not acquiesce to their demands for a more reformed order of worship. Knox's Genevan Service Book was not for her, nor was the more Prayer Book-like order of worship of the exiles at Frankfort. Indeed, as she challenged the loyalty of Puritans by keeping cross and candlesticks in her royal chapel and insisted on the retention of customary vestments, so in her Prayer Book she let it be known that if anything she favored the 1549 book over the 1552 book. And thus she approved a Prayer Book which seemingly ordered the use of "popish rags" and combined the sentences of administration at communion in the second book with those in the first, the latter appearing to some to reflect popish doctrine. In all of this, the queen was not so much recalcitrant as she was determined to preserve the aesthetic values and orderly usages of traditional worship. The *Liber Precum Publicarum*, a Latin version of the Prayer Book published in 1560 under letters patent from the queen, went even further towards the 1549 book. Unction for the sick, reservation of the holy Sacrament, and a requiem celebration of the Holy Communion were nowhere to be found in the 1559 book. This Latin book was intended for use by scholars in the universities and not for the general populace, but it was there to influence all those who were aware of its existence.

The educational program intended for the laity seemed to move in a more reformed direction. The *Primer* of Henry VIII and the Prayer Book Catechism were officially in use, but alongside the latter there appeared in 1570 a new, much more extensive and positively reformed catechism. The work of Alexander Nowell, Dean of St. Paul's Cathedral, London, this catechism emerged out of the 1563 Convocation and was thus to be considered official.[8]

Finally, out of the Convocation of 1563 there came the Thirty-Nine Articles of Religion. These were a more conservative version of the Forty-Two Articles of 1552. That they were more conservative is perhaps most clearly evident in the 28th Article, "Of the Lordes Supper" (the 29th of 1552), where the Thirty-Nine Articles have, "The body of Christ is given, taken, and eaten only after an heavenly and spiritual manner." This statement is not to be found in the Forty-Two. According to Bishop Guest of Rochester, the author of the later article, the word "only"

> did not exclude the presence of Christ's body from the sacrament, but only the grossness and sensibleness in the receiving thereof: for

Introduction

> I said [to Cheney, bishop of Gloucester, and a Lutheran in doctrine] though he took Christ's body in his hand, received it with his mouth, and that corporally, naturally, really, substantially, and carnally, as the doctors do write, yet he did not, for all that, see it, deal it, smell it, nor taste it.[9]

The Articles were endorsed by Parliament in 1571 through an Act which required clerical subscription to most but not all of them. Parliament in so acting did not please the queen who wanted no heresy trials. Indeed, while protecting Puritan consciences which were offended by certain articles, the government provided a means for hounding out dissidents in the church.

And thus it was that in a short time after the accession of Elizabeth I, those chief instruments for the reform of the church and the renewal of Christians which had first appeared during the reigns of Henry VIII and Edward VI were all recovered and all affected in various ways by the personality of the new monarch, as well as by other exigencies of the time.

Of particular interest, since what was then officially adopted was to have lasting effect, were the means for enforcement. Statutes of the realm, royal proclamations, letters patent, the efforts of officers of the crown, including bishops, were all important. But above all there looms the Royal Visitation of 1559. The Supremacy Act of 1534 had vested in the Crown "full power and authority from time to time to visit, repress, redress, reform, order...errors, heresies, abuses" in the church, and to do so by means of appointed commissioners. Thus, on top of the customary episcopal and archepiscopal visitations, there were to be royal visitations. There were two important ones under Henry VIII in 1536 and 1538, and one under Edward VI in 1547, but the most influential during the coming centuries was that of 1559. The commissioners appointed for different areas of the nation were to enforce the statutes concerning Royal Supremacy and Uniformity, including the use of the *Book of Common Prayer,* and to administer oaths as directed. Thus, for instance, the Cathedral Chapter at York took the following oath sometime between September 6 and 9 in 1559:

[handwritten margin note: Injunctions / Articles of Inquiry]

> We, the clergy of the Cathedral...do humbly confess and acknowledge the restoring again of the ancient jurisdiction over the state ecclesiastical and spiritual to the crown of the realm, and the abolishing of all foreign power repugnant to the same...We confess also and acknowledge the administration of the Sacraments, the use and order of divine service in the manner and form as it is set forth in the book commonly called the Book of Common Prayer, etc....and the orders and rules contained in the Injunctions given by the Queen's majesty, and exhibited unto us in the present visitation, to be according to the true word of God and agreeable to the doctrine of the primitive Church.[10]

The Injunctions to which the clergy at York Minster referred existed alongside Articles of inquiry used by the commissioners in their visitations. Questions were put to the clergy to be answered satisfactorily. Injunctions, based on the Articles, were distributed, to be read in public and to be obeyed. They were, indeed, treated as enforceable law. A permanent body of commissioners sat as a court after 1559, in time to be known as the Court of High Commission. There was then no further need for royal visitations such as that of 1559.

The English Bible (Inj. 6,16), *Paraphrases* (Inj. 6,16), and homilies (Inj. 27), were to be used as directed. The catechism was given special attention (Inj. 44), along with other directions concerning the education of youth (Inj. 39-42). Adults as well as children were affected by that which can easily be identified as the heart of the religious education enjoined by law: the Lord's Prayer, the Creed, and the Ten Commandments (Inj. 5). The tenor of these injunctions can be discerned where the manner in which holy days were to be kept was described:

> 20. *Item*, all the Queen's faithful and loving subjects shall from henceforth celebrate and keep their Holy-days according to God's holy will and pleasure; that is, in hearing the Word of God read and taught, in private and public prayers, in knowledging their offences to God, and amendment of the same, in reconciling themselves charitably to their neighbours, where displeasure hath been, in oftentimes receiving the Communion of the very Body and Blood of Christ, in visiting of the poor and sick, using all soberness and godly conversation. Yet notwithstanding...they

Introduction

may with a safe and quiet conscience, after their Common Prayer, in the time of harvest, labour upon the Holy and Festival days, and save that thing which God hath sent.[11]

Such an official view reflects the ideal towards which the reformers of church and nation aimed, as well as pointing to the context in which they would have the Bible read, preached and understood, the Prayer Book used, and the education of the young conducted.

By the beginning of the second decade of Queen Elizabeth's reign, the necessary instruments were all in existence and in use. It remained, as apologists of the Church of England did battle with papists and Puritans, for the meaning of it all to emerge and be accepted. But that is another story.

The Social Significance of the English Reformation

It is the contention of this study that the English Bible, *Paraphrases*, Homilies, the *Book of Common Prayer*, the *Primer* and the Catechisms, are at the heart of that which is named the English Reformation and that the English Reformation cannot adequately be understood without reference to them. Furthermore, it can be argued that these basic documents of the Reformation in England cannot adequately be understood without reference to the political and social setting in which they developed. To those who have some understanding of European history during the sixteenth century, such documents seem to be creatures of the time, as well as conservators of tradition. Thus it is that this study treats the "great books" of the English Reformation in relation to the political and social setting and not as documents simply and solely "religious" or "theological." Too often the English Bible and the *Book of Common Prayer*, the two books given the greatest amount of attention by students of the English Reformation, have been studied solely as literary or liturgical documents. The *Book of Common Prayer* is often treated simply as a liturgical text in sequence with the third-century *Apostolic Tradition* of Hippolytus, the Divine Liturgy of

St. John Chrysostom, and the Mass of the Roman Rite, with scant attention being given to the political and social setting of any of the texts. The early English Bibles are often treated in a similar fashion. Attention may be paid to the translators, men such as Tyndale, Coverdale, and Joye, and to those responsible for the authorized publication of the Bible, but the impact of the political and social ferment of the times on the text itself and the efforts of the translators and commentators to affect the course of English society are usually ignored, to the detriment of our understanding.[1]

The evidence for the social significance of the basic books is abundant, and it will occupy much of the remainder of this book, but a foretaste or sample is not out of order here. For instance, toward the end of the Injunctions of 1559 there is a bidding prayer, or prayer of intercession.[2] It was provided for use in public worship, a supplement to the *Book of Common Prayer*, and was intended for use after the Ministry of the Word where an "exhortation" is mentioned.[3]

The form of bidding the prayers to be used generally in this uniform sort.

Ye shall pray for Christ's Holy Catholic Church, that is, for the whole congregation of Christian people dispersed throughout the whole world, and specially for the Church of England and Ireland. And herein I require you most specially to pray for the Queen's most excellent majesty, our Sovereign Lady Elizabeth, Queen of England, France and Ireland, defender of the faith, and supreme governor of this realm, as well in causes ecclesiastical as temporal.

You shall also pray for the ministers of God's holy Word and Sacraments, as well archbishops and bishops, as other pastors and curates.

You shall also pray for the Queen's most honourable Council, and for all the nobility of this realm, that all and every of these in their calling, may serve truly and painfully to the glory of God and edifying of His people, remembering the account that they must make.

Also ye shall pray for the whole commons of this realm, that they may live in true faith and fear of God, in humble obedience and brotherly charity one to another.

Introduction 21

7. Finally, let us praise God for all those that are departed out of this life in the faith of Christ, and pray unto God that we may have grace so direct our lives after their good example, that after this life we with them may be made partakers of the glorious resurrection, in the life everlasting.[4]

Comparable to the prayer "for the whole state of Christ's Church militant here in earth," this bidding prayer is briefer and more openly related to the concerns of queen, Privy Council, and prelates.

1. The Church of England is here referred to as a national segment of the Universal Church. It is related to the whole while exercising a certain independence. The relation between Church and church was an issue involved in the Westminster Disputation of 1559. The second proposition to be debated said: "Every church [i.e. national or regional church] hath authority to appoint, take away, and change ceremonies and ecclesiastical rites, so the same be to edification."[5] The area of independence was limited but not unimportant. The English Church was the one, holy, catholic and apostolic Church in England, but it was the *ecclesia Anglicana*. The rising tide of national sentiment, as well as the effects of the continental Reformation, are in evidence here.

2. The temporal head of the state is the "supreme governor" of the church as well as of the state. Here the prayer for the queen calls to mind the concept of royal supremacy as enacted in Parliaments from 1534 to 1559 and interpreted in words and deeds by kings and councillors, prelates and theorists. The power and authority of the Crown over the church was very great. But here in these Injunctions of 1559 there is a further, important interpretation called "An admonition to simple men deceived by malicious," recognized as the legal exposition of supremacy in the next Parliament (5 Elizabeth I,c.1, sec. 14). The admonition denied that the queen, as some falsely accused, "may challenge authority and power of ministry of divine offices in the church," but asserted that she may challenge that authority "due to the imperial crown of this realm; that is, under God to have the

sovereignty and rule over all manner persons born within these her realms...so as no other foreign power shall or ought to have any superiority over them."[6] Thus it is made clear that the English Church, admittedly a segment of the Universal Church, is not, nor can she be, under any other like authority. The queen is the "supreme governor." The pope has no authority in England.

3. It is appropriate, next, to pray for those under her and especially for her officers in the church and in the state. The society was hierarchically arranged and so also the prayer. The queen is at the apex (under God) and the two estates of the church and the nobility are arranged side by side below her, with the commons, members of both the spirituality and the temporality, arranged on the lowest level of society. Privy councillors, dukes and earls, archbishops and curates, and the great commons of England were all joined in an hierarchical structure relating all to the Crown and to God from whom all flows, in heaven and in earth. This fact of the hierarchic arrangement of society is of great importance for an understanding of the books treated in this volume. It points to the orderly functioning of the universe beyond and reflects the Great Chain of Being and the Ladder of Perfection. The Christian's eyes were ever drawn skyward to where, in Shakespeare's words,

> The heavens themselves, the planets, and this centre
> Observe degree priority and place
> Insisture course proportion season form
> Office and custom, in all line of order....[7]

Such concepts as are mentioned here, culminating in "order," are found everywhere in the "great books" of the English Reformation.

4. The prayer "for the ministers of God's holy Word and Sacraments" is elucidated by the Ordinal and also by the prayer "for the whole state of Christ's Church." The emphasis given to Word alongside Sacraments is a reflection of the revolution caused

Introduction 23

by the Reformation. According to the medieval ordinal as used at Salisbury, the new priest was given a paten with the oblation on it and a cup with wine in it, following which the bishop said: "Accipe potestatem offerre sacrificium Deo, misamque celebrare tam pro vivis quam pro defunctis."[8] Now, as directed by the English Ordinal, the new priest received a Bible, instead of paten and chalice, after which the bishop said: "Take thou authority to preach the word of God, and to minister the holy sacraments in this congregation, where thou shalt be so appointed."[9] This was an innovation testifying to the high esteem in which the English reformers held the Scriptures, as well as indicating a very different understanding of the nature of priesthood, bringing to mind the teaching of Luther and Calvin, but also Thomas Cranmer for whom the Scripture possessed supreme authority "because," in G.W. Bromiley's words, "it is the revelation of God Himself in the concrete attestation of Jesus Christ."[10] The emphasis on Word, alongside sacraments, gave rise to many problems, not the least being the discerning of the proper spheres of temporal and ecclesiastical authority in relation to the authority of God's holy Word. Roman Catholics and Anglicans, Puritans and defenders of the Elizabethan Settlement of Religion disagreed on this issue and at times there was disagreement between the Crown and those servants of the crown whose consciences were informed by the Word causing them to defy the Crown. The ramifications were vast and can only be suggested here.

It was in the light of this Reformation revolution with its ramifications for politics and society, that the prayer "for the whole state of Christ's Church" should be read: "Give peace (O heavenly Father) to all bishops, pastors, and curates, that they may both by their life and doctrine set forth thy true and lively Word, and rightly and duly administer thy holy sacraments."[11]

5. The members of the Privy Council, together with the nobility of England, were next to receive attention in this bidding prayer. As is indicated, these persons serve the realm as called by God. They, along with the entire hierarchical structure, are God's creation and as such are intended to become anthems "to

the glory of God." God was glorified as officials of the realm labored not for their own profit but for the edification of the people of God, "remembering the account that they must make" before God at the final Judgment. The word "edify" is important here, meaning "to build up or strengthen" the people, especially in the cultivation of those moral habits which most benefit the happiness of the commonweal. And thus councillors, dukes, knights of the realm are ministers of God's edifying Word, called to be such ministers and held accountable to their calling.

6. It was natural, then, that the bidding prayer proceed to the commons, the people in general, with the prayer "that they may live in true faith and fear of God, in humble obedience, and brotherly charity one to another." The words were carefully chosen; the sequence was proper and necessary. The aim of all human existence is to "live in true faith and fear of God." God comes first, always. To define what such life under God involves is to define and describe the Christian life in detail. Here it must suffice to say that it involves mind and heart, correct belief and the right inner attitude. This inner attitude is that of awe, worship, holy fear, the obeisance of the Christian before God in order that God, through the Spirit, may rule the Christian's daily life. There follows "obedience" to the godly magistrates, with 1 Peter 2 and Romans 13 in mind: a vexed and vexing subject in the sixteenth century as it is now. Many at the time wrestled with what might happen should the ruler become a tyrant and violate God's laws and the laws of the realm. Solutions ranged from complete passive obedience to out-and-out rebellion. Yet all believed sincerely that rulers were called by God and should be obeyed—according to the Scripture and natural law. Finally, there is "brotherly charity one to another." The divine command to love God and neighbor, the neighbor in God and God in the neighbor, was impressed on all, but so too were the not unrelated societal ideals concerning love (charity), communion, and commonweal. The ideals might seem too idealistic, and unrealistic, but there is no denying their presence and their

power, as we shall have cause to observe subsequently.

7. At the end there is a remembering of the dead and prayer that the people may follow their good examples, "that after this life we with them may be made partakers of the glorious resurrection, in the life everlasting." There is no comparable section in the "prayer for the whole estate of Christ's Church." Indeed, many of those deeply committed to the Reformation argued strongly against such prayer, saying that it was founded on the popish doctrine of purgatory. But here the people are not asked to pray for the souls of the dead in purgatory; they are asked to remember the dead and to emulate them, fixing their attention on the lives they lived this side of the grave. More importantly, perhaps, is the simple reference to the dead, to their participation in the resurrection and their inheriting of life everlasting. Fifteenth- and sixteenth-century Christians were preoccupied with death. Death struck terror in their hearts. The *danse macabre* was prominent in art and literature with countless depictions of death, a skeleton, dragging off some protesting prince or pope, vain maiden or greedy merchant. Little carvings of vanity, a voluptuous and richly dressed dame, could be turned around to reveal a skeleton, naked bones, the fate which awaited her and every human being. Bones, rotting flesh, decaying bodies were reminders of human mortality and approaching judgment. The constant reminders of death, not only in art and literature, but in the streets of London and at the fires of Smithfield, and in the prayers of the people who remember the dead and seek to emulate the saints, helped cultivate and maintain the proper Christian attitude and life, building up lives in preparation for the great judgment. By the end of the century death would not so much strike terror in the human heart as arouse the believer, whether casual or sincere, to more passionate living, but in the time when the great books of the English Reformation were being produced, death was the terrible grim reaper. Hope resided in the cultivation of lives, exemplary lives, acceptable to God.

A close examination of this bidding prayer in relation to the times in which it was written indicates the degree to which it was formed by those times. In addition, such a close examination can help the student of the English Reformation achieve a more thorough and complete understanding of reform in England during the sixteenth century, reform affecting the society at large as well as the church. One fact which this volume takes seriously is that the instruments of the English Reformation, from the English Bible to the Primers and Catechisms, were viewed as means for maintaining the obedience of the citizenry. They were instruments of governmental policy as well as instruments of reform. This must be viewed in terms of the general understanding of church and commonwealth as both serving the commonweal. Beyond crass "erastianism" there were social and theological rationalizations.

Richard Hooker, the author of the great work, *Of the Lawes of Ecclesiastical Polity*, set forth the classic statement concerning the interdependence of church and commonwealth in sixteenth-century England. In 1597 the Fifth Book of the *Lawes*, a detailed defense of the *Book of Common Prayer*, was published. It began by arguing that true religion is the mother of all virtues and the "chief stay" of "all well-ordered commonweals" (V.i.5).[12] The enemies of true religion, and thus of virtue and of commonweals, are atheism and superstition. The latter is at the heart of the issue between Hooker and the Puritans against whom he wrote (V.iv.3), the impatient Englishmen regarding the Church of England and the *Book of Common Prayer* as imperfect, still riddled with superstition and thus not obedient to the Word of God.[13] The task which Hooker faced he described in the preface to the entire work as being the examination of "the causes by you [Puritans] alleged, wherefore the public duties of religion, as our prayers, our Sacraments, and the rest, should not be ordered in such sort as with us they are" (Pref.vii.6). That is, Hooker was concerned to show that the laws governing the "public duties" toward God in England were such that true religion was recognized and enforced by just laws for the sake of church and commonwealth in the one society.

Hooker's understanding of the commonwealth in the first chapter of the Fifth Book is linked to discussion in the First and Eighth Books. In the First, following Aristotle, he describes the genesis of government from the family to the nation in terms of human necessities, the need for protection against the wickedness and malice of humans and for the pursuit of the happy life (I.x.2,3).[14] With Augustine, however, he believed that government is a result of the Fall, that human nature is "disabled," and that people stand in need of supernatural law which teaches not only supernatural duties but also "such natural duties as could not by the light of Nature easily have been known" (I.xii.3). Thus true religion is necessary to fulfill the ends of the commonwealth.[15]

In the Eighth Book of the *Lawes*, published posthumously, there is recognition that the end of all societies is "living well," which involves putting spiritual things ahead of temporal, the most important of all spiritual things being religion (VIII.i.4). This applies to all societies, but in that society where true religion is revealed those who receive it are the church, and where all persons are at one and the same time members of the commonwealth and the church, while there remains a difference between the two, they constitute one society; they are not two distinct corporations as the Puritans taught (VIII.i.2).

Thus, in an argument which depends in part on Aristotle, in part on St. Augustine of Hippo, and in part on Tudor political theory as it developed from the early decades of the sixteenth century, Hooker revealed the necessary coinherence of religion and society, church and commonwealth. The *Book of Common Prayer* was viewed by Hooker as a legal means whereby the commonwealth may achieve its intended purpose: the happy life, the life well lived, the life which is virtuous and culminates in everlasting life.

From this vantage point, the so-called "erastianism" of the time can be viewed not as the state's capture and dominance of the church, but rather as the realization of a necessary coinherence, whereby the church is viewed as the "conscience" of the nation. While there is abundant evidence that the state used the church to serve its own a-Christian ends, there is also evidence that the church exercised considerable influence on the state. At its worst, this influence operated to provide sanctions for avarice and greed. At its best, it was exercised in prophetic ways, against the selfish and harmful lusts of people, nobility and yeomanry alike. It was also a means of nurturing the citizenry in the development of those virtues which served the best interests of the state.

Such Tudor theory was informed by many things and certainly by Christian humanism. Grocyn, Linacre, and Colet were prominent English humanists and Christians whose scholarly achievements influenced many persons on their way to power in church and state. Sir Thomas More was a Christian humanist who rose to prominence as Chancellor of the Realm. And King Henry himself, especially in his musical compositions, could lay claim to humanist accomplishments. But above all there was Desiderius Erasmus, the friend of Colet and More, who made two excursions into England and provided the platform for Christian humanism. His "philosophy of Christ" expressed that doctrine in Christian humanism which pervaded those circles in which political theory and ecclesiastical doctrine evolved. He expounded this philosophy in his Greek New Testament when commenting on Matthew 11:30.

> Truly the yoke of Christ would be sweet and his burden light, if petty human institutions added nothing to what he himself imposed. He commanded us nothing save love for one another, and there is nothing so bitter that charity does not soften and sweeten it. Everything according to nature is easily borne, and nothing accords better with the nature of man than the philosophy of Christ, of which almost the sole end is to give back to fallen nature its innocence and integrity... How pure, how simple is the faith that Christ delivered to us! How close to it is the creed transmitted to us by the apostles, or apostolic men. The church, divided and tormented by discussions and by heresy, added to it many things, of which some can be omitted without prejudice to the faith....
> There are many opinions from which impiety may be begotten, as for example, all those philosophic doctrines on the reason of the nature and the distinction of the persons of the godhead... The

sacraments themselves were instituted for the salvation of men, but we abuse them for lucre, for vain glory or for the oppression of the humble....[16]

There is no question that Erasmus intended this philosophy of purity, simplicity, and love to undergird and direct the activities of princes as well as citizens, for so he wrote in his *Enchiridion* (Handbook of the Christian Knight).

Erasmus' emphasis on love is also at the heart of Martin Bucer's *De Regno Christi* (Of the Kingdom of Christ), the Strasbourg reformer's treatise written in 1550 for King Edward VI. After citing the great passage from Isaiah 11:6-9, referring to the eschatological vision wherein "The wolf shall dwell with the lamb, and the leopard shall lie down with the kid," Bucer wrote:

> These words teach us three things: first, that we are in desperate condition when we are born into this world, uncultured and uncivilized, so that we deserve to be compared with lions, bears, leopards, wolves, and the most harmful serpents; secondly, if we are reborn in Christ and have become true citizens of his Kingdom, we ought to burn with such charity and eagerness to deserve well of others that no one would tolerate the discomfiture of anyone else but every individual would try, each according to all his capacity, to contribute as much as possible to the salvation and well-being of his neighbor; finally, that this humanity and love of the citizens of the Kingdom of Christ spring from faith and only from the knowledge of God (Gal. 5:5-6). For faith shows its power through love, which always manages to benefit men, and to be injurious to no one (I Cor. 13:5).[17]

The Kingdom of Christ was a *communio* for Bucer, a communion of those directed by Word and Spirit, through whom the Kingdom of Christ is realized on earth. As T. F. Torrance wrote: "The Word of God is communicated to the State through the Church, and in obedience to that Word the State creates within the world a sphere of liberty, setting bounds to the kingdom of Satan, so that the life of the Church protected by the State may freely grow in obedience to God's Word and in the exercise of love, and so assume the character of a *Respublica* or *Societas Christiana*."[18]

Such love as Erasmus and Bucer refer to involves communion with Christ and with one another in community. Here one may be reminded of the ideal of the organic unity of society professed in the Middle Ages and of the realities of community in the medieval village and monastery. Of the village, or *vill*, with its manor and its manor church, J. B. Russell has said that it largely consisted of peasants who "had come together for mutual advantage, communal living and cooperation being natural in the fertile and temperate countries of western Europe."[19] Here the Christian commandment of love of God and of neighbor sustained that community which circumstances dictated as necessary for survival. Of the religious life in community, Aelred, twelfth century Abbot of the Cistercian monastery of Rievaulx, commented: "One is able to offer more toil, another more vigil or more fasting, more prayer or more *lectio*...as (in the account of Exodus) all contributed to the construction of a single tabernacle ...so, in our case, all is to be done for the good of the community ...No one is to behave as though the gift he has received from God were merely for his own use...No, he must regard it as belonging to all his brethren. On the other hand, he cannot envy his brother if he is convinced that he benefits through whatever gift his brother has."[20]

John of Salisbury, bishop of Chartres in the twelfth century, expounded the ideal of the commonwealth in his *Policraticus*, blending Christian and Platonic elements. As C. E. Osborne comments, John believed that there was a

> foreordained harmony between the life of the commonwealth of man and that of the individual alike in his spiritual and in his physical structure. The macrocosm of society is only man's individual nature enlarged. In the latter—the microcosm—is seen the prophecy of his social life. At the basis and root of human society as its generative principles, its *Lebenskraft*, lie Justice and Reason, for man shares in the immanent Reason of which God is the spring, and without which human life would be an incoherent chaos. The social principle is not an afterthought. It has a divine root, it is an instinct not an acquisition.
>
> This common sharing of individuals in the immanence of the universal Reason leads to that idea which rules all the mediaeval

conceptions of society, i.e. that of the universal unity of the human race, a unity which transcends all social divisions, however real in their own measure and degrees. The lesser unity of the individual is regarded by John as in its organic character the representation of the various functions of man regarded as a social being. This is the anthropomorphic or biological analogy which goes back to S. Paul and even earlier, and which recurs continually in mediaeval thought.[21]

The influence of what might be called the organic theory of the commonwealth is apparent in the records of sixteenth-century England, sometimes as modified by Erasmian Christian humanism, sometimes as influenced by Bucerian or other Rhineland Protestantism, sometimes via the doctrine inherent in the laws and traditions of the nation. This latter is seen most dramatically in the Coronation Rite as found in the *Liber Regalis*. Interpreting the collect *Omnipotens sempiterne Deus creator*, as found in the coronation of Elizabeth I, E. O. Smith, Jr., puts it thus: "Through the blessings of God, the monarch would nourish the Church and people, administer the divine rule of virtue, and shape her people in the harmony of peace and faith."[22] Neither Christian humanist *per se*, nor Protestant, this statement could be endorsed by both Erasmus and Bucer, for both were inheritors of medieval tradition, even though critical of it.

The great books of the English Reformation were influenced by all that has been mentioned: by the medieval traditions which were inherited, by Christian humanism, and by Reformation doctrine and practice. Indeed, it has been suggested that the uniqueness of the Reformation in England consists in the persistence of these influences in a creative tension, represented by emphasis upon continuity with medieval tradition, reliance upon the humanist concept of right reason, and dedication to the Reformation doctrine of scriptural authority. Here, however, we are concerned to stress a common theme, that to which the bidding prayer attached to the Injunctions of 1559 refers in different ways in different places and with reference to the commons, for whom prayer is asked, that "they may live in true faith and fear of god, in humble obedience and brotherly charity one to another." In this there is reflected the divinely inspired social instinct of the Middle Ages, which produces community, the Erasmian recovery of our original innocence represented in Christ who commands us simply to love one another, and the Bucerian *communio*, the Kingdom of Christ, wherein Christians "burn with such charity and eagerness to deserve well of others that no one would tolerate the discomfiture of anyone else, but every individual would try, each according to all his capacity, to contribute as much as possible to the salvation and well-being of his neighbor."

Church and Society in the Reign of Edward VI

Given the evidence, such as that which we have reviewed, it is not at all surprising to find that the English reformers were vitally concerned for society and the socio-economic crisis as it developed in the first half of the sixteenth century. They were, after all, acting under direction of monarchs whose responsibilities encompassed the spiritual as well as the temporal realms. The monarch was importantly concerned for the nurture of godly virtues in the citizenry and for the maintenance of order, "the harmony of peace and faith," without which any commonwealth must perish. In addition, bishops were accustomed to serving the king in various ways: Chancellor of the Realm, Keeper of the Great Seal, Privy Councillors, intimates of the royal court, ambassadors, and members of the upper house of Parliament. Furthermore, many of the most prominent prelates were Protestant humanists by the end of Henry's reign. Their convictions dictated their concerns, the philosophy of Christ and the ethic of the Kingdom of God both requiring love toward God and communion with one's neighbors. A vivid example of such concern, issuing in direct involvement in societal affairs, is seen in events during the reign of Edward VI.

Some time after the appearance of the first *Book of Common Prayer*, perhaps in 1551, John Scory, bishop of Rochester, wrote King Edward reminding him of certain points made in sermons he preached at court during the past Lent. He informs us that in those sermons he charged the king, and therefore the king's agents as well, to "banish greedy avarice: the which hath by inclosures and converting tillage into sheep-pastures, contrary to the wholesome laws of this your noble realm, decayed your villages, townes, and cities, brought in an intolerable scarcity and dearth of all things that your faithful subjects should live by, diminished the number of people in the country, and therby feebled and weakened your might, power, and strength...." He argued that if the situation were not dealt with speedily and effectively the realm would be brought "unto utter ruin and desolation."[1] Scory, whose witness was representative, summing up in brief space far more detailed and lengthy indictments, proceeded eloquently:

> Oh! what a lamentable thing is it to consider, that there are not at this day ten plows, whereas were wont to be forty or fifty. Whereas your Majesty's progenitors had an hundred men to serve them with reverend obedience in the time of peace and in time of wars, with their strength, policy, goods, and bodies, your Majesty have now scant half so many. And yet a great number of them are so pined and famished by the reason of the great scarcity and dearth of all kind of victuals, that the great sheep-masters have brought into this noble realm, that they are become more like the slavery and peasantry of France, than the ancient and godly yeomanry of England.

The bishop's opinion is clear. Avaricious persons, lusting for wealth and power, have enclosed lands formerly producing food in order to raise sheep for wool. The result has been that unemployment has risen, people are starving for want of victuals, and with the dislocation and deprivation revolt is in the air, rebellion is threatening the peace and security of the land. Scory concludes with a pious and pointed observation:

> Oh! what a lamentable thing is it to behold that ground, which at this time of the year, through men's diligent labour and God's blessing, was wont to be richly adorned with corn, to be now, through God's curse, that is fallen upon us for our idleness and greedy avarice, replenished with mayweed thistles, docks, and such like unprofitable weeds. The ground, without controversy,

would be as fruitful as it hath been in times past, if it were, according to God's ordinance, and the wholesome laws of this realm, laboriously dressed and tilled, as it was wont to be. But to trust to have as much upon one acre as was wont to grow upon three, (for I think that the tillage is not now above that rate, if it be so much,) is but a vain expectation, and a wicked tempting of God....[2]

Natural disasters in Tudor England were customarily explained in terms of divine providence. A child born with a ruff, a church steeple struck down by lightning, and fields once abundant with grain now overwhelmed by useless weeds were all attributed to God's wrath against human sin. In this case, the sin was that of idleness and avarice, and avarice was believed to be at the root of the enclosures.

The enclosures which were the target of the reformers were various. There had been the enclosure of waste land and forests for the purpose of cultivation, enclosure of open field strips into hedged fields for better management, and the enclosure of village commons, denying the use of them to those who had long possessed the right to use them. But that which Scory chiefly had in mind was the enclosure of arable lands for pasture, which was seen to be the source of the greatest social evil. Enclosures had been debated for some time and it would seem that by means of laws passed in 1489, 1515, 1533-34, and 1535-36, together with the enforcement of these laws by commissions and the recession afflicting the cloth trade, the rate of enclosure had dropped severely from 1520 on and was not the chief issue by 1549.[3] Modern historians emphasize now the debasement of coinage, prices rising in an inflationary spiral, the collapse of the cloth trade, and the growing number of unemployed poor exacerbating the unstable social situation and helping to foment the rebellions of 1549.

It must be recognized, however, that for contemporary reformers the enclosures, which had not ended altogether, were weighty symbols involving much more than the enclosures.[4] The term seemed to encompass a variety of evils, including rack-renting, extortionate entry fines, engrossing, and indeed all that

Introduction 35

proceeded from avaricious and greedy opportunists of whatever class. It is true that in the process the reformers, clerical and lay alike, seemed to have little sense of the necessity of change and less appreciation of new agricultural policies and procedures. By and large they seemed intent on returning to an earlier social stability, partially factual, partially romanticized and idealized. Yet their limited knowledge need not have deterred them from attacking a practice which afflicted undeniably severe hardships on a most vulnerable segment of Tudor society.[5]

The governmental attack upon the conditions encompassed by the term "enclosure," and specifically upon the enclosers, was led by the Protector Somerset, an idealistic Protestant humanist. He was advised by such laymen as John Hales and Sir Thomas Smith and by such clerics as Hugh Latimer and Thomas Lever. Much influenced by policies developed and laws enacted under the leadership of Thomas Cromwell, with the advice of Thomas Starkey and Thomas Lupset, during Henry's reign, Somerset and those who supported him, generally called "Commonwealth Men," sought to protect the poor against the avarice of the wealthy and while so doing to restore the social and economic health of the nation. In June of 1548 a proclamation was issued which resulted in the institution of an inquiry by means of juries which then investigated social and economic problems and in particular the ways in which laws had been broken. Parliament was busy with bills concerning the care of poor men's children, ensuring farmers and lessees of the enjoyment of their leases without fear of arbitrary eviction, and preventing the decay of houses, of husbandry, and of tillage. These government actions were much opposed by those against whom they were aimed and contributed to Somerset's downfall after the rebellions of 1549.

Those guiding this governmental policy were what might be called Protestant humanists. Humanists by education, they subscribed to Erasmus' philosophy of Christ. Moral in tone, Christian humanism, as we have observed, sought to inculcate active charity and regarded the New Testament as a book of precepts for the achievement of the pure and sincere life. They were also Protestants, regarding the See of Rome as an enemy. Their humanism modified their Protestant convictions, however, inclining them more toward Melanchthon than toward Luther, more toward Bucer and the Rhineland reformers than toward Calvin and Geneva. They expressed themselves in ways which indicate that they did not altogether reject the recent past. Indeed, they were to a certain degree conservatives, seeking to restore an ideal past wherein—they believed—society was unified organically and people bound together in communities of mutual care to the great benefit of the commonwealth. It may have been John Hales, but it was perhaps Sir Thomas Smith, who wrote the *Discourse of the Common Weal* and, recalling the wisdom of Plato and Cicero, said:

> We be not born only to ourselves but partly to the use of our country, of our parents, of our kinfolk, and partly of our friends and neighbors. And therefore all good virtues are grafted in us naturally, whose effects be to do good to others, wherein shows forth the image of God in man whose property is ever to do good to others, to distribute his goodness abroad, like no niggard nor envious thing.[6]

This statement is thoroughly humanist and expresses a basic sentiment shared by all Commonwealth Men. But the reformers whose work was directed toward the defeat of the evil endangering the commonwealth were also thoroughly Protestant and this not only in opposition to the Roman See.

Hugh Latimer was the preacher of the Commonwealth Men. Converted by Thomas Bilney to the teachings of Martin Luther, Latimer had long been associated with the Protestant cause. But he followed the teachings of the Rhineland reformers and of the Christian humanists when he searched Christ's words in the Gospels, not regarding them as containing the promises of a God of mercy extended toward the sinful so much as the precepts and rules of Christ to be followed for the sake of righteousness. On the basis of his study of the Scripture and his inner convictions, Latimer set about to preach up and down the land. Preaching for him was a vital means toward specific ends. It brought forth faith, faith led to the cultivation of both individual and corporate

Introduction

righteousness, and righteousness resulted in the edification, or strengthening, of the Chrisian commonwealth.

As the most powerful preacher of his time, Latimer confronted Edward VI and his court, telling them that the commons of England

> are equal with you. Peers of the realm must needs be. The poorest ploughman is in Christ equal with the greatest prince that is. Let them, therefore have sufficient to maintain them, and to find them their necessaries. A ploughhand must have sheep; yea, they must have sheep to dung their ground for bearing of corn; for if they have no sheep to help fat the ground they shall have but bare corn and thin....[7]

He railed against greed and avarice among the small and the great, but especially the great. He attacked greedy vintners, clothiers, physicians, lawyers, and merchants. To the landlords he said:

> You landlords, you rent-raisers, I may say you step-lords, you unnatural lords, you have for your possessions yearly too much. For that here before went for twenty or forty pound by year...now is let for fifty or an hundred pound by year. Of this "too much" cometh this monstrous and portentious dearth made by man, notwithstanding God doth send us plentifully the fruits of the earth, mercifully, contrary to our deserts....[8]

Latimer was especially violent against enclosers and against the "carnal gospellers" who supported the reformation of the church for the sake of satisfying their lust for land, seizing monastic and chantry lands for their own selfish uses. As a result the poor, who had enjoyed the hospitality of the monasteries, suffered more and more. Latimer bemoaned the situation in general and in particular the ineffectiveness of the laws which were designed to curb such lusts.

> We have good statutes made for the commonwealth, as touching commoners, enclosers; many meetings and sessions; but in the end of the matter there cometh nothing forth. Well, well...from whence it cometh I know, even from the devil.[9]

Latimer and the others knew the importance of legal provisions made by Parliament and justly enforced by the officers of the law for the welfare of the commonwealth. But they also knew that the mere enactment of laws was never sufficient. What was most vitally needed was a change of heart and to this end the preaching of the Word of God was vitally important.

Thomas Cranmer, Archbishop of Canterbury, drove directly to the heart of the matter when preaching in response to Ket's rebellion in East Anglia in 1549.[10] Interrupted from his other duties, including work on the Prayer Book, recognizing the threat not only to that book but to the reform of England in general, Cranmer pointed to the "two destructions of the commonweal": the covetousness of those who "inclose and possess unjustly the commons" and the mutinous behavior of those commoners who "will be both hearers, judges, and reformers of their own causes."[11] The root cause of the trouble, as Cranmer saw it, was that "the gospel of God now set forth to the whole realm is of many so hated, that it is reject, refused, reviled, and blasphemed."[12] He was referring to the Word of God proclaimed in preaching, in daily offices, in sacraments, which devoutly received is expressed "in our manners and living."[13] The devout reception of the Word of God was viewed in terms of "true and faithful repentance." Repentance, he explained, "is a sorrow conceived for sins committed, with hope and trust to obtain remission by Christ, with a firm and effectual purpose of amendment, and to alter all things that hath been done amiss,"[14] such as those things perpetrated by the wealthy gentry who enclose arable lands for pasturage and by those commoners who revolt against lawful authority. Having thus repented, the Christian was prepared for participation in Christ who in the Holy Communion "he spiritually receiveth, spiritually feedeth and nourisheth upon, and by whom spiritually he liveth and continueth that life that is towards God."[15]

It was in the context of the socio-economic crisis, as the reformers perceived it from the 1530s on into the reign of Queen Elizabeth I, that the great books of the English Reformation appeared. They reflected the concerns of those who labored on

Introduction 39

them and they were to some extent at least—and I would say to a very great extent—designed as instruments for the effecting of social policy. In the essays which follow a two-fold task will be pursued: (1) to present the great books and to argue for their importance not only during the sixteenth century but for any understanding of the English Reformation in the present; (2) to demonstrate the social relevance of these books for the building of the godly kingdom of Tudor England. This latter shall be argued strongly, but not without criticism.

NOTES

Introduction: The Basic Theme

The Importance of the Revolution in Printing

[1] Febvre and Martin, *The Coming of the Book*, pp. 49-56. On the early decades of printing, see also Rudolf Hirsch, *The Printed Word: Its Impact and Diffusion* (London: Variorum Reprints, 1978).

[2] *Ibid.*, pp. 248-251. I rely on Febvre for the statistics given here.

[3] *Acts and Monuments of John Foxe*, G. Townsend, ed., Vol. III. Pt. 2 (London: Seeleys, 1855), p. 720. See pp. 718-22. See also Peter Heath, *English Parish Clergy on the Eve of the Reformation* (London: Routledge and Kegan Paul, 1969), pp. 192-193.

[4] *The Printing Press as an Agent of Change* (Cambridge: Cambridge University Press, 1979), 1:371.

[5] Febvre and Martin, *The Coming of the Book*, p. 288.

[6] H. C. Porter, *Reformation and Reaction in Tudor Cambridge* (Cambridge: At the University Press, 1958), p. 45.

[7] *English Books and Readers, 1475-1557*, 2nd ed. (Cambridge: At the University Press, 1969), pp. 35-36. See also M. Plant, *The English Book Trade* (London, 1939) and F. A. Mumby, *Publishing and Bookselling* (London, 1949).

[8] See Eisenstein, *The Printing Press*, 1:350-367.

The English Reformation: the story of great books

1. For the statute of supremacy, 1534, see *The Statutes of the Realm* (London: Record Commission, 1810-28), III, p. 492. See also J. J. Scarisbrick, *Henry VIII* (London: Eyre and Spottiswoode, 1968), Ch. 10.

2. See Lawrence Stone, "The Political Programme of Thomas Cromwell," *Bulletin of the Institute of Historical Research* 24 (1951), pp. 1-18, and Phyllis Hembry, *The Bishops of Bath and Wells, 1540-1640: Social and Economic Problems* (London: University of London, Athlone Press, 1967), pp. 59-61, 260-261.

3. *Certain Sermons or Homilies* (London: S.P.C.K., [1864]), p. 1.

4. Richard Hooker, *Of the Lawes of Ecclesiastical Polity*, V. 18.3.

5. For a detailed history of the articles, see Charles Hardwick, *A History of the Articles of Religion* (London: George Bell and Sons, 1895), Ch. 5.

6. *The Geneva Bible. A facsimile of the 1560 edition* (Madison, Milwaukee, and London: The University of Wisconsin Press, 1969), Sig.*** ii\v. And see F. F. Bruce, *The English Bible* (New York: Oxford University Press, 1961), Ch. 7.

7. *Certain Sermons and Homilies*, pp. 371-72.

8. See Alexander Nowell, *A Catechism Written in Latin*, G. E. Corrie, ed., Parker Society (Cambridge: Printed at the University Press, 1853). Concerning the influence of this catechism and others, see Joan Simon, *Education and Society in Tudor England* (Cambridge: University Press, 1966), espec. pp. 240-43, 307, 316-26.

9. Quoted by John E. Booty, *John Jewel as Apologist of the Church of England* (London: S.P.C.K., 1963), pp. 175-76.

10. Henry Gee, *The Elizabethan Clergy, and the Settlement of Religion, 1558-64* (Oxford: University Press, 1898), pp. 77-78.

11. W. H. Frere and W. M. Kennedy, *Visitation Articles and Injunctions of the period of the Reformation*, Alcuin Club Collections 14-16 (London, 1910), III, p. 15.

The Social Significance of the English Reformation

1. There are many examples, but see, for instance, books of a "popular" nature such as Richard M. Spielmann, *History of Christian Worship*

Introduction 41

(New York: Seabury Press, 1966), which does not entirely ignore the contexts of the various liturgical texts scrutinized, and Bruce, *The English Bible*, cited above.

[2] "Bid" in Anglo-Saxon means "pray" and thus here we may understand: the praying of the prayers but also the asking of prayers for certain persons. See J. G. Davies, *A Dictionary of Liturgy and Worship* (New York: The Macmillan Company, 1972), p. 76.

[3] At the end of the bidding prayer there is this rubric: "*And this done, show the Holy-days and fasting days.*" See John E. Booty, ed., *The Book of Common Prayer, 1559. The Elizabethan Prayer Book* (Charlottesville, Va.: The University of Virginia Press for the Folger Shakespeare Library, 1976), pp. 251, 397-8.

[4] Frere and Kennedy, *Visitation Articles and Injunctions*, III, pp. 28-29.

[5] *The declaratcyon of the procedynge of a conference, begon at Westminster the laste of Marche. 1559* (London: Richard Iugge and Iohn Cawood [1559]). Corpus Christi College, Cambridge, MS 121(21).

[6] Frere and Kennedy, *Visitation Articles and Injunctions*, III, p. 26.

[7] Ulysses' speech on degree in *Troilus and Cressida*, cited by E. M. W. Tillyard, *The Elizabethan World Picture* (London: Chatto and Windus, 1952), p. 7.

[8] William Maskell, ed., *Monumenta Ritualia Ecclesiae Anglicanae*, 2nd ed. (Oxford: At the Clarendon Press, 1882), II, p. 226.

[9] William Keatinge Clay, ed., *Liturgies and Occasional Forms of Prayer set forth in the Reign of Queen Elizabeth*, Parker Society (Cambridge: At the University Press, 1847), p. 292.

[10] G. W. Bromiley, *Thomas Cranmer Theologian* (London: Lutterworth Press, 1956), p. 19.

[11] Booty, *The Book of Common Prayer, 1559*, p. 254.

[12] The citations in parentheses are to Book, Chapter, and Section of Hooker's *Lawes*, as found in any modern edition.

[13] For Puritan objections to the Prayer Book, see W. H. Frere and C. E. Douglas, eds., *Puritan Manifestoes: A Study of the Origin of the Puritan Revolt* (London: S.P.C.K., 1907), pp. 21ff.

[14] Two classical views of the origins of government are, Aristotle,

Politics, I,i,1-12, and Cicero, *Pro Sestio,* Ch. 42.

[15] Cf. W. D. J. Cargill Thompson, "The Philosophy of the 'Politic Society': Richard Hooker as a Political Thinker" in *Studies in Richard Hooker,* W. Speed Hill, ed. (Cleveland and London: Case Western Reserve University Press, 1972), p. 36, who points out the conflicting views of the genesis of government held by Hooker.

[16] Quoted by Preserved Smith, *The Age of Reformation* (New York: Holt, 1920), pp. 58-59. See James Kelsey McConica, *English Humanists and Reformation Politics* (Oxford: At the Clarendon Press, 1965), Ch.2. For a critique, warning against putting too much weight on the influence of so-called Erasmianism, see G. R. Elton, *Reform and Renewal* (Cambridge: At the University Press, 1973), Introduction.

[17] Wilhelm Pauck, ed., *Melanchthon and Bucer,* Library of Christian Classics 19 (Philadelphia: Westminster Press, 1969), p. 196.

[18] T. F. Torrance, *Kingdom and Church: A Study in the Theology of the Reformation* (Fair Lawn, New Jersey: Essential Books, 1956), p. 87.

[19] J. B. Russell, *Medieval Civilization* (New York, London, Sydney: John Wiley and Sons, 1968), pp. 212-13.

[20] Quoted by Amédée Hallier, *The Monastic Theology of Aelred of Rievaulx* (Shannon, Ireland: Irish University Press, 1969), p. 139.

[21] C. E. Osborne, *Christian Ideas in Political History,* Holland Memorial Lectures 1925 (London: John Murray, 1929), p. 71. John Dickinson tends to confirm this view in his edition of *The Statesman's Book of John of Salisbury* (New York: Russell and Russell, 1963), pp.vxiiiff. Hans Liebeschütz presents another view in *Medieval Humanism in the Life and Writings of John of Salisbury* (London: The Warburg Institute, 1950): "John's doctrine is derived from the metaphor of the Church as a body unifying its members. But nothing of St. Paul's mystical feeling of community is transferred into John's political conception" (p. 45).

[22] E. O. Smith, Jr., *Crown and Commonwealth* (Philadelphia: American Philosophical Society, 1976), p. 13. In the Order of Coronation of King Ethelred, A.D.978, the prayer reads: "et ad veræ fidei pacisque concordiam eorum animos, te opitulante, reformat, ut horum populorum debita subjectione fultos, tuo digno amore glorificatus" (Maskell, *Monumenta,* II, pp. 14-15).

Church and Society in the Reign of Edward VI

[1] Reprinted from the Petyt MSS in John Strype's *Ecclesiastical Memorials* (Oxford: Clarendon Press, 1822), II.ii, p. 481.

[2] Strype, *Ecclesiastical Memorials*, II,ii, p. 482. There is a considerable literature reflecting the same views. For examples see C. H. Williams, ed., *English Ecclesiastical Documents, 5: 1485-1558* (New York: Oxford University Press, 1967), pp. 940-53.

[3] For a discussion of this, see W. K. Jordan, *Edward VI: The Young King* (Cambridge, Mass.: Harvard University Press, 1968), pp. 386-389. Much of that which follows has been influenced by Jordan's treatment of the subject. Concerning the earlier phase under Thomas Cromwell, see G. R. Elton, *Reform and Renewal*, Ch.5.

[4] See Whitney R. D. Jones, *The Tudor Commonwealth, 1529-1559* (London: University of London Athlone Press, 1970), p. 159.

[5] Cf. G. R. Elton, *Reform and Reformation England, 1509-1558*, The New History of England (Cambridge, Mass.: Harvard University Press, 1977), Ch.1. Elton is critical of social reformers who recognize the distress of the commonwealth and yet seem to offer no practical solutions, choosing to yearn for a past which is dead. Coming at it as he does, he is quite justified in this criticism, or so it seems to me, and his barbs could effectively pierce some of those mentioned here. Our concern, however, is not with practical results but with ideological positions reflected by the great books and which those books were meant to serve.

[6] *A Discourse of the Commonweal of This Realm of England*, Mary Dewar, ed., Folger Documents of Tudor and Stuart Civilization (Charlottesville, Va.: University of Virginia Press, 1969), p. 16. Miss Dewar attributes the work to Sir Thomas Smith, but Professor Jordan is not convinced. See his *Edward VI*, p. 395.

[7] Hugh Latimer, *Sermons*, G. E. Corrie, ed., Parker Society (Cambridge: Cambridge University Press, 1844), I, p. 249.

[8] Latimer, *Sermons*, I, pp. 98-99; and see p. 279.

[9] Latimer, *Sermons*, I, pp. 101-102.

[10] Concerning the authorship of the sermon he preached, see Jasper Ridley, *Thomas Cranmer* (Oxford: Clarendon Press, 1962), p. 297.

[11] Cranmer, *Miscellaneous Writings*, p. 196.

[12] Cranmer, *Miscellaneous Writings*, p. 197.

[13] Cranmer, *Miscellaneous Writings*, p. 198.
[14] Cranmer, *Miscellaneous Writings*, p. 201.
[15] Cranmer, *Miscellaneous Writings*, p. 173.

Part Two

GODLY AND FRUITFUL LESSONS

The English Bible, Erasmus' Paraphrases and the Book of Homilies

John N. Wall, Jr.

—II—

GODLY AND FRUITFUL LESSONS

The English Bible, Erasmus' Paraphrases and the Book of Homilies

John N. Wall, Jr.

The Reformation in England, in its decisive phase under Edward VI, began in earnest with a presentation of the Word of God, in three forms: direct translation of the Word into the language of the people, paraphrase and commentary on the Word to make it even more accessible, and homiletic interpretation of that Word to make clear its implications for those who heard it. Thomas Cranmer, Archbishop of Canterbury, when he was at last free "to issue a theological declaration precisely as he desired it...for the first time in his life,"[1] promulgated under royal authority on 31 July 1547 a set of Injunctions which required every parish church in England to have the "whole Bible, of the largest volume in Englishe," Erasmus' *Paraphrases* on the Gospels and Acts, and a collection of twelve sermons known customarily as the *Book of Homilies,* and to use them as the basis for reading, Bible study, and preaching.[2] The Great Bible was

47

already available, having been authorized for use during the reign of Henry VIII; the presses of Richard Grafton and Edward Whitchurche, official printers for the church, enabled parishes to comply with Cranmer's Injunctions by publishing the other two books within the following year and a half.[3]

Thus, even before producing the vernacular Prayer Book for which he is better known, Cranmer authorized use of these three documents, presenting in three different but closely related forms the Word of God to the people of England in their own language. Concerning this fact, I wish to make three points. First, it is worth noting, in light of recent arguments that the high water mark of Protestant humanist influence on the English Reformation was reached in the reign of Henry VIII,[4] that all three of these documents of the Word were either complete or under preparation during the later years of Henry's reign. As is well known, the conservative reaction led by bishops Gardiner and Bonner tied Cranmer's hands during that period; the rapidity with which Cranmer was able to act after the accession of Edward VI suggests that what we actually have in the reign of Edward is the completion of the reform program begun in England under Thomas Cromwell but delayed by his fall and the ascendancy of the conservative bishops. Second, Cranmer's clear intention that the presentation of the Word have such a central place in the process of reformation suggests that we must examine carefully his theology of the Word in relationship to the world if we are to understand what he was about in reforming the church. In this light, more specifically dogmatic or doctrinal questions must take second place to an effort to grasp the reasons for Cranmer's sense of urgency about simply making the Word available in the language of the people. Third, I believe that Cranmer's theology of presenting the Word was grounded in the faith that the Word, when properly presented, has the power to transform the world into which it is spoken. This theology of presentation Cranmer inherited from the northern tradition of Christian humanism, most clearly enunciated by Desiderius Erasmus.

In this context, one must acknowledge that use of the term

"humanism" is at best problematic, because there seems to be no generally agreed upon definition. William Yost is probably correct, however, in arguing that the proper question is not whether or not humanism affected the English Reformation, but how Protestantism affected the humanist culture of Tudor intellectuals in the 1530's.[5] In light of that, I can find no other source for the methods and aims of the documents under consideration here than the traditional concern of Tudor humanists with moral behavior and their faith in the power of words, rhetorically expressed, to move men and women toward what Douglas Bush has called the basic concern of Tudor Christian humanism, the "active Christian life."[6]

This is not, of course, to suggest that there was a specifically "Erasmian" party in early Tudor England, but to argue that whatever "humanism" was in northern Europe in the early sixteenth century, it was a highly complex and multi-faceted phenomenon, and that Erasmus was, at least for English humanists, a major and influential spokesman for at least some aspects of it. Instead of thinking of an "Erasmian" party, we might instead want to envision a community of men with shared educational backgrounds, shared goals, and shared methodology, for which Erasmus loomed as the most articulate spokesman.

What I do wish to argue is this: on the basis of the three documents at hand, I believe it is clear that the Reformation in England reached the culmination of its first phase during the reign of Edward VI, when the documents produced by Cranmer and his associates completed the program of reform anticipated by Erasmus and enunciated during Henry's reign in the writings of Thomas Starkey. Those documents use distinctively humanist methods — verbal and rhetorical presentation of the Word of God in the context of eucharistic action by the community — to achieve distinctively humanistic ends — the creation of *de regnum Christi*, the reign of Christ, the true Christian commonwealth — realized through humanistic education into the life of active charity. We look at the English Reformation from the wrong perspective if we look for a distinctive theology or for rigorous adherence to any continental reformed theology, for Cranmer and his associates argued repeatedly that they sought to impose no new theology, but instead to recover the ancient faith of the church. Instead, we ought to look for the reformers' distinctive use of method, and the social and ethical goals of that method. For what Cranmer and his followers *were* clear about is what they sought to do, and that was to transform the religious life of their nation. The documents of the reign of Edward VI are not essays in defining a new institution, but instruments of change, methods of transforming the life of their nation into a mirror of the true Christian commonwealth.

Trying to organize a discussion of three large and complex documents into a single chapter has proved difficult at best. What I have set out to do is to sketch some background material which seems to me essential for understanding the method and purpose of Cranmer's distinctive presentations of God's Word, and then proceed to discuss each of the documents in turn, describing their origins and suggesting how they came to be published in 1547-49, as well as relating them to my overriding argument that Cranmer's purpose in issuing them was the transformation of English society into an image of the Christian commonwealth. My stress throughout will be on language, on words used to express the divine Word, the distinctive mark of Christian humanism. The Reformation of the fifteenth and sixteenth centuries has been called an Augustinian reformation; nowhere is this more true for England than in the English reformers' explicit faith in the power of spoken and written words. Humanism recovered the classical and biblical faith in the power of oratory, the proclaimed word. Authorized by Augustine's teaching in his *De Doctrina Christiana*, the English reformers, led by Cranmer, put the theory and practice of classical rhetoric to use in their earliest plans for transforming the international, medieval, Latin Church in England into a national, Renaissance, English, Christian society.

My argument, therefore, is that Cranmer set out to domesticate the Reformation in England by using words to proclaim the Word; his goal was Christian community, "felowshyppe of life."[7] Hugh Latimer, in his contribution to the *Book of*

Homilies, makes clear that the reformers saw a link between Christian living and societal reform:

> We cannot be joyned to Christ our head, except we be glued with concord and charitie, one to another. For he that is not in this unitie, is not of the church of Christ, which is a congregacion or unitie together, and not a division.[8]

The English Reformation was profoundly social, societal, interpersonal; the Tudor reformers set out to interpret Christ's injunction to love God and one's neighbor in new terms, terms which saw the arena of that love as the human society of England. God was to be sought not above or apart from this world, but *through* this world, through journeying toward the New Jerusalem by means of building up the earthly city, of creating the true Christian commonwealth.

My purpose in this chapter is to examine in some detail the documents through which this vision of the Christian life was presented to the people who were to enact it. In a real sense, we will distort that vision by examining it apart from its liturgical setting, for Cranmer's Prayer Book was the context for reading and study of the Bible, and for delivery of the Homilies. The words that presented and expounded the Word were intended to be part of an action of prayer and thanksgiving designed to empower the transforming Word in its building-up of the Christian community. The virtue of such an approach, however, is that it will allow us to create a context for these documents, which will make clearer for us the significance both of their content and of their form.

Early Tudor Humanism: Background to the Great Books

1. Logos and Commonwealth in Early Tudor Humanism

What we are about to trace is the development, among early Tudor humanists, of a vision of the Christian commonwealth, which was the outgrowth of their basic stress on the true Christian life as one of active charity, of creative love of one's neighbor, and of a method, grounded in the use of words, to bring about the realization of that vision. In the traditional concern with Renaissance individualism, insufficient attention is given to the fact that Tudor humanists, although beginning their redefinition of the Christian life with Erasmian images of the individual Christian warrior struggling against sin in imitation of Christ, soon developed an understanding of the social contexts and implications of Erasmus' *philosophia Christi*. In the process, they revitalized the medieval view of a hierarchic society by making it a goal to be sought after, rather than merely a static description of humanity's proper place in the cosmos. The purpose of human life on earth became not simply to escape this world, or to endure its agonies through hope of deliverance through death into the next, but an active pursuit of an orderly, hierarchic, mutually interdependent society, the true Christian commonwealth, what Martin Bucer would call *respublica Christiana*,[1] to be achieved when all men and women came to direct their energies toward loving their neighbors. In these terms, the earthly city becomes not something to cast aside, but a community to transform, to build up, to restore to its prelapsarian state of order and harmony.

A convenient way to begin this survey is to clarify origins and differences, to suggest the medieval backgrounds and indicate how the humanists moved from them. We begin with two images of the Christian life drawn from early Tudor sources, one essentially medieval, the other Renaissance and humanist, which will enable us to see where in terms of community and the Christian life the humanists began, and in what directions they moved. The first image is taken from a brief work, published in 1534 on the eve of the dissolution of the monasteries, under the title *A Devout Treatyse Called the Tree and XII Fruites of the Holy Goost*. Addressed to women religious, it is evidence for the continuation into Renaissance England of essentially medieval images of the Christian life.

On the back of the title page of this book there appears a striking visual image [see Figure 2, opposite]. At the bottom, two

Illustration from *A Devout Treatyse Called the Tree and XII Fruites of the Holy Goost* (London, 1534) depicting the Christian life.

figures, one male, the other female, both in religious dress, face each other, their hands palms-together in the classic attitude of private prayer. From the chest of each figure a leafy branch emerges. The branches come together at the eye-level of the figures to form a large oval reminiscent of the outline of a tree. From this oval emerge the images of a crowned Madonna and child, surrounded by shooting flames, and attended above by two winged cherubim. The two figures, who have become trees putting forth branches and fruits of divine vision, gaze in prayerful meditation at the icon of Our Lady and her Son. The anonymous author of this work begins with the following words:

> Relygyous syster, for as moche as ye arte now planted in the gardyn of holy relygyon, yf thou wylt at the last be a tree of the hevenly paradyse, thou must vertuously growe here, and bryng forthe good goostly fruyte. For as our lorde sayeth. *Omnes arbor bona, fructe bonos facit.* Every good tree (he sayth) bringeth forth good fruyte. If a tree materyall sholde bryng forth good fruyte, it must be first depely roted, afterwarde wel watred, than sprede his branunches abrode, and at last to waxe hye. In the same wyse, if ye wylt be a good tree, and bryng forth vertuous fruyte, first thou must be veryly, and depely roted in mekenesse, which is the keper, and very true grounde & foundement of all vertues.[2]

In the emblem, and throughout the work, the image of Christian life as a tree dominates the imagination of the author. This tree must be fixed with deep roots: it must grow tall and strong, and bear fruits, which are "of the holy goost." The soil is meekness, in the "gardyn of holy relygyon," which is the religious, contemplative life. Nourished by Christ's love, the tree of the Christian life produces fruits, among which are "peas," "myldnesse," "contynence," and, of course, "chastyte." These fruits are revealed "at the last," at death, and make it possible for the Christian to become "a tree of the hevenly paradyse." This image reminds us that the medieval concept of the Christian life is profoundly and deeply private and individualistic in its orientation. Life is a pilgrimage to be endured; release from it comes not for a people but for the individual who in life has done his best, as defined in this manual, in terms of passive, private devotion.

Godly and Fruitful Lessons 55

Our second work, Edmund Dudley's *Tree of Commonwealth*, was written during the first year of the reign of Henry VIII as a work of education for the young king. It also uses, as its title suggests, the image of the tree for its concept of the Christian life, but for Dudley the emphasis is public and social, not individual:

> The comon wealth of this realme or of the subjects or Inhabitauntes therof may be resemblid to a faier and mighte tree growing in a faier field or pasture, under the coverte or shade wherof all beastes, both fatt and leane, are protectyd and comfortyd from heate and cold as the tyme requireth. In like manner all the subjects of that realme wher this tree of comon welth doth sewerly growe are ther by holpen and relyved from the highest degre to the lowest. But for a troth this tree will never long stand or growe uprighte in this realme, or in any other, withowt diverse strong rootes, and fastened sewer in the grounde.
> The principall and chief roote of this tree in every Christen realme must be the love of god, and the love of god is nothing els but to know hym and gladly observe his [lawes] and comaundymentes as his trew and faithful people.[3]

When compared to the images of Christian life in the *Tree of the Holy Goost*, some marked differences appear in Dudley's vision; instead of the stress on the individual preparing for a good death, here the emphasis is on the individual in the context of his society, whose health is based not on contemplation of divine vision but on active obedience to God's laws. In a development crucial to the humanists' concept of the Christian life, Dudley argues that obedience to God's laws has primarily social consequences. The ends sought by such obedience are no longer meekness, patience, virginity, and the like, but "justice," "troth or fydelite," "concord or Unytie," and "hospitalitie," all essentially social virtues. In contrast to the "tree of the Holy Goost," Dudley's tree is dependent for its health not on deep rooting in passive devotion, but on careful tending through active charity.

If Dudley's work marks the essential direction which the Tudor reformers were to take — from the private and contemplative toward the social and active — in their normative understanding of the true Christian life, the thought of Erasmus will move us another step closer to the actual documents of Edwardian reform, for central to Erasmus' thinking is the function of words to effect just such movement. As Marjorie O'Rourke Boyle points out in a brilliant study, for Erasmus, the Christ is God's eternally thought speech; men imitate the Father when they imitate the divine discourse made flesh in Jesus.[4] In his Latin translation of the Greek text that Tyndale used as the basis of his English New Testament, Erasmus translated the beginning of John's Gospel as *In principio erat sermo,* instead of the more familiar Vulgate *verbum;* even as the Christ is the mirror of divine discourse, so human speech, human discourse, becomes a mirror of the human spirit. The two converge when human speech is made to correspond to divine speech, when people imitate the divine speech in their imitation of Christ, so that God may admire the mirrored image of his discourse in Christ. From this basic concept emerges Erasmus' stress on the value of human speech, when Christ is put at its center as a touchstone for all that people say. The Christian orator, who speaks in imitation of God in Christ, imitates the process of God becoming incarnate in Christ the divine discourse, and thus serves as a savior of his society. Scripture, in which Christ is incarnate as divine discourse, is thus the beginning of all human speech; from its study proceeds Erasmus' understanding of the restoration of a fallen creation through oratory, in imitation of the Christ who has redeemed it through his nature as the oration of God. Through imitation of the divine speech, people come to conversation in him; as Ms. Boyle has put it:

> Erasmus plotted a conversational network which extended from the Father's utterance of his speech into creation; through the patrimonial words of men of classical and Christian antiquity, foreshadowing or witnessing the *Logos* in the world; to himself conversing with them, the reader joining in, and reader speaking with reader in a ring around the continent.[5]

Thus, human discourse, human conversation, when it is grounded in Scripture and takes Christ as its normative center, is constitutive of redeemed human society, of the true Christian commonwealth.

Thomas Wilson, a contemporary of Cranmer, echoed Erasmus at this point when he reached back over the centuries to combine Cicero, Quintillian, and other classical oratorical theorists with the teaching of Augustine to stress the transforming power of words for religious purposes. In his *Arte of Rhetorique* (1553), Wilson argues that oratory is best seen in a theological context, as God's gift so that people may overcome error by persuading others to do what is right. God's agents, Wilson states, should use rhetoric for education, "thet they myghte wyth ease wynne folke at their will and frame theim by reason to all good order."[6] The ends of persuasion through speaking the Word are thus both religious and political, or to put it more correctly, the will of God is that men and women should be persuaded to live in an ordered society. The ends of a Christian orator, therefore, are "to teache, to delight, and to perswade" so as to achieve this desired "felowshyppe of life."

We need go no further than Erasmus' theology of speech to find the reason Cranmer and his followers set out to reform England with a collection of written documents intended to be read aloud, a collection of documents including among them the Bible itself, Erasmus' own commentary on the New Testament heart of it for Christian speakers, and a collection of rhetorically constructed sermons expounding its meaning. To bridge the gap between Erasmus' theory and Cranmer's practice, however, we need to examine three works. The first is Erasmus' own *Enchiridion militis Christiani*, which will make clear the connection between verbal imitation of Christ and imitation of him through acts of active charity. The second is Thomas More's *Utopia*, which will illustrate the functioning of humanist rhetoric in instigating conversation, in impinging on the world of the reader to force him to ask questions about his society and to begin the work of reforming it. The third, Thomas Starkey's *Dialogue between Reginald Pole and Thomas Lupset*, illustrates again the humanist concern with dialogue, with conversation, but, more important, shows humanists planning a program for effecting social reform through the use of words, which we will see fulfilled in Cranmer's reform efforts under Edward VI.

2. Strategies for Change in Early Humanist Writing

Erasmus' *Enchiridion militis Christiani,* or *The Manuell of the Christen Knyght,* as William Tyndale translated its title,[1] was written in 1501 and published in Latin in Antwerp in 1503. It was his first call for the "regeneration of Christendom," directed at the international audience of learned men and women.[2] The *Enchiridion* is important for my argument because it sets forth in succinct fashion the humanist understanding of mankind's progress toward growth in the Christian life of active charity and suggests the way words may be used to effect such progress. Erasmus reaches his conclusions by translating the Socratic injunction "know thyself" into humanist and Christian terms. The *Enchiridion* begins with an exhortation to the reading of Scripture, and then outlines a way of life which Erasmus sees as following from biblical study. The first step is self-knowledge, which he defines in terms quite different from our modern psychological understanding. Self-knowledge comes not from within an individual, but from understanding of the relationship between ourselves and God, which is provided by scriptural study.[3] The next step is faith, which Erasmus says is the "onely gate unto Chryst."[4] But faith is just a beginning; the Christian must then proceed to an active life of struggle against evil in the arena of the world.[5] The rest of the *Enchiridion* outlines specific actions which Christians engaged in Christian warfare should practice or shun in obedience to the will of God. Erasmus rejects the contemplative life of the monastic, and urges instead an active life of battle with sin and evil in the everyday world of human affairs.

This paradigm, beginning with self-knowledge gained through biblical study and proceeding through faith to works of active charity, became the normative pattern for humanist discussions of the true Christian life. As we will see later in this chapter, it provided Thomas Cranmer with the structuring outline for the twelve sermons in his *Book of Homilies*. Basic to the paradigm is study of the divine Word, the Bible, which provides the

Godly and Fruitful Lessons   59

knowledge as well as the ability to live the Christian life. The end of knowledge, according to Erasmus, is learning "a certeyn crafte of vertuous lyvyng,"[6] which is our appropriate response to God's saving actions.

One additional point might well be made here about the means through which Erasmus believes the study of the Word teaches "vertuous lyvyng." At the heart of his program is *imitation*, as readers are called to "enter in to the way of spiritual helthe" by modeling themselves on the example of Christ: "have Christ alway in thy syght as the onely marke of all thy lyvyng and *conversacyon* (emphasis mine).''[7] The Christian way for Erasmus is a process of education; faith is knowledge and acceptance of the ethical law, pursued through emulation of the Christ found in the Scriptures.

If the *Enchiridion* moves its readers to discover who they are through study of Scripture and imitation of Christ, More's *Utopia* encourages them to ascertain the nature of the society in which they live. A distinctive mark of the first stage in the Tudor humanist movement is its international quality; the *Utopia*, like Erasmus' *Enchiridion militis Christiani*, was first written in Latin and directed therefore at an international audience. Published in 1516 in Louvain, More's "nowhere" has been somewhere indeed for great numbers of readers with radically disparate theologies and political allegiances who have made it their own.[8] Recent scholarship, however, has clarified More's purpose in the work, and placed it firmly in the humanist context of concern with the active life of loving one's neighbor. The portrait of Raphael Hythloday, the explorer and world traveler who reports to More and Peter Giles on the society of Utopia, is skillfully drawn as a satire on the mind of late medieval scholasticism, which would rather spend its energy in useless argument and debate than in active labor for the good of mankind.[9]

At a critical point in Book I of the *Utopia*, this point is deftly made. Peter Giles suggests to Raphael that he might aid his family and friends by putting his political skills to the use of a prince. Raphael rejects this advice:

> As for my relatives and friends,... I am not greatly troubled about them, for I think I have fairly well performed my duty to them already. The possessions, which other men do not resign unless they are old and sick and even then resign unwillingly when incapable of retention, I divided among my relatives and friends when I was not merely hale and hearty but actually young. I think they ought to be satisfied with this generosity from me and not to require or expect additionally that I should, for their sakes, enter into servitude to kings.[10]

As we come to this speech of Raphael, we must surely recognize that what his friend More wants us to hear echoed in these lines is Christ's injunction, "Give all that you have to the poor and follow me." In light of that, what we are to make of Raphael is to notice his allegiance to the letter of the law, and his distance from its spirit.[11] The contrast forces us to ask ourselves, as readers, where we are on this question; it forces us into a dialogue with the issues and images set forth by More in his work. The opening section, in fact, is in the form of a dialogue between More, Peter Giles, and Hythloday; this use of the dialogue form reminds us that every issue has two sides. When we get to Book II, with its description of Utopia presented in a monologue by Hythloday, we have been taught by example that there must be another side, which *we* are called upon to supply.

More's *Utopia* thus deals with two questions, both of which were central issues among the earliest Tudor humanists. The first is how someone trained in humanistic studies and thus possessing insight into right behavior should become active to effect change in his society; this question is dealt with directly in Book I. The second question concerns how active societal reform is to be initiated; this question is dealt with directly in Book I and indirectly in Book II. The answer to the first question, at least for the learned audience of the Latin *Utopia,* is given in terms of service to a prince. Although Raphael Hythloday refuses to take up royal service, his objections in Book I allow More and Giles to present the case for such efforts:

> Yf evell opynyons and noughty persuasions can not be utterly and

quyte pluckede owte of their hartes, if you can not even as you wold remedye vyces, whiche use and custome hath confirmed: yet for this cause yow must not leave and forsake the common wealth; yow must not forsake the shyppe in a tempeste, bycause yowe can not rule and kepe down the wyndes.... But you must with a crafty wile and a subtell trayne studye and endevoure your selfe asmuch as in yow lyethe to handle the matter wyttelye and handsomelye for the purpose and that whyche yowe can not turne to good, so to ordre it that it be not very badde. For it is not possible for all thynges to be well, onles all men were good. Which I thynke wil not be yet thys good many yeares.[12]

More's assumption of the office of Lord Chancellor upon the fall of Wolsey provides More's own assent to this answer.

More's answer to the second question, about how societal change is to be effected, is given, in part, directly in Book I. There, amid Hythloday's pointed social commentary on the dangers of enclosures and the limitations and inequities of the English system of justice, Cardinal Morton is depicted as offering the possibility of limited periods of trial for possible reforms. It is typical of Hythloday that he offers this story as an example of the *futility* of entering public service, while the story proves exactly the opposite contention.

The most interesting technique for initiating social change, however, is provided by Hythloday's famous monologue in Book II, in which he describes in detail the make-up of Utopian society. By this point in the work, we have already been taught the value of dialogue, of seeing more than one side of any issue, of verbal give-and-take. In light of this, we are called to make a dialogue out of Book II, to point out the actual injustices of Utopian society, its weak points as well as its strong points. And because Utopia contains geographical elements that remind us of England, we are drawn to examine English society from this imaginative perspective. Utopian society, as More presents it through Hythloday, is not an alternative to English society of the early 1500's, but a perspective to enable us to see that society more clearly. As we are drawn into such a comparison, into creating in our own minds a real, verbal dialogue between the society of England and the society of nowhere, we begin to initiate a process which must result in change in the real society. Having been to Utopia, at least in our minds, we can no longer be happy with the status quo in our own country. What we must notice, therefore, about More's "nowhere" is that its form, even more than its contents, is what is really important about it. Because of the way it is written, we as readers are moved to action, first to engage the work itself in dialogue, and second to initiate the process of charitable action which will transform our own society.

More's *Utopia*, then, like Erasmus' *Enchiridion*, is not a static description or definition of a state of being, but a work intended, through words, to impinge on the world of its readers, to draw them into its world and set their minds at work analyzing themselves and the world in which they live. Humanist literature always has this quality, that it seeks, through its use of language, to be an agent of change, by presenting effective images for the reader's imitation, or by making it possible for us to examine our own world, see it in a new way, and set about reforming it. The goal, and the central issue, of all humanist writing is to educate the reader in such a way that we are equipped to change ourselves and our society, and to set us in action designed to bring about that change. In so doing, it creates through words the truly Christian community, made up of those who put Christ at the center of their social discourse, and who seek by doing so to have him at the center of their society.

3. Programs for Reform in the Reign of Henry VIII

If the achievement of writers in this early stage of the Tudor humanist movement was to define the central task and method of humanist writing, the achievement of the next generation was to define the actual approaches that humanists would take toward achieving reform on the larger scale of a national society. The audience for the work of Erasmus and More was limited, for the most part, to the international audience of learned men and women, an audience wide in geographical scope but limited in each country to those fluent in Latin. After the break with the papacy under Henry VIII, attention shifted to reaching the widest possible national audience; this necessitated a shift in approach from the use of Latin to the use of the vernacular, a step Erasmus had anticipated, as we have seen. It also meant the creation of programs of education through the persuasive use of language which would reach out from the centers of religious and political authority to touch the lives of every citizen in the country.

Much has been made of the execution of Thomas More as a result of his inability to go along with Henry VIII's claims to be supreme head of the church; in fact, the old tradition saw this as the death of Tudor humanism itself.[1] Recent studies, however, make clear that such conclusions are based on a very narrow definition of humanism and do not reflect the fact that many humanists, men with educational backgrounds and religious and social convictions similar to those of More and Erasmus, saw the cleavage between Rome and Canterbury not as a tragedy but as an opportunity to advance the cause of religious and societal reform.[2] While Erasmus and More were unable to follow Henry VIII instead of the pope, other humanists responded vigorously to seize this opportunity to break with the past and, unencumbered with the weight of papal tradition, to strike out boldly toward achievement of the humanist vision of religion and society. Among those humanists who chose to side with the king were Richard Taverner, Thomas Elyot, Thomas Starkey, Richard Morison, and, of course, Thomas Cranmer. These men formed the leadership of a second generation of Tudor humanists. Their works reveal a concern to find practical ways to effect the vision of society described by Dudley, Erasmus, More, and other members of the first generation.

Thomas Starkey, who along with Richard Morison had been a member of Richard Pole's humanist household in Padua, was rewarded for his decision to follow the king with an appointment as one of Henry's chaplains.[3] In the period 1533-36 he produced two works, *An Exhortation unto the People Instructynge theym to Unitie and Obedience* and the *Dialogue between Reginald Pole and Thomas Lupset,* both on the general subject of reformation of the church and state in England. The former work is important for the history of the English Church, because it enunciates decisively the doctrine of *adiaphora,* or "things indifferent," in matters of church polity. The second work, though not printed until modern times, circulated in manuscript form.[4] Written before Pole made his final decision to remain on the side of Rome, Starkey's *Dialogue* presents a humanist understanding of the state, and an ambitious, visionary program of reform; it reveals the growing humanist concern with active reform of the body politic, with the formation of a Christian commonwealth, a concern which was to culminate in the reform program of Edward VI. Starkey's work uses throughout the dialogue form we noted in Book I of More's *Utopia;* it also involves the reader through presenting a searching criticism of the England that exists and a tantalizing image of the England that might be. Starkey's aim is to enlist the reader's support for those reforms necessary for the transition from the old to the new.

Starkey's *Dialogue* is cast as a conversation between Pole and Thomas Lupset, another English humanist and member of Pole's household. The chief topics of their conversation are those raised by More in *Utopia:* what is the best sort of commonwealth, and what is the role of the humanist in bringing about the reform needed to achieve this end? Starkey's work does not deal with these concerns abstractly, but applies them to a real situation. In the *Dialogue,* the realm under discussion is England, and the humanist in the role of Hythloday is Pole himself, a positive rather than a negative *exemplum,* who has been asked by Henry VIII to join the service of the king. Both men are agreed that everyone is called to an active life, for the good of "the weal of their country":

> [Lupset] to this all men are born and of nature brought forth: to commune such gifts as be to them given, each to the profit of other, in perfit civility, and not to live to their own pleasure and profit.
>
> [Pole] Indeed it cannot be denied but it is a goodly thing to meddle with the matters of the common weal, and a novel virtue to do good to our friends and country, to the which, as you say, we are

born and brought forth... to the end of all man's studies and acts, and best thing in this life to be attained unto.[5]

Here, in a development crucial for Cranmer's reform program, the concern of Erasmus for a life of Christian action, grounded in faith and created through words, extended by him to society through the example of the Christian prince, is broadened to involve all people working together for the same ends. *De Regno Christi*, the rule of Christ,[6] is presented as a model for all to aspire to for their country:

> [Lupset] all labours, business and travail, of wise men handled, in matters of the common weal, are ever referred to this end and purpose: that the whole body of the commonality may live in quietness and tranquility, every part doing his office and duty, and so (as much as the nature of man will suffer) all to attain to their natural perfection.
>
> To this every honest man meddling in the common weal ought to look chiefly unto; this is the mark that every man, prudent and politic, ought to shoot at: first to make himself perfit, with all vertues garnishing his mind, and then to commune the same perfection to other. For little availeth virtue that is not published abroad to the profit of other; little availeth treasure closed in coffers which never is communed to the succor of other. For all such gifts of God and nature must ever be applied to the common profit and utility; whereby man, as much as he may, shall ever follow the nature of God, Whose infinite goodness is by this chiefly declared and opened to the world, that to every thing and creature He giveth part thereof according to their nature and capacity. So that virtue and learning, not communed to other, is like unto riches heaped in corners, never applied to the use of other.[7]

The note of imitation is struck here as well. To "follow the nature of God" is to follow God's commands for personal conduct — "first to make himself perfit, with all vertues garnishing his mind" — and then to work to the betterment of order in the commonwealth, "to commune the same perfection to other," even as God gives to every part of his creation some of his riches. Starkey's language, appropriately, echoes Jesus' parables of those who do and do not use their talents, and of those who do not hide their lights under a bushel. The active life of giving to others of what one has been given is in imitation of the nature of God.

Starkey's vision of the ordered commonwealth is described in images which compare it to the human form, with the people composing the body, and the civil law, the soul.[8] He asserts that things which are wrong with the "body politic" are analogous to various diseases; the society is healthy only when all people live in it in concern for others, rather than in concern for themselves alone. The social virtue of charity, grounded in Christ's command to love one's neighbor, is the highest duty and calling of humanity. Such conditions do not prevail in England because people do not do their duty to themselves and to each other. Instead, people are idle, and, as a result, cities, towns, and the crafts which support them are all in decay. The nobility luxuriates in idle wealth, the monastic communities are too large, fat, and lazy; in short, an idle selfishness produces too much disharmony among social groups. As a result, there is a general lack of justice in the society. Finally, there is the problem of the pope, who has usurped inappropriate authority over the people, and the problem of the regular clergy, who are, for the most part, too ignorant to do their jobs well.[9] Because of these diseases, which are failures of duty, the health and good order of the commonwealth of England are disturbed.

To correct this state of affairs, Starkey presents, through the opinions of his conversationalists, several remedies. At the heart of all his proposals is education of the people, each according to his station in the hierarchy of society. The nobility should be trained in letters, but also in discipline and virtue, so they will be better rulers of the society.[10] A national system of education should be set up for them, which would be better than the private tutors now in charge of their instruction. Such education of the nobility should be grounded in Scripture. Without this new educational system, "all the rest of our device will little avail."[11] The end of this system would be to produce men who would insure order and justice in the society through just rule and able administration. People on lower levels of society should be educated in crafts and trades, and instructed to learn them and pursue them diligently. All lazy people, and all who do wrong, should be cast out of the "body politic" as diseased members. For the entire society, good preachers, trained according to Erasmus' ideas, should instruct in doctrine and manners. In all things, Christ is the supreme model; he is to be imitated so as to live a good life. For this program of active imitation of Christ to succeed, all divine services and all readings from Scripture should be "wholly in our tongue." Regular clergy should be allowed to marry, though some celibate monastic houses might remain, if they fulfilled their duty in imitation of Christ. Starkey specifically presents Erasmus' *Enchiridion* as the basic guide to the Christian life.[12] Erasmus' pattern of action rooted in faith is to be taught to all men by educated clergy, through both their words and their deeds. Indeed, instruction in "Christian life and evangelical doctrine," reading of Scripture, and religious services conducted in the vernacular make up the heart of Starkey's humanistic program for the reform of the commonwealth. In this work, the Christian life of charitable action instigated by word and grounded in faith is developed in great detail by Starkey as the basis for a sweeping reform of English society.

In the work of men like Starkey, early Tudor humanists articulated their vision of what God called people to do in this world. This vision was of an ordered, hierarchic society, in imitation of God's self-revelation in the order of nature, to be achieved through educating everyone to live lives of active charity, grounded in faith. This vision was radical, in that it substituted worldly activity aimed at changing the society for the passive devotion typical of medieval images of the Christian life. At the same time, it was conservative, in that it sought no major change in the structure of society, only the perfection of a structure implicit in the existing state of affairs. Such perfection would be, simultaneously, the achievement of a vision and the restoration of human society to its prelapsarian condition. Having developed this vision, Tudor humanists then had to create means to effect its realization.

The official acts and publications of Henry's reign, at least under Cromwell's chancellorship, manifest the earliest official steps toward reforming the developing English Church along humanist lines. Reforms effected through the *Ten Articles*, the Bishops' Book, the Great Bible, and Cromwell's *Injunctions* of 1536 and 1538 all move in the direction charted by Starkey in his *Dialogue*: "an abolition of what they had come to regard as unreasonable or antiquated, and an accentuation of what could give room for a new spirit, a new interpretation of what was retained from the old."[13] Cromwell's *Injunctions* call for the Bible in English to be placed in every parish, for required instruction in the *Pater Noster*, the Creed, and the Ten Commandments, and for support for scholars in grammar schools and universities. In these works, the humanist program of reform through education emerged as official church policy.

The fall of Cromwell in 1540, however, provoked yet another crisis in English humanist circles, as a major source of patronage and official support was lost. In addition, the period of Stephen Gardiner's domination of church affairs was one of retrenchment and reduced toleration for variety of opinion within the leadership of the church. The role of chief patron for the humanist community was transferred again, this time falling to Thomas Cranmer and Queen Catherine Parr.[14] The Archbishop, trained at Cambridge when it was becoming an important center for the New Learning, gathered to himself a number of humanist scholars. At Cambridge, he helped to continue the humanist tradition by supporting Thomas Becon and John Ponet in their residency. Perhaps under his auspices, Morison and Starkey deeply influenced the next generation of humanists through their relationships with Roger Ascham and John Cheke.[15] Under Queen Catherine Parr's direction and leadership, the court school for the children of the royal household was established, with humanists Richard Coxe, Cheke, and William Grindal, a student of Ascham's, as tutors. As we will see in more detail later in this chapter, this group undertook as one of its projects the translation of Erasmus' *Paraphrases* which was to be an important part of Cranmer's program of reform for the church under Edward VI.

With these events in the background, it becomes clear that the accession of Edward VI in 1547, especially under the Protector-

Godly and Fruitful Lessons

ship of Somerset, presented to the English humanist community an opportunity unequalled even by Henry's earlier break with Rome to move forward toward full realization of their program for reforming England into the true Christian commonwealth. The intervening years had seen the development of humanist ideas from general statements of belief in the efficacy of education for improving the moral character of personal action to a major and fully articulated vision of what the education of all people into such a Christian life could mean for the whole of society. Also developed had been a humanist methodology, from the initial efforts of Erasmus and More to explore the efficacy of rhetorical techniques to move men and women to action through imitation of ideals and examination of realities toward a full set of programs to present models for imitation through rhetorical persuasion to the entire nation. Since everything was now in place, Cranmer was able to move with remarkable speed once the death of Henry cleared the way.

"GOD'S TRUE WORD, SETTING FORTH HIS GLORY":
The English Bible

Of the three documents in Cranmer's reform program which we consider in this chapter, the Great Bible will receive the most cursory attention, since its contents are the best known, and its story is the most carefully documented. Nevertheless, a few points are well worth making. First of all, a reform program proceeding out of Erasmus' theology of language would certainly have a vernacular Bible at its center. Erasmus himself argued that the Gospels and Epistles of Paul ought to be in the common tongue, so that "the farm worker might sing parts of them at the plough, that the weaver might hum them at the shuttle, and that the traveller might beguile the weariness of the way by reciting them."[1] If Christ is incarnate in the text of the New Testament, if Scripture is the norm for human discourse, and if human speech in imitation of divine speech reforms society, then the text of

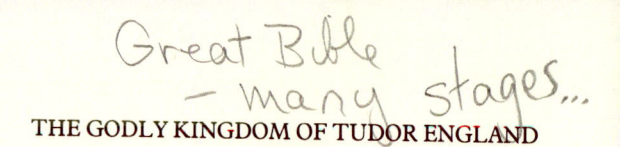

Scripture must be in the hands of all. And so it was, from 1539, when the Bible that became known as the "great" Bible, because it was "of the largest volume in Englishe," was published and authorized for reading in all English churches.

The second point that bears making is that the actual text published in 1539 was not a fresh translation, but a revision of an earlier text, which itself already had a long and somewhat checkered history. We will review that history in a moment, but what will be of significance are the changes which the contents of this translation underwent on the way from its inception as a translation intended for private distribution to its final use as a translation intended for public use with official authorization. These changes do not affect the actual text of the translation so much as they do the accompanying apparatus of commentary and explanation. What we will notice is that the original editions of this translation came with commentary of a decidedly partisan nature, which was, for the most part, eliminated before the translation achieved official status.

The story of the Great Bible begins in 1516,[2] when William Tyndale, having achieved the degree of Master of Arts at Oxford, moved to Cambridge, where the study of Greek was more advanced than it was at Tyndale's *alma mater*. Erasmus himself had been professor of Greek at Cambridge from 1511-15; while there, he had done much of the work for his Greek New Testament, which was first published in 1516, along with his Latin translation of the Greek text, with its famous use of *sermo* for *verbum* in the translation of John I:i. After six years of absorbing an advanced knowledge of Greek at Cambridge, Tyndale moved, in 1522, to Little Sodbury in Gloucestershire, where he became tutor to the children of Sir John Walsh. While there, Tyndale translated Erasmus' *Enchiridion*, with its stress on the centrality of the New Testament for the Christian life, and conceived for himself the task of preparing a vernacular text. When he found no support for his work at home, he set off for the continent in 1524 and completed his translation by August of 1525. After some difficulty in securing a printer, Tyndale finally saw his English New Testament through the press in Worms toward the

Godly and Fruitful Lessons

end of February, 1526.
 Two points must be made about this text. First, it was based on Erasmus' edition of the New Testament in Greek. Second, the ordering of the books, as well as a number of the marginal comments, indicates that Tyndale was also influenced, in his reading of the text, by the German edition of the New Testament published in 1522 by Martin Luther. Although Tyndale toned down many of Luther's more polemical annotations, the reading of many points in the commentary on the text clearly reflects a Lutheran cast to Tyndale's own theology. It is this commentary, with its Lutheran tendencies, which gradually came to be omitted as the Tyndale text moved toward inclusion in the Great Bible, leaving behind the essentially Erasmian text of the New Testament, made over into English.
 Tyndale's translation was, initially, opposed in England, at least in official circles. Cuthbert Tunstall, bishop of London, had burned as many copies as he could find: owners were ordered to hand them over on pain of excommunication or worse. The appearance of Tyndale's English New Testament in England sparked the well-known controversy between Thomas More and Tyndale. In the midst of all these controversies, Tyndale turned to the Old Testament, and prepared translations of the Pentateuch, published in 1530, and Jonah, published in 1531. Translations of the historical books of the Old Testament, from Joshua to 2 Chronicles, were also prepared by Tyndale, but were not published until they were included in the so-called "Matthew's Bible" of 1537.
 Tyndale published revisions of his New Testament in 1534 and 1535; he also translated those Old Testament passages appointed to be read as "Epistles" on certain Holy Days, according to the Sarum calendar, which were included with his revised edition of the New Testament, published in 1534. The next major step forward toward the Great Bible, however, was the work of Myles Coverdale, who finally produced a complete translation of the Bible into English in 1535. Coverdale was not the scholar of biblical languages that Tyndale was; so, for the parts of the Bible that Tyndale had not translated, Coverdale was dependent on the

Vulgate and other Latin versions, as well as Luther's German version for the text of his translation. It might be worthwhile to point out that Coverdale's translation was the first to group the books of the Old Testament included in the Septuagint text, but not included in the Hebrew Bible, in a separate grouping as an appendix to the Old Testament, a practice followed by Anglican Bibles to this day.

The next step was the production of what is called "Matthew's Bible," in 1537. This text, a combination of all of Tyndale's translations of the Old Testament, Coverdale's translations of the Old Testament where Tyndale's were lacking, and Tyndale's New Testament, was the work of one John Rogers, a former assistant of Tyndale's. Cranmer had, from the mid-1530's, sought a translation of the Bible into English to serve as an official Bible for the Church of England; to speed this process along, he secured royal authority for Matthew's Bible and for the 1537 revision of Coverdale's Bible. Finally, Coverdale completed a revision of the Matthew's Bible, which was published with royal authority in April of 1539. In 1540, a second edition was printed, containing revisions by Coverdale, notably in the poetic passages in the Old Testament, and a preface by the Archbishop himself; at the foot of the title-page there appeared this simple phrase: "This is the Byble apoynted to the use of the churches." Thus, the Great Bible had finally made its appearance. Cranmer's Preface echoes Erasmus' plea that "the farm worker might sing parts...at the plough, that the weaver might hum them at the shuttle":

> Here may all manner of persons, men, women, young, old, learned, unlearned, rich, poor, priests, laymen, lords, ladies, officers, tenants, and mean men, virgins, wives, widows, lawyers, merchants, artificers, husbandmen, and all manner of persons, of what estate or condition soever they be, may in THIS BOOK learn all things, that they ought to believe, what they ought to do, and what they should not do, as well concerning Almighty God, as also concerning themselves, and all other.[3]

In this context, Cranmer's comments suggest he saw this official

Godly and Fruitful Lessons

document as achieving one of the goals of Erasmus' program of imitation of divine discourse. The fact that the official publication of Tyndale's translation of Erasmus' Greek New Testament retained its dependence on Erasmus' text, while leaving behind Tyndale's own theological leanings in the omitted marginalia, suggests the importance of Erasmus' philological theology for Cranmer's own theological aims. This conclusion is strengthened by the fact that when Cranmer was able to achieve the full reform program he desired under Edward VI, he had reprinted the 1540 text of the Great Bible. When, at the same time, he desired to include a commentary on the New Testament, and make it an official commentary by insisting that every parish church in England have and use a copy, he chose an English translation of Erasmus' *Paraphrases,* rather than any commentary out of Germany, Switzerland, or Geneva.

"THE FRUITION OF HONEST AND GODLY STUDIES":
Erasmus' *Paraphrases*

The Great Bible had been a part of Cromwell's reformation; to it, Cranmer began his pioneering efforts to complete the humanist program by adding the *Paraphrases* and the *Book of Homilies* as significant interpretations of the Bible and by giving the full weight of royal and ecclesiastical authority to the concept of the religious life they embody. The purpose of authorizing use of the *Paraphrases* was to provide a standard interpretive guide to the New Testament for both clergy and laity. Through commanding use of the *Paraphrases,* Cranmer sought to bring the whole nation of England to understand the New Testament as Erasmus read it.

For this reason, a brief description of Erasmus' approach to the Scripture is in order. The unifying theme of Erasmus' Christian humanism seems clearly to have been his *philosophia Christi*. This perspective helps to locate Erasmus' biblical scholarship at the center of his work and to unite it with his devotional and satiric writings. It is the Christ, found through study of the New Testa-

The paraphrase of Erasmus vpon

The texte. Judge not, and ye shal not bee iudged: condemne not, and ye shall not bee condemned: forgeue, and you shalbee forgeuen: giue and it shalbee geuen vnto you, good measure and preßid downe, and shaken together, and runing ouer, shall men geue into your bosomes. For with the same measure that ye meate withall, shall other men meate to you agayne.

Thys also forsoothe that foloweth is a poynte of christian myldenesse, and also of plainnesse vncounterfeict, that ye enterprete and construe in the better parte, all the sayinges and doynges of your neighboure, as many as maye bee doubtefull of what minde they are dooen. For an herte that is pure from all corruption, is alwayes more enclined to thinke the best, then to mistrust or deme euill. As for in manifeste naughtye thynges (of whiche sorte are these, slaunderous backebiting, filthye talke of ribauldie, open robberie, and aduoutrie, it shalbe of youre goodnesse to remedie and cure the faultes as muche as in you doeth lye: but the mennes selfes neyther to hate, ne to take vengeaunce on them. Judge ye therefore no man: so shall it come to passe, that ye shall not agayne bee iudged youreselues. Condemne ye no man: so shal it come to passe, that ye shall not agayne on youre owne partes bee condemned. Forgeue ye in case any offence or trespace hath bene doen agaynst you: and God shall agayne on hys partie forgeue your sinnes vnto you.

Geue and it shalbe geuen vnto you Bee ye liberall and beneficiall towardes youre neyghbour, and the good turne that ye dooe, shall returne to you agayne with a bauntage and encrease. For there shal be poured in your lappes backe agayne a good measure, a measure brimfull, a measure turned and shaken together euery where, that all the lappe maye be full, and no corner thereof emptie or voyde, and a measure that shall runne ouer the sides for fulnesse, although no recompence at all of the good turne that ye haue doen, shal returne to you agayn at the handes of men.

For with the same measure, &c. For after the selfesame measure with the whiche ye shall haue measured your liberalitie towardes your neighboure, after the same measure shal the reward be returned home to you agayn at Goddes hande. If ye haue bene pynching & niggishe towardes your neyghboure, of the same sorte shall ye feele youre rewarde agayn to bee.

The texte. And he putte foorth a similitude vnto them. Can the blinde lede the blynde? doe they not bothe falle into the dicke? The disciple is not aboue hys maister, euerie man shall be perfeicte, euen as his maister is. Why seest thou a mote in thy brothers iye, but considerest not the beame that is in thyne owne iye: Either how canst thou saie to thy brother: Brother let me pull out the mote that is in thyne iye, whan thou seest not the beame that is in thine owne iye? Thou hypocrite, caste out the beame that is in thyne owne iye first, then shalt thou see perfeictly to pull out the mote that is in thy brothers iye.

And to the ende that the Lorde Jesus woulde the better emprieute the premisses in the heartes of his disciples, he added moreouer this similitude or parable. Can a blynde manne bee guyde to an other that is blynde? That if he assaye the mattier, dooeth it not come to passe that bothe fall into the pitte? Requisyte it is that he bee pure hymselfe from all manyer cryme, whiche will take vpon hym to leade an other the righte waye of innocencie. How shall one teache an other man what is to bee dooen, if himselfe be faste entangled in errour, and bee clene out of the waye? But it is an harde thyng (ye will saye) throughlye to endure the obstynate malice of some persones. Why are ye agrieued to endure, that I my selfe dooe endure? Is it reason that the dyscyples state or case bee better then the state of hys mayster? He shall bee in perfeicte

A page from Erasmus' *Paraphrases Upon the New Testament* (1548) concerning Luke 6:37-42.

ment, who is to be "embraced... in the innermost feelings of [the] heart and... emulated by... pious deeds." As we have noted, for Erasmus it is only through imitation of Christ that one is truly Christian, regardless of dogmatic definitions and traditional interpretations. This view of the essence of Christianity put Erasmus at once in opposition to both scholastic theology, with its interest in precise definition of the faith, and medieval piety, with its emphasis on contemplative devotion. Faith in the Christ of the Gospels, culminating in active charity through loving one's neighbor, is the distinctive mark of Erasmian efforts at religious reform. In this light, the *Paraphrases* on the New Testament are a logical outgrowth of his basic concern to imitate Christ through teaching by bringing the image of the biblical Christ to the attention of all men and women.

Erasmus' Greek New Testament was published in 1516; two years later, Erasmus stressed in his dedication of the *Enchiridion militis Christiani* the need for a layman's guide to the Scriptures. Devereux argues convincingly that the *Paraphrases* represent Erasmus' own response to this need.[1] Significantly, they were prepared and published (1517-24) during the same period that Erasmus was at work on two revised editions of the Greek and Latin New Testaments (1519, 1522), and a Latin commentary on his work (1520).[2] Thus, the *Paraphrases* are clearly the product of the most intense period of biblical scholarship in Erasmus' career; as an outgrowth of that scholarship, they represent one concrete attempt to link that scholarship, through words, to the active practice of the imitation of Christ.

Erasmus' interest in Scripture was inspired by his belief that reform in the church was possible only through return to the original sources of Christianity. Erasmus' biblical scholarship C. A. L. Jarrott calls a "combination of philological criticism with a religious purpose,"[3] in that its goal was not only to establish an accurate text but also to explain it in such a way that the Christ of the apostles and evangelists might be heard clearly and plainly. Erasmus' annotations in his textual notes sometimes extend beyond mere explanation of difficult passages and take on the character of full-fledged commentaries. At these points, Erasmus rejects the traditional medieval "four senses" of Scripture in favor of attention to the "spiritual sense," the practical message of Christ, closely related to the grammatical sense of the passage.

This emphasis suggests the importance of Erasmus' work for Cranmer and the English reformers. The various Paraphrases represent, in light of their content and their close chronological link to Erasmus' edition of the New Testament, a more fully developed and extensive use of this approach to Scripture, which Jarrott terms "characteristic of humanistic exegesis." One of the chief interests of Erasmus' editorial work with the New Testament is in those controversial aspects of the text in which certain interpretations had come to have special doctrinal significance. Jarrott points, as an example, to his exploration of the notion of penance in the context of commentary on John the Baptist's injunction, "Repent ye of your former lyfe. For the kingdome of heaven is at hande" (Matthew 3:1-2).[4] Jarrott notes Erasmus' dissatisfaction with the Vulgate *poenitentiam agite,* and his concern to stress that what is meant in the original suggests an internal change of heart, or mind, rather than the medieval conception of penance as an external act of painful contrition. Such an interpretation is emphasized more fully in Erasmus' paraphrase of this section of Matthew. The purpose of John's mission is said to be "to prepare mennes myndes that they myght be the more able to recyve the benfyte that should furthwith ensue."[5] Man's state is of "the filthines of the mindes"; to correct it a man should "knowledgeth his disease and hateth it." The *Paraphrases* have been called "the Gospel according to St. Erasmus";[6] this is certainly true to the extent that they provide more extensive examples of Erasmus' exegetical method in practice.

Roland Bainton has provided a convenient summary of various techniques used by Erasmus in these expanded commentaries.[7] One is simple elaboration of the biblical details, often with the addition of lively judgments about what is going on. In his commentary on Luke's account of the sick man let down through the roof (Luke 5:19-20), Erasmus' imaginative response to the situation is evident:

Godly and Fruitful Lessons

> Therefore marke me nowe, what a bolde and aventurous parte these carryers of the sicke man plaied.... Up thei gotte their heavie carriage to the house roufe in the outside, and the tilyng pulled awaie, thei leat down the sicke man with chordes, as it had been in at a wyndoore,... directly before the feete of Jesus. What a more shamelesse or sawcie pranke coulde there bee, then to take down the tylyng of an other mannes house, and to tumble in suche a lothely syghte before suche a presence to beholde it?... And what dooeth the moste jentil and mylde physician therewhyle? He casteth not them in the teeth with their shamelesse facion and their importunitee, he maketh no railyng nor bittur chyding that his preachyng was interrupted with a sight muche to bee lothed and abhored. The bearers of the sicke bodye lookyng down from the house toppe asked nothyng of hym, the man selfe that had the paulsey, asked nothyng neither, from whom the great disease had taken awaie the use of his toungue also. And yet all the more did he speake to this merciful physician in that he could not speake at all.... Jesus therefore whan he had thoroughly perceived and seen their woondrefull assiaunce in hym, did accomplishe more unto theim, then thei looked for (sig. ² K3ᵛ).

In addition to this expansion of details, there is also frequently an exploration of the psychological states of biblical characters. Bainton points to Erasmus' discussions of Mary and Martha; another example is the response of the Sanhedrin to the preaching of Peter and John (Acts 4:13-17):

> Whan Peter had spoken these wordes as many as were in that counsel, beholding bothe in Peter and John, free courage and stedfastnes of mynde, whiche appered in their very countenaunce: and perceyving also, that they wer of the comens, men unlearned, wondered greatly, wherupon they should beare themselves so bolde, howe they came by suche eloquence, and so perfit understanding of the prophetes. In conclusion, they came into remembraunce of them, how they had kept cumpany with Jesus, whome they them selfes knewe certaynly to be slayne of envye. They were in a great perplexitie, by reason that they, being of the base sorte of men, and unlearned, were so bold spirited, and so free of tong and lyberall, who neyther for the deadly paynes whiche their maister suffred, neyther for the honour and aucthoritie of so famous assembly, were troubled any thing at all in mynde (sig. ³ C4ᵛ).

..., Paraphrases ...

Bainton also points to Erasmus' interpretations of biblical material in a fashion which Jarrott calls "spiritual," and which Bainton relates to traditional allegorical or typological techniques of exegesis. In such passages, Erasmus relates biblical detail to the larger issues of the Gospel message, or to the present-day significance of such details. The essence of this technique, in Bainton's words, is that "the corporeal always typifies the spiritual." Thus, Jesus' delay of four days in raising Lazarus from the dead signifies that the resurrection of the soul is frequently a lengthy process. In this light, the loaves and fishes' miracle (Mark 6:30-44) suggests the bread of the Gospel, which has the power to take whatever a man has and use it for the glory of God:

> By thys myracle Jesus bothe prescrybed unto hys dysciples a fourme or rule howe to feede a multitude with the foode of the Gospell and also pulled oute of their myndes all pensyve carefulnesse to provide for corporal sustenaunce. Therfore whosoever thou be that arte a Bishop, Curate or pastour of Christes flocke, thynke not thus with thy selfe: I am a Doctoure of divinitie: I am an excellent cunnyng expounder of holye scripture. I have great store of learning wherwith to enstruct the people and may take inough out of my riche storehouse stuffed with cunning to feed them with all, be they never so hungry. Yea rather loke, and acknowledge howe small store of vitalyles thou hast at home, for the whiche, what so ever it be, thou arte a debtoure unto the Lorde. But bryng such store as thou haste unto the handes of Jesu. Desire hym to vouchesafe to handell, and breake it. That done, what he hathe delyvered thee, the same dooe thou... minister unto the people as the Lordes meate, and not thyne... not trustyng to thyne owne strength: and so in conclusion shal it be a very evangelike banket (sig. Gg⁶).

Often the two techniques of amplification of detail and "spiritual" reading are combined, as when Erasmus comments on the blind man partially restored to sight (Mark 8:24):

> They that have not yet perfitely receyved the lyght of the Gospel, whatsoever they see in this worlde, seemeth muche greater then it is in dede. Thei see a ryche man, he semeth a plane tree. They see

Godly and Fruitful Lessons 79

> an heade officer or a prince: they thinke they see an Apple tree, or a Cypresse tree. They see a stoicke philosopher, with a great beard, or a Pharisey trimmed with brode hemmes and phylacteries: they believe he is a figge tree. Now yf their iyes were clensed, and thinges would shewe and appeare unto them in their propre likenes, and as they be in dede, then should they perceive what maner of trifles and vanities suche thynges were, as semeth so great unto him whiche is halfe blynd (sig. Ii4^v-Ii5).

In light of Erasmus' desire to present the philosophy of Christ to people of his day through calling them back to its Gospel sources, the *Paraphrases* are best seen as a logical extension of the enterprise which produced his Greek New Testament. As Etienne Gilson has reminded us, Erasmus' New Testament is primarily a work uniting theology with philology, in which Erasmus sought to restore Christian thought "to a genuinely patristic type of sacred learning."[8] His annotations are an integral part of that work, for they make explicit the presuppositions of translation. The *Paraphrases,* seen as extensions of these annotations, are thus fuller statements of Erasmus' understanding of his text.

The earliest English versions of the *Paraphrases* were of the Epistles to Jude and Titus, prepared early in the 1530's as part of the humanists' efforts to popularize Erasmus' writings under the patronage of Cromwell.[9] For our purposes, however, the significant translations are those of the Gospels and Acts, carried out late in the reign of Henry VIII under the patronage of Queen Catherine Parr and published at Cranmer's direction in 1548. While the degree of Catherine's active commitment to the cause of reformation before her marriage to Henry is a controversial issue,[10] it is clear that she provided an important source of patronage for humanists during the period between the fall of Cromwell and the accession of Edward VI. Much of this patronage centered on the royal nursery and school, which, as we have already noted, she set about reorganizing immediately upon her marriage to the king. An educational establishment for certain of the nobility as well as the royal family, the royal school, staffed with such proponents of the New Learning as John

Cheke, Thomas Sternhold, Richard Coxe, and Roger Ascham's pupil William Grindal, took its direction and spirit from the personal involvement of the queen herself. Her learned pietism, as McConica puts it,[11] contributed to her ability to reunite the royal children, so bitterly divided by their father's changes in policy, in a period of domestic harmony almost unique in Henry's reign.

If her patronage was her greatest contribution to the continuity of English humanism, then the translation of the *Paraphrases* on the Gospels and Acts is the most significant result of her efforts. She seems to have set about the preparation of it soon after her marriage. Strype, in his *Ecclesiastical Memorials*, suggests that she was the translator of Matthew; this would seem to be disputed by Udall's statement in his dedication of Acts to her that he edited the translations of Matthew and Acts but not John because he knew the translators of that text. What *is* clear is that Catherine knew a number of the works of Erasmus.[12] Her call for a translation of the *Paraphrases* must have gone out soon after her marriage; most of the work was done on the Gospels and Acts by 1545, within two years of that date. Her special concern seems to have been with only this section of Erasmus' larger work; although her patronage is sometimes loosely extended to include the volume containing the Epistles, the best evidence is that she had nothing to do with it.[13]

At the outset, the work lacked a general editor. Each of the Paraphrases was prepared by a different translator, who turned his work over to Catherine either in response to her request or in the hope of her patronage. Four of these translators are known, while the translators of Matthew and Acts remain anonymous. One of the most interesting aspects of this translation is that the basic work on the Gospel of John was prepared by the Princess Mary, at Catherine's direct invitation.[14] This effort at English translation by the woman who was later to work so hard at the suppression of the Englishness of the English Church is one of the ironies of history; it is striking testimony both to the conciliatory power of Queen Catherine and to the more ambiguous state of religious affairs in the reign of Henry VIII.

Mary became ill before finishing her section; the Gospel of

John was completed by Frances Malet, her chaplain. The Gospel of St. Mark was translated by Thomas Key, a "Registrary of Oxford," at the suggestion of Dr. Owen, Henry's physician.[15] He is also responsible for the Preface to his translation, the only one of the five Prefaces not by Nicholas Udall. Udall, more famous for his play *Ralph Roister Doister*, translated the Gospel of St. Luke, which he presented to Catherine on 30 September 1545.[16] Udall was then appointed general editor, with responsibility for "addyng, digestyng, and sortyng the texte with the paraphrase thoroughly perused, and conferryng the same with the Latine . . . to make the Englishe aunserable to the Latine book" (sig. ⁶₵2ᵛ). In this description of his editorial labors, given in his Preface to the Paraphrase of Acts, Udall is careful to qualify his role in the case of Mary Tudor's efforts: "In Jhon I have in manier dooen nothyng at al saving only placed the texte, and divided the paraphrase, because I knew the translatours thereof, with whose exquisite dooynges I might not without the cryme of great arrogancie and presumpcion bee buisie to entremedle." A clear case of sixteenth-century tact, Udall's comment indicates one of his qualifications for editorship of the *Paraphrases*.

Tact, however, was not his only qualification. Udall was, by this time, an experienced hand at translations of Erasmus. In 1542 he had prepared a translation of Books III and IV of the *Apophthegmata* of Erasmus in conjunction with Richard Grafton, the printer who had issued the first edition of the Great Bible in 1539. Devereux suggests that Udall and Grafton may have intended a series of translations of Erasmus' work for popular consumption;[17] at any rate, Udall was deeply interested in the publication of the *Paraphrases*. In his dedication of the Paraphrase on Luke to Queen Catherine, he expresses the hope that Henry "wil not suffer it to lye buiryed in silence, but will one daie, whan his godly wisedome shall so thinke expedient, cause the same paraphrase to bee published & set abrode in prient" (sig. ⁴₵3ᵛ).

The conservative reaction in the English Church after the fall of Cromwell, which at its high point threatened the queen herself, prevented any such publication during the closing years of Henry's reign. When printing finally took place in 1548, during the second year of the reign of Edward VI, the hand of Udall was clearly present throughout. As his comments indicate, Udall checked and on occasion revised the various translations against the Latin original, and incorporated into the text the Gospels and Acts according to the Great Bible translation, an act which tied the *Paraphrases* volume closely to the central document in Cranmer's reform program. He also prepared a Dedication of the whole work to Edward, and Prefatory dedications to Catherine for each of the Paraphrases, except for Matthew, where the work was done by Thomas Key, translator of that Paraphrase.

Udall's comments in these Prefaces reflect the spirit and intention behind the preparation and publication of the English translation of the *Paraphrases*. In his Dedication to Edward, after thanking God for giving England so excellent a king, Udall praises him for making "so precious a treasour common to as many as maie take profite or fruicte thereby" (sig. 77 B3ᵛ). Nothing is better for the commonwealth than such publication, "for what hath been or is in any common weale the foundacion of spredying abrode the knowlage of Goddes woorde, but onely the settyng foorth of the Bible with other good and godly traictises for the declaracion of the same?" In his Preface to the Reader, Udall makes clear the connection in his mind between the good of the commonwealth on the one hand, and the writings of Erasmus on the other: "whosoever is in his herte a favourer of the trueth... hath no lesse cause but to embrace Erasmus, whose doctrine the most & best parte of all Christian Royalmes and universities hath evermore allowed & judged to be consonant to the trueth: & also is bound with immortall thankes to praie for the kynges moste excellent Majestee for this his moste gracious settyng foorth and publishyng this present weorke to the use of suche as have nede therof" (sig. 77 B7-B7ᵛ). "Such as have need," in Udall's terms include all men, but especially those clergy who lack training or books "for the enstruccion & teachyng of eche other in common."

In Udall's view, Erasmus takes his place among the great church fathers, for in the *Paraphrases*, he "bryngeth in and briefly conpriseth the pith of all the myndes & menynges of all the good Doctours of the churche, that ever wrote in justificacion of feith, in honouryng God onely, in repentaunce and puritie of a Christen mannes lyfe, in detestyng of imagerie and corrupte honouryng of Sainctes, in openyng and defacyng the tyrrannie, the blasphemie, Hypocrisie, the ambicion, the usurpacion of the See of Rome,...in teachyng obedience of the people towardes their rewlers and Governours,...and finally in all other poynctes or articles of our religion havyng now of late yeres been in controversie" (sig. $\pi\pi$ B3). No clearer statement of the central place of Erasmus in the thinking of the English reformers could be asked; at the same time it must be admitted that Udall passes over in silence Erasmus' dislike of threats to Christian unity.

Two final points must be made about Udall's editorial comments. First, he locates the importance of this translation within the humanist vision of an ordered society characterized by mutual interdependence and public service:

> The partes of devout readers are with immortal thankes to receive and take the fruicion of honeste and godly studies: the office of learned men is without depravyng or derogacion of other mennes diligence, and without any arrogancie on their owne behalfes, to emploie their good talentes to the publique behouf of their countrey, and to the fertheraunce of godly knowelage: the office of everie studious and diligent wryter is to have his yie directed to the publique utilitee onely, and than to think his upright well dooynges a sufficient price and rewarde of themselfes, and so without respect of any worldly rewarde or thanke to referre the fruicte and successe of his labours to God the mocioner, the autour, & the weorker of all goodnesse (sig. ₡1ᵛ).

If this is the ideal of Christian service, then Erasmus is a model for he "hath with comparable studie and travaill shewed himself a diligent labourer in Christes vineyearde." If Erasmus sought to call everyone to the imitation of Christ, so he too became a model to be imitated in the pursuit of that goal. The note Udall strikes here of the public consequences of such imitation reflects once again the distinctive aspect of English humanism, as will be made clear in the final section of this chapter.

Second, in his Preface to the Paraphrase of Luke, Udall develops an image of the importance of reading Scripture, and the part of Erasmus' *Paraphrases* in such reading, which is central to the humanist understanding of biblical translation. Perhaps taking his lead from Erasmus' own Preface to Luke, in which the Gospel is seen as medicine for the soul, or from Erasmus' *Enchiridion militis Christiani,* in which Scripture is seen as meat set before a hungry man,[18] Udall compares Scripture to "good and holsome foode," although it is occasionally "hard of digestion." Erasmus' *Paraphrases,* translated into English, however, are "everie English mans meate, though his stomake bee never so weake or tendre... liquide to renne pleasauntly in the mouth of any man whiche is not to muche infected with indurate blindenesse of herte, with malicious cancardenesse, and with to muche perverse a judgemente" (sig. ₵3). The centrality of this image is demonstrated by its use in Cranmer's Preface to the Great Bible, and in his homily, "A Fruictfull Exhortation, to the Readinge of Holy Scripture," from the *Book of Homilies* of 1547. In this latter case, the image is put eloquently: "as drinke is pleasaunt to them that be drie, and meate to them that be hungrie, so is the readinge, hearing, searchyng, and studying of holy scripture" (sig. leaf 1).

Thus it was that under the patronage of Queen Catherine Parr and the editorship of Nicholas Udall, the first English translation of Erasmus' *Paraphrases* on the Gospels and Acts took the form in which we have it. One purpose for this enterprise was surely to support the distinctively English direction of reformation. But to stop here is to ignore a larger purpose. If the heart of Erasmian humanism is to educate men and women in the imitation of Christ by bringing them into contact with the New Testament image of his nature, and the purpose of Erasmus in making these *Paraphrases* was to further that goal, then too the overriding aim of translation into English was to achieve the same ends within English society. While the nature of English humanism is not identical to that of Erasmus, it is surely an outgrowth of that aspect of Erasmian humanism which stresses the importance of education into the Christian life of active charity not just for individuals but for the society in which they live. Yet a conservative reaction meant the work could not be published in the reign of Henry VIII; ready for the press in 1545 or 1546, it had to await the return to power of men more hospitable to the ends for which it was prepared. When that time came, early in 1547, Cranmer thus ordered use of the Great Bible to make God's word available to all Englishmen in their own language, as well as to provide them with the fruits of humanist biblical scholarship. He also ordered use of Erasmus' *Paraphrases* to ensure that the heart of that Bible would be read as the great instigator of humanist reform had read it. Finally, he added a volume distinctively English, to provide instruction in the Tudor humanists' vision of the Christian life, a work to which we now turn.

"THE TRUE SETTING FORTH AND PURE DECLARING OF GOD'S WORD":

The Homilies

Of the three documents Cranmer ordered to be used in the parish churches of England through the Injunctions of 1547, the third volume, the *Book of Homilies,* is most fully a product of the new regime; that is to say, the evidence suggests it was not finished in the form that we have it until after the death of Henry VIII. Cranmer not only brought this collection of twelve sermons together with dispatch in the spring and early summer months of 1547, but indicated the importance for the book in his overall program of reform by arranging for its publication simultaneously with the Injunctions which commanded its use. Nevertheless, there are even here clear connections with the Henrican period. Cranmer had conceived and begun work on just such a collection of sermons as early as 1539. During the meetings of Convocation in 1542 and 1543, he organized the production of sermons for a book of homilies, for the purpose, he announced, of preventing ignorant preachers from spreading their errors.[1] On 27 January 1542, he called for this work to be prepared, and the matter was discussed at least once, at the

¶An homilie of christian loue, and Charitie.

Of all thinges that be good to be taught vnto Christen people, there is nothynge more necessary to be spoke of, and dayly called vpon, then charitie, aswel for that all manner of workes of righteousnes be conteined in it, as also that the decaye therof, is the ruyn of the worlde, the banishment of vertue, & the cause of al vice. And forsomuche as almost euery man maketh and frameth to himself charity after his owne appetyte, and howe detestable so euer hys lyfe be, bothe vnto god and man, yet he perswadeth with hym selfe styll that he hathe Charitie: Therfore you shal heare nowe a true and playne descripcion of Charitie, not of mennes ymaginacion, but of the very wordes & example of our sauiour Jesus Christe. In whiche description euery man, (as it were in a glasse) maye consyder him self, and see plainly without errour, whither he be in the true charitie or not.

Charitie is to loue god with al our harte, all our lyfe and al our powers & strength. With all our hart, that is to say, ỹ our hartes, mynde & studye be set to beleue his worde, to trust in hym, and to loue hym aboue all other thinges ỹ we loue best, in heauen or in yearth. With all our lyfe, that is to say, that our chiefe ioye, and delite be set vpon hym

What charitie is.

The loue of God.

A page from *Certaine Sermones* or *Homilies* (1547).

meeting of 3 April of that year.² During the meetings of Convocation, work must have progressed on the project, because the final entry of the Convocation records, dated 16 February 1543, contains this note: "there were produced the Homilies composed by certain prelates of divers matters: the which books were delivered to Mr. Hussey to be kept."³ Kept they were: nothing more was recorded of this project until the reign of Edward.

Although Convocation may well have been at the point of issuing this early collection of homilies, Henry VIII decided, perhaps at Gardiner's suggestion,⁴ to block publication of any work which might be in conflict with the King's Book, then also in preparation.⁵ Gardiner later recalled, in a letter to Cranmer, that Henry said he feared homilies devised by "divers men might injender diversity of understandings," a problem the King's Book avoided by sustaining one voice throughout.⁶ Such criticism might have influenced the final form of the *Book of Homilies*, which presents its sermons anonymously, with no indication that they are the work of more than one man.

Any direct relationship between the "books delivered to Mr. Hussey" in 1543 and the *Book of Homilies* of 1547 is impossible to mark precisely, since no copy of the 1543 material is known to exist. Some observations are possible, however, on the basis of other evidence. It is clear that Thomas Cranmer was the motivating figure behind both efforts to produce a book of homilies. On each occasion, his stated purpose carried the same educational intent. In 1542, he proposed the work as a curb on the influence of ignorant preachers. In the Injunctions of 1547, he stated his belief that as a result of ignorant preachers, "the people continue in ignoraunce and blindenes," thus he was requiring the reading of homilies.⁷ At the same time, however, the two collections of sermons were not identical, since Cranmer made personal appeals to Tunstall, Gardiner, and others for additional sermons in the spring and early summer of 1547.⁸

At any rate, the final product of Cranmer's labors for a standard homiletic anthology is a collection of twelve sermons which were by royal and ecclesiastical decree read over and over "in suche ordre as they stand in the boke" in every parish church in

England during most of the reign of Edward VI. After the Great Bible and the *Paraphrases,* the *Book of Homilies* must be seen as the major document in Cranmer's initial reform program, a concrete attempt to put humanist educational theories into actual practice on a national scale. It embodies the vision developed by English humanists during the reign of Henry VIII concerning the relationships between church and society, between humanity and the world order, which should exist in an ideal Christian commonwealth. At the same time, it sets forth this vision in such a way that its hearers are intended to be moved to emulate its images of the ideal society through action aimed at transforming the actual nation into a concrete manifestation of those images. By requiring the reading of the *Book of Homilies,* Cranmer and his supporters sought nothing less than the realization of the ideal Christian society in England.

The *Book of Homilies* begins with a preface, which is a short address by "The Kynges most excellent Majestie, by the prudent advise of hys moste deere beloved uncle" (sig. +2). While it is unlikely that Edward VI actually wrote this preface, its inclusion is crucial for the *Book of Homilies* because it gives royal authority to the work it introduces. Otherwise, the book had no authority at all, except that of Cranmer himself. Unlike the religious documents of the reign of Henry VIII, and especially the King's Book, which the *Book of Homilies* legally replaced late in 1547, the *Book of Homilies* did not receive approval by Convocation or by Parliament before the Crown required its use in every parish in the land. Instead, it was an act of the king, in consort with his Archbishop, which closed dramatically one of the last remaining divisions between church and Crown. While Henry may always have procured what he wanted in religious affairs, he was careful to go through the motions of having religious pronouncements approved by the church assembled in Convocation. With the *Book of Homilies,* the monarch simply assumed the role of chief agent for regulating and reforming church affairs. In this one act, the twin pyramids of medieval society, the two parallel hierarchies of church and state, became, openly, one hierarchy.

The *Book of Homilies,* is therefore, both a political and a religious document. It represents a move toward greater reform in the church, and at the same time a greater consolidation of power in royal hands. It suggests the profound connections which its framers saw between church and state: on the one hand, the political meaning of religious change; and on the other, the religious meaning of power. This thoroughgoing link between the two is presented by the Preface to the *Book of Homilies* in its argument for issuing these sermons. Two reasons are given: first, "manyfolde enormities, whiche...have crepte into hys graces Realme, through the false usurped power of the bishop of Rome, and the ungodlie doctrine of his adherents," bringing about a "great decaye of Christen religion," and, second, "the ernest and fervent desire, of [Edward's] deerly beloved sujects, to be delivered from al errors and supersticion, and to be truly and faithfully instructed in the very worde of GOD," which is "that lively foode of mans soule" (sig. +2). These reasons are strongly religious reasons, but the Preface proceeds to give them equally strong political dimensions. What is sought by the issuers of the *Book of Homilies* is that all English people "maye learne unfaynedly...to honor GOD, and to serve their Kynge, with all humilitie and subjeccion, and godly and honestly, to behave them selfes towarde all men" (sig. +2-+2ᵛ). Giving honor to God and service to the king are thus closely linked. They are so closely joined that the Preface calls everyone to perform both duties in the same way, "with all humilitie and subjection." To achieve these goals, "the next moste redy waye" is as follows:

> to expell and avoyde, as well all corrupte vicious, and ungodly livinge, as also erronious doctrine, tendinge to supersticion and Idolatry, and clerely to put awaye all contencion, whiche hath heretofore rysen throught diversitie of preachinge, is the true setting furthe, and pure declaringe of GODS woorde, whiche is the principall guyde and leader unto all godlynes and vertue (sig. +2ᵛ).

What is sought is for men and women to live better, but also that they "put awaye all contencion." Improvement in the religious lives of all people has clear political consequences; it is defined as meaning an end to disruption in society. The religious basis of political disruption is also recognized; blame for this disorder is placed on "diversitie of preachinge." What is important to grasp here is not just that the *Book of Homilies* is a religious work with political consequences, but that those responsible for this work saw the active political life of their society to be identical with the religious life of that society.

The *Book of Homilies* is presented as a means of countering "diversitie of preachinge." It provides all clergymen "of what learninge soever they be" with "some godly and fruictfull lessons in a redynes to reade and declare unto their parishyoners, for their edifiynge, instruccion, and comforte," which will "move the people to honor and worshippe almightie GOD, and diligently to serve hym, every one accordynge to their degree, state, and vocacion." In its role as a religious and political work, the *Book of Homilies* is a means of education through the rhetorical use of words, which seeks to bring people to act in certain ways toward God. But this honor, worship, and service of God does not take place in a vacuum. Instead, it is seen in the context of a hierarchy, a society in which each person has a place and should act in a manner appropriate to it. The sermons in the *Book of Homilies* are to be read "in such ordre as they stande in the boke":

> And when the foresaide boke of Homilies is redde over, the Kynges Majestis pleasure is, that the same be repeted, and redde agayn, in suche like sorte, as was before prescribed, unto such time, as his graces pleasure shal further be knowen, in this behalfe (sig. +3).

In these terms, therefore, the people of England were put to the rigorous discipline of the *Book of Homilies*.

I find this Preface suggestive of several conclusions about the intent of Thomas Cranmer and those who helped him prepare the *Book of Homilies*. First of all, this collection of sermons is not simply an unrelated assortment of moral lessons. Its contents are, quite specifically, to be read in order, "as they stande in the boke"; in some sense, they form a unit, a collection specifically arranged to move in a progression of argument from a beginning toward a particular end. Second, they emerge as a way to meet specific needs — the "decaye of religion" and the "desire of sujects to be delivered from al errors" — and to achieve specific goals — "to honor GOD, and to serve their kynge, and to behave them selfes" — by specific means — "the true setting furth of GODS woorde." The Preface also defines the ends of the work in terms of moving "the people to honor and worshippe almightie GOD, and diligently to serve hym." It describes what this means in terms of honoring God, serving the king "with all humilitie and subjeccion," and "godly and honestly, [behaving] them selfes towarde all men." What is being evoked here is that vision of the *respublica christiana,* the true Christian commonwealth, that humanist vision of national life, which goes beyond matters of religious ceremonial or devotional practice to embrace total reform of all aspects of human society.

The basis for the ideal Christian commonwealth which Cranmer sought by issuing the Homilies is thus what we have already termed the life of active charity in imitation of Christ which Erasmus called his *philosophia Christi.* In carrying out the program of social and religious reform outlined by Starkey, Cranmer organized the *Book of Homilies* around the Erasmian pattern of the Christian life, as set forth in the *Enchiridion militis Christiani.* The First Homily is Cranmer's "Fruictefull Exhortacion, to the Readinge of Holy Scripture," which calls for universal study of the Bible.[9] The Second Homily, Harpesfeld's "Of the Miserie of all Mankynde," describes the self-knowledge to be obtained from reading the Scriptures. The Third Homily, Cranmer's "Of the Salvacion of all Mankynde," declares that the Christian life begins in faith. The next two homilies, also by Cranmer, "Of the True and Lively Faithe" and "Of Good Workes," argue that the saving faith is a faith which reveals itself in deeds of active charity. The remaining seven homilies, including one each by Edmund Bonner, Thomas Becon, and Hugh Latimer, as well as four sermons of unknown authorship, describe specific works of charity which people should do, or evil deeds which they should avoid, in living the active Christian life. As in Erasmus' work, the life of active charity is affirmed and the passive devotional life of the medieval church is rejected. Each time the sermons in this collection are read "in suche ordre as they stande in the boke" the hearer is led step by step through instruction into the humanist paradigm of the Christian life.

At the same time the later sermons in the *Book of Homilies* demonstrate how English humanists developed the implications of Erasmus' *philosophia Christi* on the social as well as on the personal level. Thomas Starkey had enunciated these implications in his *Dialogue* by positing that pursuit of the active Christian life would result in an ideally ordered society in which each person contributed to the good of all by fulfilling the role assigned him by his place in the social hierarchy. This image of an ordered Christian society is constantly before us in the later sermons in the *Book of Homilies,* as various goods and ills are defined in social, rather than personal, terms. Edmund Bonner, bishop of London, argues in his homily "Of Christian Love and Charitie" that the nation is analogous to the human body, and must be treated for disease:

> charitie requireth [evil-doers] to be cut of from the body of the commen weale, lest they corrupt other good and honest personnes: lyke as a good surgyne cutteth awaye a putrified, and festred membre, for love he hath to the whole body, least it infecte other membres adjoyning to it (sig. F4^v).

The anonymous homily "Agaynst Swerynge and Perjury" indicates the importance of lawful oaths for the ordered society:

> By lawfull othes, mutuall societie, amitie, and good ordre is kept continually in all communalties, as borowghes, cyties, townes, and villages. And by lawfull othes, malefactours are serched oute, wrong doers are punisshed, and they whiche sustayne wronge, are restored to their right. Therfore lawfull swearyng can not be evel, whiche bryngeth unto us, so many godly, good, and necessarie commodities (sig. G3^v).

This vision of the ideal society is the goal of all the arguments presented in the *Book of Homilies*. It is the context for Cranmer's sermons on faith and works and the end toward which the Christian life of active charity, originating in faith, should move. The *Book of Homilies* is at once the fullest Tudor expression of the vision of a Christian commonwealth attainable through universal humanist education and the basic work in a program of universal education aimed at realizing this vision.

The *Book of Homilies* thus embodies what Starkey's work outlines, an extension of the ideas of Erasmus developed by early Tudor humanists, which includes a significant social function for the *philosophia Christi*. It seeks to realize this vision of an ideal Christian commonwealth through means also distinctively humanistic. At the heart of Erasmus' thought is the belief that men and women can be educated through imitation of models; the true Christian is "the man who has embraced Christ in the innermost feelings of his heart, and who emulates Him by his pious deeds." A similar faith in the power of imitation is reflected in the First Homily, which argues that Christian teaching proceeds through imitation of the Word, which has the power to transform its imitator. Cranmer says of the Bible:

> This worde, whosoever is diligent to reade, and in his harte to prynte that he readeth, the great affeccion to the transitorie thinges of this worlde, shalbe minished in him, and the great desire of heavenly thinges, (that be therin promised of God) shall encrease in hym.... For that thinge, which (by perpetuall use of reading of holy scripture, and diligent searching of the same) is depely prynted, and graven in the harte, at length turneth almoste into nature (sigs. leaf 2^v-leaf 3).

If Elyot's *Governour* and Ascham's *Scholemaster* are private "courtesy books" which seek to educate Christian princes through imitation, then the *Book of Homilies* is a national "courtesy book" which presents an image of a Christian society so that all Englishfolk could realize the Christian commonwealth by imitating it. By repeated readings of these sermons, the vision of that commonwealth was presented over and over again for imitation.

In fact, the homilists themselves followed the concept of imitation as they wrote the sermons in the *Book of Homilies*. As a work designed to educate, the *Book of Homilies* reflects Christian humanist beliefs about the language, style, and structure of didactic literature. A close look at this aspect of the Homilies not only reveals the pervasiveness of humanist influence at the middle of the sixteenth century; it also raises serious questions about the traditional evaluation of early Tudor literature. C. S. Lewis finds it "drab"; for him, the Prayer Book is the "one glory of the Drab Age; so glorious indeed that it would throw doubt on the justice of the epithet 'Drab' if we forget that it was principally a work of translation."[10] But the anonymous author of the Tenth Homily "On Good Ordre and Obedyence" has advanced in skill far beyond the prose efforts of English writers at the beginning of the century. The lines which open this sermon are the fullest statement in the *Book of Homilies* of the ordered Christian commonwealth in harmony with the divine order; they are among the finest examples of sixteenth-century prose:

> ALMIGHTY God hath created and appoynted all thinges, in heaven, earth, and waters, in a moste excellent and perfecte order. In heaven he hath appoynted, distincte orders and states of Archangelles and Angelles. In earth he hath assynged kynges, prynces, with other governours under them, all in good and necessary order. The water above is kepte, and rayneth doune in dewe tyme and season. The Sonne, Mone, Sterres, Raynebowe, Thundre, Lyghtnynge, cloudys, and al byrdes of the ayer, do kepe their ordre. The earth, trees, seedes, plantys, herbys, corne, grass and all maner of beastes, kepe theym in their order.

The macrocosm in its order embodies the divine will which is also reflected in the microcosm of the inner hierarchy of human anatomy and psychology. This divine ordering is both implicit in God's creation and necessary for its perpetuation:

> And man himselfe also, hath all his partes, bothe within and without, as soule, hart, mynde, memorie, understanding, reason, speache, withall and singular corporal membres of his body, in a profitable, necessary and pleasaunt order. Every degre of people,

in their vocation, calling, and office, hath appointed to them their duetie and order... and every one have nede of other, so that in all thinges, is to be lauded and praysed, the goodly order of God, without the which no house, no citie, no common wealth, can contynue and endure (sigs. N1-N1ᵛ).

No translation but instead a brilliant development of a medieval commonplace which describes the underlying order of the created universe and the interdependency of its different levels, this passage establishes the context for the argument of the sermon, that people should obey their superiors not simply because it is expedient or commanded of God, but because imitation of God's order as seen in the cosmos is the way to achieve a truly Christian commonwealth. At once eloquent and intelligible, this passage is typical of the style of the *Book of Homilies* in its plainness and clarity.

In using a plain style, the homilists followed humanist rhetorical theories which held that for didactic literature to write "plainly and nakedly after the common sort of men in a few words, then to overflowe wyth unnecessaire and superfluous eloquence"[11] was the appropriate means of expressing what was to be taught. In religious writing this was supported by the belief that the plain style of Christ's own speech, and of the Bible as a whole, served as the appropriate model for style as well as the source for content. Influenced by both these attitudes, the authors of the *Book of Homilies* rejected the ornate style characteristic of late medieval sermons; instead they worked to bring their use of language into harmony with the "simplicity of the Gospel."[12] Plainness and simplicity of style do not, however, necessitate uniformity or dullness; the sermons in the *Book of Homilies* exhibit a great variety and flexibility in the use of the plain style. On the one hand, there is the lofty eloquence of the opening lines of the Tenth Homily. Against this fine but restrained statement of the world order might be placed for contrast the brusquely vigorous and physical voice of Hugh Latimer in his homily "Against Strief and Contencion." In a typical passage choked with emotion, he laments the divisions produced by disharmony in the church:

Oh how the church is divided. Oh howe the cyties be cutte and mangled. Oh how the coote of Christ, that was without seame, is al to rent and torne. Oh body mistical of Christ, where is that holy and happy unitie, out of the which, whosoever is, he is not in Christ? If one membre be pulled from another, where is the body? If the bodye be drawn from the heade, where is the life of the body? (sig. S3).

These passages define the limits of restraint and emotion found in the style of the *Book of Homilies,* but they do not exhaust the possibilities within these limits, possibilities explored by the authors of the other homilies. W.G. Crane has pointed to the extensive use of comparisons in early sixteenth-century prose and has suggested that they are at the heart of rhetorical wit so praised by More and Erasmus.[13] Two passages from other homilies, both rich in comparisons, explore further possibilities within the plain style. The first, from Becon's "Agaynst Whoredome, and Adultery," has strident and insistent qualities:

the outragious seas of adultry, whoredome, fornicacion, and unclennes, have not onely braste in, but also overflowed, almost the whole worlde, unto the great dishonoure of God, the exceading infamie of the name of Christ, the notable decaye of true religion, and the utter destruccion of the publique wealth, and that so abundatlye, that through the customable use therof, this vice is growen into such an heyght, that in a maner, emonge many, it is coumpted no synne at all, but rather a pastime, a dalliaunce, and but a touche of yoghte, not rebuked, but winked at, not punished, but laughed at (sig. P2ᵛ).

The second, from the anonymous homily "Agaynst the Feare of Deathe," has a more peaceful and reassuring tone:

For now we be mortal, then we shalbe immortal, now infect with divers infirmities, then clerely voide of al mortal infirmities, now we be subject to all carnall desyres, then we shalbe al spiritual, desiring nothinge but Gods glory, and thinges eternall. Thus is this bodiely death, a doore, or entring unto lyfe, and therfore not so much dreadful, (if it be rightly consydered) as it is comfortable, not a mischief, but a remedy of all mischief, no enemy, but a frende, not a cruel tyraunt, but a gentle guyde, leadyng us not to mortalitie, but to immortalitie, not to sorowe and paine, but to joy and pleasure, and that to endure for ever (sigs. L1-L1ᵛ).

Such examples reveal the richness of the plain style found in the *Book of Homilies*. Its range includes restrained and formal eloquence and strident denunciation, fervent exhortation and tranquil reassurance. In the hands of Cranmer and his fellow homilists, the possibilities of an English plain style for didactic prose were fully explored.

The rhetorical structure of these homilies also accords with the precepts of humanist educational theory. To carry out their goal of moral education, Tudor humanists had studied classical manuals of rhetoric and prepared instruction books which repeat classical instructions for constructing an oration but surround these rules with distinctively humanist arguments for their use. Thomas Cranmer and his fellow homilists put into practice the prescriptions for form, or *dispositio*, of the classical oration as set forth by Cicero and Quintillian, and as taught in England by humanists from the time of More and Erasmus. If English churchmen needed any support in their choice, they had recourse to the authority of St. Augustine, who gave the aims of preaching as *"docere, delectare, et movere,"*[14] thus anticipating Christian humanists in borrowing from classical rhetoric to enrich the resources of Christian oratory.

Use of the classical oration as a model for sermon construction represents a rejection of the more elaborate so-called "modern" sermon form devised in the university schools of the late Middle Ages.[15] This general pattern of sermon construction with its sevenfold division into parts is followed in the sermons of the *Book of Homilies,* with one exception. The Second Homily "Of the Miserie of all Mankynde" by John Harpesfeld consists chiefly of an extensive compilation of biblical verses chosen to illustrate its main point, that a person should be humble rather than proud in his miserable state of sin. This homily shows the influence of the classical oration only in a striking "enteraunce," or opening statement of its theme, and in a final summary of its main points. Between these two passages are quoted many biblical texts, some of which describe humanity's sorry condition while others hold up biblical characters as models for people to imitate so that they will act in a properly humble fashion once they are aware of their sinfulness. Still others remind of God's mercy in sending Jesus Christ to make salvation possible. Mixed with these verses are summaries and exhortations employing vivid imagery:

> Wherefore good people, let us beware of suche hypocrisy, vainglory, and justifyng of our selfes. Let us look upon our fete, and then, doune pecockes fethers, doune proude harte, doune vile claye, frayle and britle vesseles. Of our selfes, wee be crabbe trees, that can bryng furth no apples. We be of our selfes, of such yearth, as can bryng furth, but weedes, nettles, brambles, briers, cocle and darnell (sig. two leaves 4).

This sermon departs from the "modern" sermon form of the Middle Ages, as well as from the classical form of an oration. J. W. Blench, in his study of the sixteenth-century sermon, identifies the structure of this sermon as an imitation of the "ancient" sermon form exhibited in the homilies of the patristic age.[16] In this case, Harpesfeld adhered to the concept of imitation, but chose a uniquely Christian form of ancient literature as his model. His sermon is little more than a collection of biblical *exempla*, presented so that his auditors could imitate them and thus behave with proper humility in response to the human condition of sinfulness.

The remaining sermons in the *Book of Homilies* follow, though not inflexibly, the rhetorical structure of the classical oration. While the First Homily, Cranmer's "A Fruictefull Exhortacion, to the Readinge of Holy Scripture," exhibits the full seven-part form, others modify or shape it freely to make a more forceful presentation of their subjects. Thus the "confutacion" of Bonner's homily "Of Christian Love and Charitie" is not a refutation of those who object to charity, but is instead a treatment of the question of possible conflicts between charity and the need for public justice. Cranmer's homily "Of Good Workes" uses this section to attack various forms of piety to which the Archbishop objected. In each case, the rhetorical form is modified to fit the needs of the argument, but the negative quality of this section of the classical oration is preserved. Hugh Latimer's "Against Strief and Contencion" is such a vigorous attack on religious disputes that it is almost all "confutacion." In addition, it uses biblical quotations so freely that it seems closer in many ways to the Second Homily and to the patristic sermon. Yet the sevenfold structure, though heavily adapted, is still clearly present.

The images used in the *Book of Homilies* reveal another way in which these sermon authors continued humanist rhetorical practice. Tudor humanists took from classical rhetoric not only its prescriptions for form, but also its instructions for ornamentation of a formal oration. Thomas Wilson stresses the importance of the "figure," or, "a certaine kinde, either of sentence, oration, or worde, used after some new or straunge wise, muche unlike to that, which men communely use to speak."[17] Wilson maintains the importance of using such figures: "By all whiche figures, everye Oration maye be muche beautified, and without the same, not one can attaine to be counted an Oratoure, thoughe his learninge otherwise be never so greate." The most important figure is the *trope*, which encompasses metaphors, circumlocution, similes, and other related techniques of imagery. Interest in this rhetorical device in the early sixteenth century gave rise to collections of similes and other *tropes* drawn from classical literature.[18] As a technique of style, such figures were of interest in that they increase the writer's or speaker's ability to move and delight, and thus augment his teaching skill. These homilies, appropriately, abound in such *tropes*, but in keeping with their authors' desire to have a plain, easily intelligible style, they make use of extremely commonplace, though vivid, language. Becon's homily "Agaynst Whoredome, and Adultery" is rich with strong figurative language:

> And surely, if we wolde weye the greatnes of this synne, and considre it in the right kinde, we shoulde fynde the synne of whoredom, to be that most fylthy lake, foule puddle, and stinkyng

synke, wherinto all kynds of synnes, and evils flow, whereaslo, they have their restinge place, and abydinge.... What synne or kynde of synne is it, that is not joyned with fornicacion and whoredome? It is a monstre of many heades (sigs. Q3ᵛ-Q4).

Hugh Latimer's sermon characterizes an objection to his argument against contention in equally vivid imagery:

But thei that be so full of stomacke, and sette so muche by themselfes, that thei maie not abide so muche as one evill worde to be spoken of theim, peradventure will saie: if I be evill reviled, shal I stand still like a goose, or a foole, with my finger in my mouth? Shal I be suche an idiot and diserde to suffre every man to speake upon me, what thei list, to raile what thei list, to spewe out all their venyme against me, at their pleasures? (sig. T1ᵛ).

Significantly, the *Book of Homilies* uses the Bible, rather than classical literature, as its chief source of figurative language. In the First Homily, Scripture is "heavenly meate of our soules," "a lighte lanterne to our fete," and "more sweter than hony or hony combe." In the homily "Of the True and Lively Faithe," also by Cranmer, good works are "as the light [which] can not be hid" (sig. A2ᵛ). He who has faith "is like a tree, set by the water syde, that spreadeth his rotes abrode toward the moysture." Christ went to his death, says Bonner in his homily "Of Christian Love and Charitie," "as a shepe that is led unto the shambles to be slayne, and as a lambe that is shorne of his flese" (sig. F2). A complete catalogue would be lengthy, but the significance is clear. Tropes are used in the *Book of Homilies* after the prescription of the classical model, to render the sermons more forceful and vivid, but always in keeping with the plain style of language to increase the clarity and immediacy of what is being said. The language of the *Book of Homilies,* like its teaching and examples of moral living, is grounded in biblical example.

To the framers of the *Book of Homilies,* their vision of an ordered society was in fact the goal of a Christian life; it was their understanding of what Christians should do to obey the will of God in order to achieve salvation. This vision, presented in the *Book of Homilies* to be imitated by those who heard it, was itself

Godly and Fruitful Lessons

an imitation of what its authors believed to be God's own ordering of his creation. These homilists visualized their society achieving an ordered hierarchy of charity and obedience, with the king as its earthly head, which would take its rightful place in the hierarchy of nature. Behind their call for England to realize this vision lay the urgency of obedience to God's will. In his homily, Hugh Latimer summarizes this vision, and at the same time expresses the urgency felt by him and his fellow homilists:

> We cannot be joynted to Christ our head, except we be glued with concord and charitie, one to another. For he that is not in this unitie, is not of the church of Christ, which is a congregacion or unitie together, and not a division (sig. S3).

Behind Latimer's comments lies the Pauline image of the church as the body of Christ. Latimer equates the "body politic" of England with the church and with the body of Christ. In his view, the needs for order and harmony in the church and in society are not separate issues, but one requirement, which carries with it all the weight of the issue of salvation. In other words, achieving individual salvation requires membership in the church, which is the body of Christ. Yet the church cannot be the body that has Christ as its head unless it is a unified body. At the same time, the political entity which is England is coterminous to the church. Therefore, political strife as well as religious dissension deprives the church of the Lordship of Christ. From this view, the Tudor passion for order in society takes on consequences that are not limited by the grave.

According to the homilists' theory of education, however, something could be done to restore this critical loss of unity in society if the right images of church and society could be put before the people for their imitation. To this end, they prepared the educational program called for in the Injunctions of 1547, in which the *Book of Homilies* plays a crucial part. We will now review the content of these homilies, to see what images Cranmer and his supporters chose to present through classical and patristic form and vernacular, forceful, plain style to educate the people of England in the Christian life.

The First Homily, "A Fruictefull Exhortacion, to the Readynge of Holy Scripture," makes clear that the *Book of Homilies* is a Bible-centered work, which draws its teachings and inspiration for its style from this central document of the Christian Church. Appropriately, Cranmer composed a sermon to open his collection which urges that "nothinge [is] either more necessarie or profitable, then the knowledge of holy scripture." The Bible contains "Gods true worde, setting furth hys glorie, and also mannes deutie" (sig. leaf 1). Scripture is described in gastronomic terms, as appropriate meat and drink for all Christians, "the heavenly meate of our soules" (sig. leaf 2), the difficult parts being "strong meate" (sig. leaf 5). They who read the Bible humbly and persistently will be turned into what they read about, will be empowered to understand it and to do what it says each person should do to obtain salvation:

> The wordes of holy scripture...have power to convert through Gods promise, and they be effectuall, through Gods assistence (sig. leaf 2^v).

The Christian life is, therefore, one of imitation of the moral examples given in Scripture. In addition, the words of Scripture have the power to enable men and women to carry out this imitation.

The Second Homily, by Harpesfeld, "Of the Miserie of all Mankynde," begins by identifying humanity's chief problem as the sin of pride. This, asserts Harpesfeld, is where human self-knowledge begins. His homily follows closely from the First Homily by making heavy use of scriptural quotations to illustrate its point. We know of human pride, says Harpesfeld, because "The holy Ghoste, in writinge the holy scripture, is in nothing more diligent, then to pull doune mans vainglory, and pride, which of all vices, is moste universally grafted in all mankinde, even from the first infeccion of our firste father Adam" (sig. 2 leaves). He then gives numerous examples, from both the Old and New Testaments, to illustrate this point, and to show appropriate responses of men and women to their knowledge of it.

Godly and Fruitful Lessons 103

> ALSO the holy patriarke Abraham, did wel remember this name and title, duste, earth, and asshes, appointed and assigned by God to al mankynde: and therefore he calleth him selfe by that name, when he maketh hys earnest prayer for Sodom and Gomore (sig. 2 leaves 1ᵛ).
>
> ....
>
> Sainct Paule in many places paynteth us out in our colours, callinge us the children of the wrathe of God, when we be borne: saiynge also, that we cannot thinke a good thoughte of our selfes, much lesse we can saye well or do well of our selfes (sig. 2 leaves 2ᵛ).
>
> ....
>
> Let none of us be ashamed, to saie with the holy saincte Peter, I am a synfull man (sig. 2 leaves 4ᵛ).

Self-knowledge begins when people acknowledge their sinfulness, and realize that by themselves they can do no good. Thus, men and women realize how dependent they are on God's mercy and forgiveness. This, says Cranmer in an editorial addition, is the subject of the next homily.

The Third Homily, "Of the Salvacion of all Mankynde," is the first of three by Archbishop Cranmer which move the argument through the difficult issues of faith and works. They also begin to expand the scope of concern expressed by these sermons. The First Homily stressed the importance of reading the Bible for each individual, while the Second Homily pointed out that each individual reader of Scripture would find that he was a sinner. The next three sermons describe what God and mankind, working together, can do about humanity's sin. In doing so, however, they point the individual sinner beyond himself, toward God and toward his neighbor. Thus, they open the way for considering the social implications of Christian living.

Cranmer's sermon on salvation deals with the acts of God for the salvation of mankind. This homily stresses that human works, without God, can do nothing to effect our justification. Rather, mankind is totally dependent on God's redeeming act in the life, death, and resurrection of Jesus Christ, which served as a ransom for everyone.

> Because al men be sinners, and offenders against God, and breakers of his lawe and commaundementes, therfore can no man by his awne actes, woorkes, and deedes (seme thei never so good) be justified, and made righteous before God: but every man of necessitie is constrained, to seke for another righteousnes, or justificacion, to be received at Goddes awne handes, that is to say, the remission, pardon, and forgevenesse of his synnes and trespasses, in suche things as he hath offended. And this justificacion or righteousnes, whiche we so receive by Goddes mercie, and Christes merites, embraced by faithe, is taken, accepted, and allowed of God, for our perfecte and full justificacion (sig. 3 leaves 3).

Cranmer argues that three things are involved in human justification: first, God's mercy and grace; second, Christ's satisfaction of God's justice in the offering of his body; and third, on humanity's part, a "true and lively faithe" (sig. 3 leaves 4ᵛ). This faith, which is also a gift of God, is the essential element which each person must contribute to his justification. Cranmer marshals quotations from SS. Paul, Hilary, Basil, and Ambrose to provide biblical and patristic support for his assertion that "if justice come of workes, then it cometh not of grace, and if it come of grace, then it cometh not of workes" (sig. 4 leaves 1ᵛ). Having made this claim, Cranmer then quickly rejects any suggestion that the faith which is required of us is ever present without good works, that "the said justifynge faith is alone in man, without true repentaunce, hope, charitie, dread and feare of GOD, at any tyme or ceason" (sig. 4 leaves 2ᵛ). Instead, the point of this argument is to stress human need for God, and God's great power and mercy toward all mankind. All people are called to recognize their true condition, in which none of their good acts, being imperfect, can help toward justification. Having understood this, men and women are called to "truely repent and convert unfaynedly to [Christ] agayne" (sig. 4 leaves 4).

> we putte oure faythe in Christ, that we be justified by hym onely, that we be justified by Goddes free mercie, and the merites of our saviour Christe onely, and by no vertue or good worke of our awne, that is in us, or that we can be able to have or to do for to deserve the same, Christe hymself onely, beyng the cause

Godly and Fruitful Lessons

meritorious thereof (sig. 4 leaves 4-4ᵛ).

Justification is a free and merciful act of God, made effective for an individual through recognizing his own insufficiency when totally on his own, through turning in trust and faith to God, and through giving all the glory for his justification to Jesus Christ.

Having elaborated this point, Cranmer then turns to a discussion of what duty mankind owes to God in return for his mercy. But this duty is more than just an adjunct or a product of faith. It is nothing less than the mark, the defining indication, of the "true and lively faithe" which is required for justification:

> For that faith, whiche bryngeth furth... either evill workes, or no good workes, is not a right, pure, and lively faith but a dedde, devellish, counterfaite, and fained faithe (sig. 5 leaves 1ᵛ).
> ....
> For the right and true Christian faithe is, not only to beleve that holy scripture, and al the foresaied articles of our faith are true, but also to have a sure trust and confidence in Goddes mercifull promises, to be saved from everlastyng dampnacion by Christ: wherof doth folowe a lovyng hart, to obey his commaundementes (sig. 5 leaves 2).

Although devils can believe in God and in Christ, only a Christian can have a true and lively faith, which reveals itself in trust in God and in the performance of good works, "whiche cannot be doen without a lively faith in Christ" (sig. 5 leaves 2ᵛ). Good works, therefore, are both the sign and the products of a true and lively faith. Such works consist both of seeking God's glory and honor in all things, and of being "ever ready to geve our selfes to our neighbors, and... to do good to every man" (sig. 5 leaves 3). The proper sort of works are, therefore, active works done in a social context, a point which is developed at length in the later sermons.

Cranmer's next sermon, however, deals with the importance of distinguishing between a faith which shows itself in good works and a faith which does not. In this Fourth Homily, "Of the True and Lively Faithe," he distinguishes between the two by saying that the latter is a dead faith, "not properly called fayth" (sig.

A1). The true faith, necessary for justification, is a "quicke or lively faith, [which] worketh by charity" (sig. A1ᵛ), "lyvely and fruitful, in bringing furthe good workes" (sig. A2ᵛ). This necessary faith has three characteristics, only the first of which is dealt with in this homily. The last two are treated in the last of Cranmer's three homilies of doctrine.

The first characteristic of a true and lively faith is that it is revealed in good works, and the degree to which this is understood by an individual is a test of the depth of his knowledge and apprehension of faith. True faith "will shew furth it self, and cannot long be ydle" (sig. A3):

> Al holy scripture agreably beareth witnes, that a true lively fayth in Christe doeth brynge furth good workes, and therfore every man must examine him self diligently, to know whether he have the same true lively fayth in his hart, unfaynedly or not, whiche he shall knowe by the fruites thereof (sig. B1ᵛ).
> ....
> For the tryall of all these thinges, is a very godly and christian lyfe (sig. B3).

The thrust of this homily is to direct people toward an active Christian life, filled with good works toward their neighbors. Cranmer here develops the biblical image of the tree, or vine, and its fruits, which are the good works brought forth by a true faith, in a manner which expands on Edmund Dudley's usage we mentioned earlier in this chapter:

> Christ him selfe speaketh of this matter, and saieth: The tree is knowen by the fruite. Therefore let us do good workes, and therby declare our faith, to be the lively christen faith (sig. B4).

The life of good works of active charity is not just the Christian's duty, or thanksgiving, to God for the gift of justification, but is first of all an essential component and test of the faith required of someone for justification. Although faith alone justifies, a faith without good works is not the "true and lively faith" required for justification:

Thy deedes and workes must be an open testimonial of thy faith: Otherwise thy faith being without good workes, is but the devils faith, the faith of the wicked, a phantasie of fayth, and not a true christian fayth (sig. B4ᵛ).

People are called to examine their faith to see if it produces good works, which are defined as an "encrease of love and charitie by it toward God and your neighbor" (sig. C1). Only if men and women engage in such works can they have any hope of being in God's favor.

Cranmer's argument also points beyond the initial act of justification toward the quest for salvation during the rest of one's life. Justification and salvation are not identical. Instead, justification is Cranmer's term for the overcoming of original sin by God's free act of grace, obtained by men and women in their earthly lives through this "true and lively faithe," which reveals itself in good works. After justification before God, people then enter lives of faith and good works which lead beyond justification toward salvation at the end of life on earth. Cranmer urges, "Endevour your selves to make your calling and election certain by good workes" (sig. B4). The "true and lively faithe," proven by evidence of ever-increasing love and charity, achieves not only justification in this life, but also the eventual salvation of the human soul.

The Fifth Homily, "Of Good Workes," is the last of Cranmer's three sermons of doctrine. In it, he discusses his last two points about the true and lively faith. In so doing, he describes in more detail the sorts of works which are the products and evidence of this faith. He also outlines the life lived in faith and good works which proceeds from initial justification to final salvation. Cranmer's first point is that good works which are acceptable to God are dependent on faith, which gives life to the soul, "for true faith doth geve life to the worke, and out of such faith come good workes, that be very good workes in dede, and without it no worke is good before God" (sig. C2ᵛ). Here, Cranmer picks up from the preceding sermon the image of the tree and its fruits. He argues that works are the fruits of faith: people require nourishment by faith to bring forth such fruits.

Faith is prior to good works, and is necessary before they can be pleasing to God. At the same time, faith and good works are so closely connected that one cannot be separated from the other.

Cranmer's final point about this "true and lively faithe" is that the good works which spring from it "and leade faithful men unto eternal life" (sig. C4) are those works done in obedience to God's commandments. He says that he must argue this point because, since mankind's first disobedience of God's first commandment, people have tended to fall from God and his laws. They have instead tried to find salvation by other means, especially by setting up their own laws and customs on an equal or superior footing with the commandments of God himself. Yet God calls men and women to put his laws above all other laws. The human laws are "good and necessary for every common weale" (sig. D3), and should be obeyed. Yet such human laws should be framed only in such a way that they bring people into accord with the laws of God, and help men to serve God better. Above all, religious laws and customs which are devised by human beings should not be put before things commanded by God for his honor and glory. On these grounds, Cranmer launches the one major attack in the *Book of Homilies* on the religious laws and customs of Jews and papists. These human inventions, argues Cranmer, are put between a person and his proper first duty to God. The Roman Catholics are worse in this regard than the Jews whom Christ attacked, because the pope and his followers have many more customs that people are instructed to follow in place of obeying God's commands.

Cranmer is especially hard on those who take up the vows of the contemplative life. He claims that these vows commit a person to violating the God-given order of society. "Obedience" to the pope and monastic superiors is in reality a violation of God's command to obey father, mother, and the temporal rulers of the state. "Chastity" is only a shield to hide violations of God's commands in sexual matters. "Poverty" is only an excuse for the monastic order to amass great wealth, in avoidance of Christ's command of charity toward one's parents and toward the poor. The contemplative life itself is no more than a means of gaining support and power from the ignorant and helpless, who are led to seek the ineffectual prayers of the monastics. Henry VIII is to be thanked, says Cranmer, for delivering his people from these and other papal enormities:

> of beades, of lady psalters and rosaries, of .xv. Oos, of sainct Barnardes verses, of saynct Agaths letters, of purgatory, of Masses satisfactory, of stacions and Jubilies, of feyned reliques, of halowed beades, belles, bread, water, palmes, candelles, fire and such other (sigs. E2-E2^v).

The prime fault of these practices was that they left men and women in ignorance of God's commandments. Through such human inventions, people were brought to honor God by human devices, rather than "to searche out Gods holy commaundementes and to kepe them" (sig. E2^v).

Two points must be made about this section of Cranmer's homily "Of Good Workes." The first is that the practices which he singles out as abuses and human inventions are precisely those which take people away from social acts of charity and put them to private acts of devotion. Cranmer here rejects the whole medieval system of devotional piety, the life of contemplation, and the notion that the Christian life is essentially a passive life. For this understanding of the Christian life, he substitutes the idea that the Christian life is an active life, spent in works of charity empowered by faith. The second point is that Cranmer here suggests that the active Christian life has implications for all of society. The monastic system was wrong because it went against God's commandments for the ordering of society. This argument presupposes an understanding of society which the monastic system works against. To this point, the *Book of Homilies* follows Erasmus' argument in his *Enchiridion,* but now it enlarges the perspective from which that argument is viewed. Erasmus' Christian warrior engaged in an active life is now taken up into a larger context, in which this vision of the Christian life is given consequences for the society as a whole. The Christian life is one of charity towards one's neighbors. While this concept remains central to the *Book of Homilies,* from Cranmer's sermon

"On Good Workes," the concept of neighbor takes on ever larger meanings.

The homily concludes with an exhortation to keep God's commandments:

> as you have any zeale to the righte and pure honouring of God: as you have any regard to your awne soules, and to the life that is to come, which is bothe without pain and without ende, applye your selfes chiefli above al thing to reade and heare goddes worde, marke diligently therin what his will is you shal do, and with all your endevour applie your selfes to followe the same (sig. E3).

What people are to do, says Cranmer, is to have faith in God, love him in prosperity and adversity, love everyone, both friends and enemies, do good to everyone and hurt none, obey all superiors and governors, obey parents, and so on. The organization of his exhortation is that of the Ten Commandments. Cranmer's vision of the Christian life remains close to its biblical base, even in the organization of its rhetorical passages.

In its interpretation of history and in its call for obedience to God's commandments, Cranmer's homily "Of Good Workes" states the heart of the matter and summarizes the plan of the *Book of Homilies*. God's will is that people live lives of active charity. By taking "mens commaundementes for Godes commaundementes, yea, and for the highest, and most perfite and holy of all Gods commaundementes," the Church of Rome has caused to "growe muche error, supersticion, ydolatry, vaine religion, preposterous judgement, great contencion, with al ungodly living" (sig. E3^v). On the grounds of humanity's most important concern — the state of one's soul — we should cast off the commandments of human devising and return to the life of active charity in obedience to God's will.

The *Book of Homilies*, therefore, is a call for Christian action. Since people can be brought to act better by giving them the right models for imitation, and since good actions are the test of the required true and lively faith and the way to salvation, people are called to knowledge of Scripture, which tells of human sin and God's redeeming acts, requiring faith, revealed in and ex-

Godly and Fruitful Lessons 111

pressed through good works done in accordance with God's own commandments. The *Book of Homilies* begins with a call to Scripture and then rehearses what is said there about the problem between God and mankind. In this way, each person comes to know his true nature, and what he can do about the state of his soul. First, he must be justified, through faith expressed and proven in good works. Then, he enters into a life of Christian action, nourished by faith, which leads, at the end, to eternal life. In this, the *Book of Homilies* follows Erasmus closely. But it moves beyond Erasmus to suggest that the Christian life has consequences for the nation as a whole, that the Christian life contributes to an order in society which imitates God's order in his creation.

At this point, we need also to remember that when Cranmer completed his reform program with the publication of the *Book of Common Prayer* in 1549, he declared the context for the delivery of these Homilies to be the service of Holy Communion. After the recitation of the Creed, the rubrics there call for "the Sermon or Homely," to be followed by an exhortation to "the worthy receivyng of the holy Sacrament." In that service, the action of reception, so central to Cranmer's eucharistic theology, is followed by language that echoes his sermons on faith and works. Through receiving "these holy Misteries," the congregation is assured that they are "very membres incorporate in thy Misticall bodye, whiche is the blessed companye of all faythfull people." They also pray for "thy grace, that we may continue in that holy fellowship, and doe all suche good workes, as thou hast prepared for us to walke in." Cranmer thus established the source for that which would enable the pursuit of the life of active charity and the building-up of the Christian commonwealth in the two-fold action of hearing the Word in Bible reading and the Homilies and receiving the Word in Communion. Only when we think of these two forms of "reception" together as two parts of a single liturgical action can we fully grasp the significance of the sermons in the *Book of Homilies* as not just expositions of theology but part of a process of enabling the very Christian life they describe.

The remaining seven homilies deal with the specific actions which Christians are called by God to do, or to avoid. They also describe in more detail the larger perspective of the Christian society, the arena in which the individual Christian life participates through good actions and to which such works contribute. Thus, Homily VI, "Of Christian Love and Charitie," by Bishop Bonner, asserts that charity is the most important good work "as well, for that all maner of workes of righteousnes be conteined in it, as also that the decaye therof is the ruyne of the worlde, the banyshment of vertue, and the cause of all vice" (sig. E4). Charity thus has definite social implications; the decay of charity is not a matter of merely personal or local consequences, but is the "ruyne of the worlde." Charity contains all good works; it has two aspects. The first is love of God as "our chief joye and delite" (sig. E4). The second is love of every person, both friend and foe. Thus, Bonner's definition of charity is organized by Christ's summary of the Law of God. Charity is what men and women must do to be obedient to God's commandments, as called for in the preceding homily. Christ is presented as the supreme model of this loving relationship between God and his human creatures:

> And as a shepe that is led unto the shambles to be slayne, and as a lambe that is shorne of his flese, make no noyse or resistence, evenso went he unto his death, without any repugnaunce or opening of his mouthe, to saie any evill. Thus have I described unto you, what charitie is, aswel by the doctrine, as by the xample of Christ hym self. Wherby also every man may without error know hym self, what state and condicion he standeth in, whether he be in charitie (and so the child of the father in heaven) or not (sig. F2).

If people love Christ, they will keep his commandments. Christ is both teacher and example to be imitated: knowledge of his charity gives self-knowledge, and also a guide to the charitable acts commanded of all people.

Having thus presented Christ as a model for imitation, Bonner turns to an objection, not on the personal level, but on the level of government: if we are to love our enemies, how can magistrates punish evil-doers? In response, he asserts that charity has two offices. The first is to encourage good men and women and to protect them. This is the office of the bishops and the clergy, in which they use the power of the word. The second office of charity is to "rebuke, correct, and ponyshe vice, without acceptacion of persons" (sig. F3ᵛ). This second office is the duty of the magistrate, using the power of the sword. It must be performed for the good of society, "that God and the commen welth may be the lesse hurte and offended" (sig. F4ᵛ). Bonner describes criminals in terms of diseased parts of the body in need of amputation:

> charitie requireth [them] to be cut of from the body of the commen weale, lest they corrupt other good and honest persons: like as a good surgyne cutteth awaye a putrified, and festred membre, for love he hath to the whole body, least it infecte other membres adjoyning to it (sig. F4ᵛ).

Civil crimes are not just crimes against society; they are also offenses against God. Bonner thus gives religious sanction to the civil legal system.

Bonner uses in this passage, for the first time in the *Book of Homilies*, the analogy, or "correspondence," between the commonwealth and the human body. This image is the central one for the remaining homilies, as they expand the perspective of the Christian life of active charity to include all of society in its scope. Bonner here makes a key link between the earlier homilies, with their concern for the Christian life at the individual level, and the later homilies, with their concern to bring all men and women into one body under the headship of Christ. He does so by connecting the Christian life of charity in active obedience to God with the well-being of the body politic. This connection is direct and intimate; it has both positive and negative aspects. If God's call to charity is not followed, the result will be infection and sickness in the commonwealth. If it is followed, the result will be a healthy commonwealth. In the same way that obedience to God in faith leads to salvation for the individual, it also leads to a kind of salvation for the society in which the individual lives. The rest of the homilies develop in more detail this vision of a "saved" society, organized in obedience to the will of God.

Clearly, it is possible to read passages such as this one as self-serving propaganda for a monarchy in less than firm control of the country. I grant that if these passages do nothing else, they bring the threat of divine wrath on those who disobey the government. At the same time, the religious commitment of those who wrote these sermons must be taken seriously. If they were not naive, neither were they necessarily cynical. The movement in the *Book of Homilies* from interest in individual salvation to concern with the state of society is carefully arranged. The social consequences of charity are deeply rooted in Cranmer's discussion of salvation, faith, and works, and proceed naturally from it. Indeed, the whole thrust of the English Reformation, with its establishment of one hierarchy, at once religious and political, under the headship of the king, its rejection of monasticism and monastic devotional practices, and its stress on vernacular Scriptures, points clearly toward the notions of active charity and its social consequences enunciated in the *Book of Homilies*. All of these elements suggest a developing vision of the society which might be achieved if all men and women loved God and their neighbors.

The Seventh Homily, "Agaynst Swerynge and Perjury," deals with the social implications of active charity from a different point of view. The purpose of this sermon, perhaps influenced by the work of Becon, is to demonstrate when it is lawful to swear, so that God's name will be honored, instead of being taken in vain. The proper use of swearing is essential for "conservation of common wealthes" because it confirms relationships of trust among members of society. Thus, it is essential for judges in pursuit of truth, for Christian princes in making peace treaties, for clergy in preaching the Gospel, and for individuals engaged in causes necessary and lawful. At every level of society in public matters of order and justice, oaths are necessary for the common good. The stress on public oaths is crucial, because

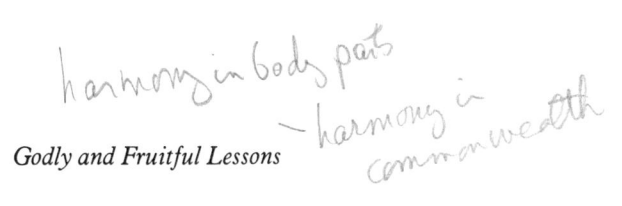

Godly and Fruitful Lessons [handwritten margin note: "harmony in body parts — harmony in commonwealth"]

people in private business matters and in private daily conversation only swear in an ungodly manner. All public swearing must be truthful, done with judgment, and in righteousness. Lawful oaths are taken by God's command, but <u>for specific social purposes only</u>:

> BY lawful othes, mutuall societie, amitie, and good ordre is kept continually in all commonalities, as boroughes, cyties, townes, and villages. And by lawful othes, malefactours are serched oute, wronge doers are punisshed, and they whiche sustayne wronge are restored to their right. Therfore lawfull swearyng can not be evel, whiche bryngeth unto us, many godly, good, and necessarie commodities (sig G3ᵛ).

In short, lawful and godly oaths are those which help preserve the good and ordered commonwealth. Oaths violated, oaths taken unadvisedly, and perjured oaths incur the wrath of God. Here again, the central argument is that <u>actions taken in obedience to God's will are healthful for the commonwealth</u>, while actions taken in violation of divine commandments are destructive to the social order. But this homilist advances the argument by suggesting that whatever is good for the commonwealth must be in accordance with the will of God.

These two homilies, therefore, enlarge the arena of conduct undertaken in faith and in obedience to God. They suggest that such actions have implications beyond the mere proving of an individual's having the "true and lively faithe" necessary for justification and eventual salvation. In fact, such actions are necessary for and contribute to the well-being of the society in which the individual lives. Bonner's homily uses the analogy of <u>the body</u> to suggest the <u>organic unity of society</u> and to argue that disobedience to God's will is like a sickness which can affect the entire society. Following this analogy, he suggests the social implications of sin as clearly as he indicates the importance of obedience. Homily VII, "Agaynst Swerynge and Perjury," goes even further in this direction to suggest that only those acts which are good for the society are in keeping with the will of God, while those acts which are not good for society bring about individual damnation, as well as a decrease in the health of the society. If, for Bonner, the commonwealth is like a human body, then for the anonymous writer of Homily VII, the essential thing to be preserved in the commonwealth is order among the parts. Only in an ordered society can justice prevail. Disorder, or violations of order, become the diseases which can attack the "body politic." Even as society is like a human body, so the pursuit of individual salvation is a pursuit of order, and the pursuit of salvation for the commonwealth. The religious life of the individual is indistinguishable from the social life of the commonwealth in which he lives.

Homily VIII, "Of the Declyninge from God," deals with the negative side of this concept by discussing people who, through pride or other sin, turn away from God. To do this is a dangerous thing, because it leads men and women to forsake God and to disobey his commandments. If this happens, God will forsake those who turn from him, and will take all his goodness with him. The anonymous homilist argues that this will result in great misery for the individual, but that the ensuing ill does not stop with the sinner. Instead, it affects the nation as a whole: "grevous plages of famine, and battaile, derth, and death" will result if individuals do not do good works (sig. I3). Thus each person has an urgent need to obey God's commandments, not only for his own religious concerns, but for the charity he owes his neighbors, who also will suffer for his sins. This homilist picks up the image of good works as good grapes, or fruits of faith, from Cranmer's sermons on doctrine, to suggest what is required of every Christian. He also uses the image of Israel and her fate to suggest an example to all of the social consequences of failure to do God's will. Since the New Testament Church thought of itself as a new Israel, this image in Homily VIII again makes the nation of England equal to the church in England. God's mercy applies only to those in the church and nation who turn to him: to sinners, only the law and the divine wrath apply. Again, while good works determine the well-being of the commonwealth and its favor with God, lack of good works results in great ill both to the individual sinner and to the commonwealth.

Godly and Fruitful Lessons 117

Homily IX, "Agaynste the Feare of Deathe," is the only homily in this second group which deals almost exclusively with an individual and personal problem. At the same time, it restates firmly the earlier assertion that the Christian life is one of active charity. This anonymous homilist argues that worldly people fear death because it means for them the loss of worldly honors and possessions, the fear of death's pains, and the threat of God's judgment upon them. Yet, because of the promises of God, such fear is needless for the true Christian, because for him death is "a doore, or entring unto lyfe, and therfore not so muche dreadful ...as it is comfortable" (sig. L1). The best way to prepare for death is through education in the Christian life:

> THERFORE, seeynge, that when we have in earth, our carnall fathers to be our correctors, we do feare them, and reverently take their correccion, shal we not much more be in subjeccion to God our spiritual father, by whome we shall have eternall life? And our carnal fathers some tyme correct us, even as pleaseth them, without cause: but this father justly correcteth us, either for our synne, to the intent we should amend, or for our commoditie and wealth, to make us thereby partakers of his holinesse (sig. L4-L4^v).

This homily, therefore, reinforces the whole concern for education expressed in the program for Christian education that Cranmer presented in the Injunctions of 1547. This education consists of the practice of active charity towards everyone's neighbors:

> let us studye dayly and diligently to shewe our selves to be the true honorers and lovers of God, by keping of his commaundements, by doyng of good deedes unto our nedy neighbours, relevyng by al means that we can, their povertie, with our aboundance, their ignorance, with our wisedome and learnyng, and comfort their weakenes, with our strength and authoritie, callyng all men backe from evil doyng, by godly counsall and good example, perseveryng styll in well doyng so long as we live. So shall we not nede to fear death.
> ....
> THUS makyng poore wretches our frendes, we make our saviour

Christe our frende, whose membres they are (sig. M3ᵛ-M4).

The call to a life of active charity thus resolves for the *Book of Homilies* the problem presented by nominalism concerning assurance of salvation, to which Luther responded with his understanding of justification as both the beginning and the end of salvation. Here, certainty lies in the promises of God to those who turn to him in faith and keep his commandments of active charity. In anticipation of the language of the Council of Trent, the *Book of Homilies* suggests that the Christian life is one of friendship with Christ. At death, therefore, the Christian does not go to the presence of a stern and wrathful judge, but to a friend, "to whose gracious presence, the Lorde of his infinite mercy and grace, bring us to reyne with him, in life everlasting" (sig. M4ᵛ).

Although Homily IX does not discuss the social implications of the fear of death, it does present, in eloquent language, a picture of the Christian life of charity. This life is, above all else, a social life, in which the Christian gives to his neighbor of whatever he has that the neighbor needs. At the same time, this life of charity is the life of the educator, for all Christians are called to correct evildoers "by godly counsall and good example." The Christian life is the cohesive force in the ordered body of the commonwealth. It binds the members together in mutual concern and assistance, for the salvation of the members and the good of the society.

Homily X, "An exhortation to Obedience," deals precisely with the nature of the Christian commonwealth. As we have already noted, its anonymous author opens with one of the great descriptions of the rightly ordered commonwealth, and its place in the divinely ordered cosmos (see above, p. 94). Both are creations of God, but while the cosmos is sustained directly by him, the commonwealth depends on man's cooperation with God in imitation of the divine order. The homilist carefully describes the divine order at every level of the creation, and reveals humanity's participation in it.

In this view, the human order of society is the equivalent of the

Godly and Fruitful Lessons

natural order and the angelic order, each on its appropriate level in the cosmos. In addition, as the water "rayneth doune," the various levels in the cosmos cooperate with each other to preserve the greater order of the entire creation. Human beings are integral parts of this order, both in their physical and psychological beings, and in their social organization. The homilist continues his description:

> And man himselfe also, hath all his partes, bothe within and without, as soule, hart, mynde, memorie, understanding, reason, speache, withall and singular corporal membres of his body, in a profitable, necessary and pleasaunt order. Every degre of people, in their vocacion, calling, and office, hath appointed to them their duetie and order. Some are in high degre, some in lowe, some Kynges and Princes, some inferiours and subjectes, Priestes, and laimen, Masters and servantes, Fathers and children, Husbands and wyves Riche and poore, and every one have nede of other, so that in all things, is to be lauded and praysed, the goodly order of God, without the which no house, no citie, no common wealth, can contynue and endure (sigs. N1-N1ᵛ).

Here, the notion of order, achieved through charity on the human level, becomes the unifying quality in the cosmos. Even as each level of creation cooperates with other levels, so each group in human society of necessity cooperates with all other groups. Indeed, this cooperation is essential to the health of society, or "there must nedes folowe all mischiefe and utter destruccion, bothe of soules, bodies, goodes, and common wealthes.... For where there is no righte order, there reyneth all abuse, carnall libertie, enormytie, synne, and Babylonical confusion" (sig N1ᵛ). The arena of the Christian life here reaches its widest possible expression. To do the will of God in faith is necessary for everyone's individual salvation, for the salvation of the community, the nation, and by extension, for the salvation of the cosmos itself. Against the background of the whole range of creation, each person is called to active charity, so as to cooperate with the divine order. Not to do the will of God is to disrupt not just an individual's progress toward salvation, but to endanger the whole of human society.

On earth, God gives authority for maintaining this order to magistrates "which do exercise Gods role in judgement, and punishynge, by good and Godly lawes, here in earth" (sig. N2ᵛ). All people, clergy and laity alike, owe "obedience, submission, and subjection" to these rulers, whose authority comes from God. Resistance is not only unlawful, but is also against God's commands. Even wicked rulers are to be obeyed, since God gives them their authority and will himself punish them for their misdeeds. But God will also punish all rebels; treason will never go unanswered. Such injunctions against rebellion do not apply, of course, to the rejection of the authority of the bishop of Rome, since he is a usurper of the King of England's rightful and God-given authority. The homilist's argument here is, in effect, that the divine order also contains a divine economy. There is only one hierarchy visible in the cosmos; thus, human society, if it is to imitate this hierarchy so as to complete it, must compose one hierarchy also. There is no room for the medieval dualism of a secular hierarchy headed by the king, and a religious hierarchy headed by the pope. Since the whole of English society makes up the church in England, both must arrange themselves in one ordered hierarchy under the authority of the monarch.

This homily ends with an appeal to pray for the king, that he may use his authority rightly, to the glory of God and the good of the commonwealth. People, too, are to be prayed for:

> that we maye lyve Godly, in holy and christian conversacion: So we shal have God of our side. And then let us not feare what men can do agaynst us: So we shall lyve in true obedience, bothe to oure most mercifull Kynge in heaven, and to oure most christen Kynge in earthe: So shall we please God, and have the excedinge benefite, peace of conscience, reste and quietnes here in this worlde, and after thys lyfe, we shall enjoye a better lyfe, rest, peace, and the eternall blisse of heaven (sigs. P1ᵛ-P2).

The point here is the same noted before; the call to obedience to God's commands, the test of a "true and lively faithe," is not just a call to personal action for one's own salvation, but an exhortation to cooperate in the great, godly enterprise of the Christian commonwealth, which is God's creation for the well-being of his people on earth. The order of the cosmos, given expression in human society as the ordered commonwealth, provides a model for imitation, so that people can see how to shape their society. The goal of a Christian society is to achieve an order, in imitation of God's order in his creation, so that the commonwealth will take its appropriate place in the hierarchy of the cosmos.

The divine order, which is to be obtained in the human society of the commonwealth through charity, is something to be achieved. At the same time, it is something already present which must be conserved. The *Book of Homilies* speaks of this order both in the present and in the future tense. Even as for Aquinas, grace does not destroy human nature, but rather perfects it, so here grace does not overturn the order implicit in human society from its creation by God, but permits men and women to restore the original order disrupted by human sin. To correct human disordering, God gives grace so that people may again participate in the divine order of creation. By grace, through faith, mankind is empowered to obey the commands of God and his earthly agents, and thus to achieve a society ordered in imitation of the cosmic order. But such a society would not be new; instead, it would be a realization of the order implicit in all human society. This order is not an invention of man, but is the relationship in which God created mankind in the first place. Thus, the *Book of Homilies,* in its call for the creation of a Christian society, is at once revolutionary and conservative. To achieve this vision would be to create a radically new society, and at the same time, to restore human society to its original condition.

The next-to-last homily, Becon's "Agaynst Whoredome and Adultery," is another sermon which deals with a personal sin, but it does so against the full perspective of the consequences of this sin for the well-being of the commonwealth. Adultery is a grave sin which has "overflowed, almoste the whole worlde, unto the great dishonoure of God, the exceading infamie of the name of Christ, the notable decaye of true religion, and the utter destruccion of the publique wealth" (sig. P2v). Adultery has a serious impact on society because it disrupts the God-given laws for regulating the relationships between men and women, and thus upsets the ordering of the commonwealth. Adultery is also a grievous sin because all other sins flow from it. It is "that most fylthy lake, foule puddle, and stynkyng sinke, wherinto all kyndes of synnes and evills flow" (sig. Q3ᵛ). This language is another echo of Erasmus' *Enchiridion,* for Erasmus also singles out adultery as a grave sin which reduces a person to "fylthy swine, to gotes, to dogges," since "no vyce stynketh more carrenly than the name of lechery." Both are agreed that God's punishment for this sin will be severe indeed. All are called to put it aside in love of "chastitie, and clennes of life" (sig. S1ᵛ), and in obedience to God's law for the ordering of married life.

The last homily, Hugh Latimer's "Against Strief and Contencion," deals with yet another way in which the divine ordering of the commonwealth is upset by human pride and disobedience and needs to be restored. Strife and debate destroy the unity of church and state which is basic to the *Book of Homilies'* vision of the rightly ordered Christian society. People should study God's Scriptures to learn how to lead better lives, but not to learn how to be better disputers in religious arguments. Such contentiousness only leads people into greater error. The proper Christian life is one of quietness, meekness, and good deeds, rather than one of picking quarrels, spreading evil division, or disputing other private interpretations. In such a quiet Christian life lies true humanness, effective overcoming of evil, and achievement of well-being in the commonwealth. Men and women should seek to order themselves according to God's will, and avoid vices of dissension which are "so muche hurtful to the societie of a common wealth in all well ordred cyties" (sig. U3). Those who disrupt the godly order are brawlers who "be unworthy to live in a common wealth, the whiche do as muche as lyeth in them, with braulinge and scholdynge, to disturbe the quietnes and peace of the same" (sig. U3). Latimer argues that the best response to "brawlers," and the true Christian one, is not to respond in kind, but to work for the proper ordering of the Christian commonwealth. If people do this, then God will pro-

Godly and Fruitful Lessons

vide the grace for this vision of an ordered Christian society to be achieved:

> above all thynges, kepe peace and unitie, be no peace breakers, but peace makers. And then ther is no doubt, but that God, the aucthor of comfort and peace, wyll graunt us peace of conscience, and suche concord and agrement, that with one mouth and mynd, we may glorify God, the father of oure Lorde Jesus Christ (sig. U3^v).

The goal of the Christian life is to live in obedience to God's commands, which means to live in harmony and peace, in imitation of the divinely ordered creation.

On this note of peace and harmony, the first *Book of Homilies* comes to an end. Latimer adds a final set of details to the picture of the Christian commonwealth. Charity results not just in order but in tranquility and harmony for the society. When this harmony is achieved, human society will realize the two images of the "body politic" and the body of Christ, and make them one. This society-as-church would achieve that community of conversational fellowship sought by Erasmus; with "one mouth and mynd," it would unite with the Father in the unity of his discourse in Christ. Its ordering would be to the honor and glory of God, from whom comes the grace to achieve such harmony. Latimer repeats the quality of looking both forward and backward; his image of the Christian commonwealth is already implicit in human society, although human sinfulness detracts from its harmony, so that human lives of active charity can work to make its potential presence actual in England.

Latimer's final vision of the peaceful and unified society is the goal toward which the whole argument of the *Book of Homilies* moves. As we have seen, the work begins, according to the Erasmian paradigm, with a call for all people to know their true condition. Such knowledge is obtained only through reading Scripture, which reveals that everyone is a sinner, incapable of doing anything on his own to improve his relationship with God. Thus, mankind is totally dependent on God's mercy, revealed in the biblical accounts of Jesus Christ. This mercy is obtained for humanity's justification by a "true and lively faithe," which is revealed through the doing of good works. Justified people are called to express their faith in good works, which are defined as acts of Christian charity in the world, by obeying God's commandments. These works are thus done in cooperation with God and in fellowship with Jesus Christ; the life lived in doing them is one of community with God and one's fellow human beings, a community of conversation, in harmony with God's discourse in Christ. Grounded in traditional Christian understandings of the relationship between God's grace and human free will, this conception of the Christian life departs from medieval notions in its abandonment of devotional piety as the normative act of Christian living in favor of the life of active charity as the basic meaning of the term *good works*. In this key departure from medieval Christianity, the *Book of Homilies* follows closely the movement of Erasmus' vision of the Christian life, from knowledge of self to faith to action, as outlined in his *Enchiridion militis Christiani*.

The *Book of Homilies*, in fact, expresses fully Erasmus' theology of human discourse in the way it develops the implications of its model for Christian living. The work is a collection of sermons, essays in the rhetorical use of language with Christ at their center, aiming at the creation of a society harmoniously united in Christian conversation. In Cranmer's sermon-collection, good works of active charity not only show forth the true and lively faith of an individual, but also restore human society to its proper order and thus to its appropriate place in the divinely ordered cosmos. The end of human life on earth, in obedience to God's commandments, is to reorder and restore the well-being before God of his society, or commonwealth. This Christian commonwealth would be characterized by order and harmony, as its members act in charity toward each other, the strong aiding the weak. All would obey those in authority, so that they could carry out their divinely given duties of preserving order and establishing justice. In this ordered society, peace and tranquility prevail, as church and state become one to glorify God.

The Christian commonwealth, as envisioned by the writers of

the *Book of Homilies*, would be in harmony not just with itself, but with all of God's creation. The argument of these homilists is that God initially created all things, in heaven and earth, in perfect order; human sin, however, disrupted this order in human society. To this point, the homilists agree with medieval theologians, who saw the divinely ordered creation as revealing the glory of God, which should be perceived and contemplated in passive devotion. But the *Book of Homilies* goes beyond this to argue that the order of creation reveals not only the way in which human society *was* ordered, but also the way it *should be* ordered. In the divine order is a model for human imitiation; through the rhetorical use of language, when Christ is at the center of the discourse, men and women can be moved to imitate that order. Acting in the faith that God will give humanity the grace to restore the divine order to the human commonwealth if mankind will turn to God in faith and obey his commandments, the homilists put forth their vision of human society and human behavior within that society. The *Book of Homilies* presents the image of the Christian commonwealth as a "true and lively image" of what is possible in human society if men and women imitate the divine order of creation in the faith that the method of presentation itself has the power to move people to action. Thus, the vision of a Christian commonwealth, as presented in the *Book of Homilies*, becomes itself an object of imitation, an agent of change, to move men and women to bring it into being through active charity, to the greater glory of God. To this end, Cranmer and his supporters presented their vision of a Christian commonwealth to the people of England to enable them to understand and act out the humanist vision of the Christian life.

Conclusion

What should be clear by now is the appropriateness of considering the three initial documents of the Edwardian reformation — the Great Bible, the English translation of Erasmus' *Paraphrases*, and the *Book of Homilies* — as a group, not randomly chosen, but carefully selected and prepared as three parts of a single effort to achieve a single end. The Great Bible presents the Word of God directly to the people in their own language, to provide them with the appropriate images of the Christian life for their imitation. The *Paraphrases* of Erasmus offers a specific reading of that Word, or at least its central narratives, aimed at insuring that people would read that Word according to humanist precepts. The *Book of Homilies* expounds that Word, suggests its implications for all people everywhere in terms of the life of active charity and the Christian commonwealth to result from pursuit of that life, in such a way that the people are to be moved to imitate the images given in that Word. What is at work here to unite all these documents, along with their common purpose, is a theory of biblical language, tied up in the humanist, the Erasmian, concept of the Word. If the story of Jesus presented in the Gospels is the central story, not just of the biblical narrative, but of all human history, and if the stories of the Old Testament prefigure that story, then all human history since the period of Jesus' life must *refigure* that story if it is to be included in the history of human salvation. That is to say, the stress in Erasmus' writings on imitation of Christ and in the Homilies on the life of active charity in imitation of Christ serves to call the readers and hearers of these documents to make their lives over into the image of Christ along the lines of the pattern established by the events of his life. It is through this refiguring of the Christ-story for the individual and for his society, seen as the Body of Christ on earth, that the promises of salvation made in the Bible become effective for the individual at a later point in human history. And it is the transforming power of the Word, in its biblical, homiletic, and liturgical expressions, that makes such refiguring possible.

Thus Cranmer set the whole nation of England to the discipline of hearing and reading God's holy Word, of inwardly digesting it and being inwardly transformed by it, to the end that charitable action would result in creating the true Christian commonwealth.

In a letter to the Protector Somerset from John Hales, written while Hales was acting in the name of the Crown to enforce the

Injunctions of 1547, we get a sense of the enthusiasm, optimism, and idealism which nourished the humanists' vision of the Christian community and kept it alive into the reign of Elizabeth. Hales writes:

Hales to Somerset

> If there be any way or policy of man to make the people receive, embrace, and love God's word, it is only this, — then they shall see that it bringeth forth so goodly fruit, that men seek not their own wealth, nor their private commodity, but, as good members, the universal wealth of the whole body... and what wealth will thereby universally grow to the whole realm, albeit these worldlings think it but a money matter, yet am I fully persuaded, and certainly do believe in your Grace's sayings, that, maugre the Devil, private profit, self-love, money, and such-like the Devil's instruments, it shall go forward, and set such a stay in the body of the commonwealth, that all the members shall live in a due temperament and harmony.[19]

In this spirit, therefore, Cranmer and his associates set out to rebuild the earthly city, a building to usher in God's true reign on earth. In light of the fires Queen Mary was to set at Oxford, their quest for the earthly commonwealth cost them no less than everything. Although the short reign of Edward, as well as controversies with Edmund Bonner, Stephen Gardiner, and others over secondary theological issues, prevented Cranmer's experiment in national Christian education from running its full course, the humanist vision embodied in that experiment did endure into the reign of Elizabeth. Then, as part of the Elizabethan settlement of religion, Cranmer's Prayer Book and his *Book of Homilies* became once again official documents of the national church which Cranmer had created through use of them in Edward's reign.[20]

Thus, the importance of the Great Bible, the *Paraphrases,* and the *Book of Homilies* is as a witness to the continuing vitality of Tudor humanism in the middle years of the sixteenth century, as well as to the integrity and idealism of the Edwardian reformation. In the Injunctions of 1547, Cranmer insured the continuing centrality of the Bible for religious reform in England, enshrined the Erasmian approach to the Bible as a touchstone for English interpretation, and incorporated humanist rhetorical and educational theory to create a collection of sermons to embody and express a humanist vision of the Christian commonwealth to be reached through the Christian life of active charity. As a result, the reform program of Edward VI occupies a central place in the history of sixteenth-century thought and writing. On the one hand, it made available to the majority of Elizabethans a summary of literary and intellectual developments, while on the other, Cranmer's reform program served as a mid-century nexus, a collector and disseminator of the best that early Tudor humanism had to offer. In fact, the humanists of Henry's reign effected both a revolution in English thought about the meaning and purpose of people's lives and a restocking of the linguistic and imaginative resources of English writers. Only when the contributions of these early Tudor humanists are taken into account is it possible to understand the flowering of English literary and religious life in the Age of Elizabeth. For what the early Tudor humanists bequeathed to their successors was no less than the religious, intellectual, and imaginative foundations on which the glories of the Elizabethan Age were built.

NOTES

Godly and Fruitful Lessons:
The English Bible, Erasmus' Paraphrases, and the Book of Homilies

[1] Jasper Ridley, *Thomas Cranmer* (Oxford: Clarendon, 1962), p. 266.

[2] *Injunccions Geven by the Moste Excellente Prince Edwarde VI* (London: Richard Grafton, 1547), sigs. A4-C4.

[3] The *Book of Homilies* was published by Grafton simultaneously with the Injunctions on 31 July 1547, and by Whitchurche on 20 August 1547. Thirteen separate editions, with minor revisions, were pub-

lished during the reign of Edward. Erasmus' *Paraphrases* were first published by Whitchurche on 31 January 1549; for further information, see E. J. Devereux, "The Publication of the English *Paraphrases of Erasmus*," *Bulletin of the John Rylands Library*, 5 (1969), 346-52 and my facsimile edition of the work (Del Mar, N.Y.: Scholars' Facsimilies & Reprints, 1975).

[4] Thus James K. McConica, *English Humanists and Reformation Politics* (Oxford: Oxford University Press, 1965), esp. pp. 236-37, and G. R. Elton, *Reform & Reformation: England, 1509-1558* (Cambridge, Mass.: Harvard University Press, 1977), esp. pp. 338-75. Both writers ignore, I believe, the clear links between the reform efforts under Henry VIII and Cromwell and those under Somerset. While Elton's research into the years of Cromwell's ascendancy has been monumental, he seems to denigrate the efforts of Cromwell's successors; Cromwell does not need that sort of treatment for his importance to show through. The crux of my disagreement with Elton may be seen in his comment that Cranmer moved slowly after the death of Henry VIII (p. 339); considering what Cranmer was able to have through the presses within six months of the end of Henry's reign suggests to me a different conclusion. Elton clearly underestimates the importance of the documents Cranmer added to his revisions of the Henrican Injunctions; to him they are minor (p. 339, "neither extensive nor revolutionary"), while to me they are the heart of the matter.

[5] See his essay, "A Reappraisal of How Protestantism Spread during the Early English Reformation," *Anglican Theological Review*, 60 (1978), 437-46.

[6] "Tudor Humanism and Henry VIII," *University of Toronto Quarterly*, 8 (1938), 175.

[7] The phrase is from Thomas Wilson; see note 6 below under "Logos and Commonwealth in Early Tudor Humanism."

[8] *Certaine Sermons, or Homilies, Appoynted by the Kynges Majestie, to be Redde* (London: Richard Grafton, 1547), sig. S3. STC 13638.5. This edition, the first to be printed, will be used for all quotations from the *Book of Homilies*, which will be cited by signature in the text. In quoting from this, and all other sixteenth-century books in this chapter, I have normalized "j" for "i," "v" for "u," and silently expanded all contractions.

Early Tudor Humanism: Background to the Great Books

Logos and Commonwealth in Early Tudor Humanism

[1] Bucer, *De Regno Christi*, Wilhelm Pauck, trans., in *Melancthon and Bucer*, Wilhelm Pauck, ed. (Philadelphia: Westminster, 1969), p. 188. Bucer's work, written while he was in residence at Cambridge under the patronage of Somerset and Cranmer, is an important *apologia* for and description of the reform movement under Edward VI. Bucer's work stresses throughout the role of each man and woman in society to put personal interest aside in favor of ushering in the *regno Christi*, the reign of Christ, through self-giving service to neighbor and society.

[2] (London: R. Copland, 1534), sig. A2. STC 13608.

[3] Dudley, *The Tree of Commonwealth*, D. M. Brodie, ed. (Cambridge: Cambridge University Press, 1948), pp. 31-32. For a different view of Dudley, see Elton, *Reform & Reformation*, pp. 1-3. Elton faults Dudley for the inadequacy of his plans for reform, a view not shared by later Tudor humanists.

[4] Boyle, *Erasmus on Language and Method in Theology* (Toronto: University of Toronto Press, 1977), p. 53.

[5] *Ibid.*, p. 129.

[6] Wilson, *Arte of Rhetorique* (London: Richard Grafton, 1553), sig. A3^v. STC 25799.

Strategies for Change in Early Humanist Writing

[1] (London: Wynken de Worde, 1533). STC 10479.

[2] Thus Enno van Gelder, *The Two Reformations of the Sixteenth Century* (The Hague: Martinus Nijhoff, 1961), p. 134.

[3] *Enchiridion*, sig. C4^v.

[4] *Ibid.*, sig. F4.

[5] *Ibid.*, sig. F5^v.

[6] *Ibid.*, sig. F2^v.

[7] *Ibid.*, sig. G4^v.

[8] For a summary of scholarship on More's *Utopia*, see the introduction

to the Yale edition, Edward Surtz, SJ and J. H. Hexter, eds., in *Works,* vol. 4 (New Haven: Yale University Press, 1965), xv-clxxxi; and Judith Paterson Jones, "Recent Studies in More," *ELR,* 9 (1979), 442-458.

[9] See especially A. R. Heiserman, "Satire in the *Utopia," PMLA,* 78 (1963), 163-74; and R. C. Elliott, "The Shape of Utopia," *ELH,* 30 (1963), 317-334.

[10] *Utopia,* Surtz and Hexter, eds., p. 55.

[11] I am grateful to my colleague at North Carolina State University, M. Thomas Hester, for pointing this out to me.

[12] *Utopia,* Ralph Robinson, trans. (London: A. Vele, 1551), sig. F6-F6^v. STC 18094.

Programs for Reform in the Reign of Henry VIII

[1] See especially J. S. Philimore, "Blessed Thomas More and the Arrest of Humanism in England," *Dublin Review,* 63 (1913), 26; Frederic Seebohm, *The Oxford Reformers of 1498* (London: Longmans, Green, 1867); and R. W. Chambers, *Thomas More* (London: Cape, 1935).

[2] See especially McConica, *English Humanists and Reformation Politics;* Gordon Zeeveld, *Foundations of Tudor Policy* (1948, rpt. London: Methuen, 1969); Arthur B. Ferguson, *The Articulate Citizen and the English Renaissance* (Durham, N. C.: Duke University Press, 1965); Fritz Caspari, *Humanism and the Social Order in Tudor England* (Chicago: University of Chicago Press, 1954); and Whitney Jones, *The Tudor Commonwealth, 1529-1559* (London: Athlone, 1970), and *The Mid-Tudor Crisis, 1539-1563* (London: Macmillan, 1973).

[3] Zeeveld, p. 89.

[4] *A Dialogue Between Reginald Pole and Thomas Lupset,* Kathleen M. Burton, ed. (London: Chatto & Windus, 1948). p. 19.

[5] *Dialogue,* pp. 22-23. See Zeeveld, pp. 39-81, for a detailed and well-drawn portrait of Pole's humanist household in Padua, and Starkey's place within it.

[6] The term is, of course, Bucer's. See note 1 above, under "Logos and Commonwealth in Early Tudor Humanism."

[7] *Dialogue,* pp. 24-25.

[8] *Ibid.*, p. 55.

[9] *Ibid.*, pp. 77-79, 81-85, 118.

[10] *Ibid.*, p. 169.

[11] *Ibid.*, p. 170.

[12] *Ibid.*, pp. 140-46, 151, 186-87.

[13] van Gelder, *Two Reformations*, p. 329.

[14] Zeeveld, p. 236; see also McConica, p. 201.

[15] Zeeveld, pp. 237-38.

"GOD'S TRUE WORD, SETTING FORTH HIS GLORY":
The English Bible

[1] From the Preface to Erasmus' Greek New Testament of 1516, rpt. in F. F. Bruce, *History of the Bible in English*, 3rd ed. (New York: Oxford University Press, 1978), p. 29.

[2] For a recounting of this story in more detail, see Bruce, pp. 24-80. See also *The Cambridge History of the Bible*, 3 vols. (Cambridge: Cambridge University Press, 1963-70), especially Vol. III, *The West from the Reformation to the Present Day*; J. F. Mozley, *Coverdale and His Bible* (London: Lutherworth, 1953); W. T. Whitley, *The English Bible under the Tudor Sovereigns* (London: Marshall, Morgan & Scott, 1937); C.C. Butterworth, *The Literary Lineage of the King James Bible* (1941, rpt. New York: Octagon, 1971); H. Wheeler Robinson, ed., *The Bible in Its Ancient and English Versions* (Oxford: Oxford University Press, 1940); and T. R. Henn, *The Bible as Literature* (New York: Oxford University Press, 1970).

[3] Rpt. in *Cranmer, Miscellaneous Writings*, John Cox, ed. (Cambridge: Cambridge University Press, 1846), p. 121.

"THE FRUITION OF HONEST AND GODLY STUDIES":
Erasmus' Paraphrases

[1] E. J. Devereux, "The Publication of the English *Paraphrases* of Erasmus," *Bulletin of the John Rylands Library*, 5 (1969), 349.

Godly and Fruitful Lessons

2. B. Hall, "Erasmus: Biblical Scholar and Reformer," in *Erasmus,* T. A. Dorey, ed. (Albuquerque: University of New Mexico Press, 1970), pp. 104-05.

3. In "Erasmus' Biblical Humanism," *Studies in the Renaissance,* 17 (1970), 123.

4. All biblical quotations are from the Great Bible translation.

5. Desiderius Erasmus, *The First Tome of the Paraphrase Upon the Newe Testamente* (1548, rpt. Delmar, N. Y.: Scholars' Facsimiles & Reprints, 1975), sig. B4^v. STC 2854. All further references will be by signatures in the text.

6. Anonymous, quoted in Roland H. Bainton, "The Paraphrases of Erasmus," *Archiv fur Reformationsgeschichte,* 57 (1966), 67.

7. *Ibid.,* pp. 68-75.

8. In "Erasmus and the Continuity of Classical Culture," *Erasmus in English,* 1 (1970), 4.

9. The Paraphrase on Jude was translated privately by John Caius in 1530; the Paraphrase on Titus was translated by Leonard Cox and published in 1534 or 1535 (STC 10503). Erasmus' "Preface to the Reader" from the beginning of the *Paraphrases* volume was translated and published in 1534 (STC 10494). For a fuller discussion, see Devereux, "Publication," pp. 349-50, and McConica, pp. 106-99.

10. While McConica argues that Catherine was active in the reformers' cause before becoming queen (p. 215), William P. Haugaard, "Katherine Parr: The Religious Convictions of a Renaissance Queen," *Renaissance Quarterly,* 22 (1969), believes McConica here "far outdistances the evidence" (p. 350). Both, however, are in general agreement on her influence after her marriage to Henry VIII.

11. McConica, p. 215.

12. She owned copies of the English translations of the *Enchiridion militis Christiani* and *De Praeparatione ad Mortem;* see F. Rose-Troup, "Two Book-Bills of Catherine Parr," *The Library,* 3rd ser., 2 (1911), 40-48.

13. Thus McConica, p. 246, and Haugaard, p. 348. The patron of the second volume of the *Paraphrases* was Anne Seymour; the translations were by Miles Coverdale, Leonard Cox, and John Olde. It was published in 1549 by Whitchurche.

[14] MS. Cotton Vespasian F. III, no. 35, fol. 37 in the British Museum is a Latin letter from Catherine to Mary, dated 20 September 1544 or 1545, in which the queen praises Mary's work in the translation and urges her to let it be published under her name.

[15] McConica, p. 241.

[16] *Paraphrases,* sig. 4¢6ᵛ.

[17] Devereux, "Publication," p. 352.

[18] *Enchiridion,* sig. B3ᵛ.

"THE TRUE SETTING FORTH AND PURE DECLARING OF GOD'S WORD":
The Homilies

[1] Stephen Gardiner, *Letters,* James A. Muller, ed. (New York: Macmillan, 1933), pp. 296-97.

[2] In *Concilia Magnae Britanniae et Hiberniae a Synodo Verolamiensi A.D. CCCCXLVI ad Londinensem A.D. MDCCXVII* (London: Gosling, et al., 1737), III, 860-63.

[3] Quoted in J. T. Tomlinson, *The Prayer Book Articles and Homilies* (London: Elliot Stock, 1897), p. 230.

[4] Gardiner, *Letters,* p. 303.

[5] Ridley, *Cranmer,* p. 265.

[6] Gardiner, *Letters,* p. 303. For a lamentably brief recounting of the events surrounding publication of the *Book of Homilies,* see R. B. Bond, "Cranmer and the Controversy Surrounding Publication of *Certaine Sermons or Homilies,*" *Renaissance and Reformation,* 12 (1976), 28-35.

[7] *Injunccions,* sig. C4.

[8] Ridley, *Cranmer,* pp. 265-66.

[9] The attributions of authorship given here are conjectural; for a fuller discussion of this point see my doctoral dissertation, "The Vision of a Christian Commonwealth in the Book of Homilies of 1547," Harvard University, 1973.

[10] C. S. Lewis, *English Literature in the Sixteenth Century* (New York:

Oxford, 1954), p. 204. But see James A. Devereux, SJ, "The Collects of the First Book of Common Prayer as Works of Translation," *SP*, 66 (1969), 719-38, for an evaluation which demonstrates Cranmer's skill as a prose stylist in his translations.

[11] Thomas Wilson, trans., *Three Orations in Favour of the Olynthians* (London: H. Denham, 1520), sig. *4ᵛ. STC 6578. For a discussion of the 1559 revisions in the *Book of Homilies,* aimed at making the style even plainer, see R. B. Bond, "The 1559 Revisions in *Certayne Sermons or Homilies:* For the Better Understandyng of the Simple People," *ELR*, 8 (1978), 239-55.

[12] J. W. Blench, *Preaching in England in the Late 15th and 16th Centuries* (Oxford: Basil Blackwell, 1964), p. 142.

[13] In *Wit and Rhetoric in the Renaissance* (New York: Columbia University Press, 1937), pp. 20-21.

[14] In *De Doctrina Christiana;* lib. IV, cap. xvii, in *Patrologiae Latini,* 34 (1861), 103.

[15] For a discussion of the "university" or "modern" sermon of the Middle Ages, see W. O. Rose, ed., *Middle English Sermons,* EETS, 209 (Oxford: Oxford University Press, 1940). For a more general discussion, see G. R. Owst, *Literature and Pulpit in Medieval England,* 2nd ed. (Oxford: Basil Blackwell, 1966).

[16] Blench, *Preaching in England,* p. 71.

[17] Wilson, *Arte of Rhetorique,* sig. z2.

[18] Crane, *Wit and Rhetoric,* pp. 22-32.

[19] Quoted in P. F. Tytler, ed., *England Under the Reigns of Edward VI and Mary* (London: R. Bentley, 1839), I, 114-17.

[20] For a demonstration of the continuity between the Reformation of Edward VI and the Elizabethan Settlement of Religion, see Winthrop S. Hudson, *The Cambridge Connection and the Elizabethan Settlement of 1559* (Durham, N.C.: Duke University Press, 1980). For a discussion of the impact of the early Tudor humanists' emphasis on the life of active charity on the thought of Elizabethan and Stuart followers of John Calvin, see R. T. Kendall, *Calvin and English Calvinism to 1649* (New York: Oxford University Press, 1979).

Part Three

COMMUNION AND COMMONWEAL

The Book of Common Prayer

John E. Booty

—III—

COMMUNION AND COMMONWEAL

The Book of Common Prayer

John E. Booty

The Book of Common Prayer was constructed, enacted and published as an instrument for the reform of the English people and the perfection of the Christian commonwealth. So it was understood in the sixteenth century by Thomas Cranmer, its architect, by the Protector Somerset and Queen Elizabeth I, acting through Parliament to make it the official and sole order of public worship in England, and by Richard Hooker, its defender against the attacks of the Puritans. However, except for Hooker, whose task it was to explain the meaning and utility of the Prayer Book, people generally did not talk or write about the importance of the book to the safety and prosperity of the commonwealth. They assumed its worth and promoted its use, unless like the Puritans they considered it subversive and ungodly, or like the Roman Catholics they condemned it as heretical.

Richard Hooker (1554-1600), Master of the Temple, the "parish church" of the Inns of Court, wrote the fifth book of his eight book masterpiece, *Of the Lawes of Ecclesiasticall Politie* (1597),[1] specifically in defense of the *Book of Common Prayer*, against the Puritan charge that it was "an unperfecte booke, culled and picked out of the popishe dunghil, the Masse booke full of all abhominations,"[2] and thus containing "much superstition."[3] Hooker refuted this charge, and in the process explained the intent and meaning of public worship as contained in the *Book of Common Prayer,* intent and meaning, as we shall see, such as conforms essentially to that guiding Thomas Cranmer in his work. Hooker, indeed, provides us with a unique opportunity for understanding the Prayer Book and Prayer Book worship. He began with the statement that "religion unfainedly loved perfecteth mens habilities unto all kindes of virtuous service in the common wealth" (V.1.4).[4] In the promotion of such religion we have designated places, persons, and liturgies. The church building, properly adorned and cared for, has "great vertue force and efficacie, for that it serveth as a sensible help to stirre up devotion, and *in that respect* no doubt *bettereth* even our holiest and best actions" (V.16.2). In discussing the designated person—the priest—Hooker points out again "that everie mans religion is in him the wellspring of all other sound and sincere vertues." It is manifest, therefore, that

> the verie worldlie peace and prosperitie, the secular happines, the temporall and naturall good estate both of all men and of all dominions hangeth chieflie upon religion and doth evermore give plaine testimonie that as well in this as in other considerations the Priest is a pillar of that commonwealth wherein he faithfullie serveth God (V.76.1).

The priest—or presbyter, as Hooker preferred to call him—is engaged in "actions tendinge immediatelie unto Gods honour and mans happines." These actions are chiefly *"contemplation"* and *"administration,"* the latter being work which consists "in doinge the service of Gods house and in applying unto men the sovereign medicines of grace allreadie spoken of the more largelie" (V.76.10).[5] These "medicines" or means of grace include preaching, which covers teaching as well. Preaching involves the public reading of Scripture, teaching the Catechism, and delivering sermons. Hooker described sermons as "the blessed ordinance of God," being "unto the sound and healthie as foode, as physicke unto diseased mindes" (V.22.1). Such preaching Hooker presents as the descent of doctrine from on high. Prayer is the ascent of angels, carrying our responses to that doctrine to the throne of God:

> For what is thassemblinge of the Church to learne, but the receivinge of Angeles descended from above? What to pray, but the sendinge of Angels upward? His heavenly inspirations and our holy desires are as so many Angels of entercorse and commerce betweene God and us (V.23.1).

Public liturgy, such as that of the *Book of Common Prayer*, has been provided to enable this holy commerce between earth and heaven; "that verie sett and standinge order it selfe, which framed with common advise hath both for matter and forme prescribed whatsoever is herein publiquely don" (V.25.5) to promote true religion and thus to promote the secular and spiritual welfare of the commonwealth.

Preeminent among "the sovereign medicines of grace allreadie spoken of" are the sacraments of Baptism and Holy Communion. Such sacraments are the *necessary* means not only of the bestowal of saving grace upon the faithful but of that participation in Christ which has great ramifications. That is to say, sacraments

> serve as bondes of obedience to God, strict obligations to the mutuall exercise of Christian charitie, provocations to godliness, preservations from synne, memorialls of the principall benefites of Christ (V.57.2).

The consecrated bread and wine of the Eucharist are Christ's body and blood "because they are causes instrumentall upon the receipt whereof the *participation* of his boodie and bloode ensueth" (V.67.5). It is evident that for Hooker the purpose of the sacrament is not the transformation of the elements of bread and wine but the transformation of the recipients of those elements. That transformation, which is participation in Christ, is such that true religion is fostered, charity and godliness promoted, sin prevented, and, thus, the secular as well as the spiritual well being of the commonwealth advanced.

Hooker expressed in his own words and ways the convictions of many in sixteenth-century England, including those responsible for producing the *Book of Common Prayer* in 1549 and 1552. This assumption is based in part on our understanding of Hooker's concern to avoid novelty and to represent the prominent leaders of the church in Elizabethan England. But there is also evidence derived from other sources, such as the sermons of Hugh Latimer, bishop of Worcester when the Prayer Book was first published, John Jewel, bishop of Salisbury when the Elizabethan Prayer Book was introduced, and Thomas Cooper, bishop of Lincoln in the 1580s when the Puritans were seeking to displace the Prayer Book with one of their own.[6] One of the most prominent indications that Hooker's views as described above were in tune with the thinking of the church's leadership, including that of the persons responsible for the construction of the Prayer Book, consists of answers Cranmer drafted in response to the fifteen articles (or demands) made by the rebels in Devon and Cornwall during the so-called Prayer Book Rebellion of 1549. We have referred to Cranmer's sermon against the rebellion in which he exposed the "two destructions of the commonweal," the one being the covetousness of the landlords, the other the rebelliousness of the commons.[7] In that sermon, the archbishop espoused the cause of the Commonwealth Men.

In his answers to the articles, Cranmer speaks specifically of the Prayer Book, against the background of the kind of thinking represented by the sermon. Here Cranmer views true religion as the worship of Christ, whom the believer "spiritually receiveth, spiritually feedeth and nourisheth upon, and by whom spiritually he liveth, and continueth that life that is towards God."[8] The emphasis is on worship that affects life. The Prayer Book is the instrument of the Word of life, for Cranmer claims that

> in the English service appointed to be read there is nothing else but the eternal word of God: the new and old Testament is read, that hath power to save your soules; which, as St. Paul saith, 'is the power of god to the salvation of all that believe;' the clear light to our eyes, without which we cannot see; and a lantern unto our feet, without which we should stumble in darkness.[9]

At the heart of the Prayer Book are the scripturally warranted sacraments of Baptism and the Holy Communion. Cranmer's statements here are especially important, for they place emphasis on the sacraments as *moral* instruments of grace, which transform lives so that they avoid both covetousness and rebelliousness. He wrote:

> our Saviour Christ ordained the water of baptism to signify unto us, that as that water washeth our bodies outwardly, so be we spiritually within washed by Christ from all our sins. And as the water is called water of regeneration, or new birth, so it declareth unto us, that through Christ we be born anew, and begin a new life towards God; and that Christ is the beginning of this new life. And as the body that is new born, although it have life within it, yet can it not continue without meat and drink; even so can we not continue in the spiritual life towards God, except we be continually nourished with spiritual food: and that spiritual food is Christ also. For as he is the first beginning of our spiritual life, so is he the continuance and ending thereof. And for this cause did Christ ordain in the holy communion to be eaten bread, and drunken wine, that we should surely believe, that as our bodies be fed with bread and wine in these holy mysteries, so be we out of doubt that our souls be fed spiritually with the lively food of Christ's body and blood; whereby we have remission of our sins and salvation.[10]

Because participation in the sacraments constitutes the means of participation in Christ, Cranmer insists upon emphasizing participation. Baptism is to take place—normally—when the congregation meets, on "the holy-day, when the most number of the people be together," that all may rejoice in receiving "new members of Christ into" the church, and remember the promises made by godparents on their behalf, "and be more earnestly stirred to perform the same."[11] He also stresses participation by all persons in the Holy Communion. The sacrament should be received often. When the Spirit was most active in the early church, the communion was received daily, but "when the Spirit of God began to be more cold in men's hearts, and they waxed more wicked, the more people withdrew themselves from the holy communion."[12] Not only should participation in the Holy Com munion be more frequent—as frequent as possible—but the sacrament should be understood and be found in the language of the people. The change from Latin to English in the orders of worship was a sign of the growing national sentiment in England, but it was also both realistic and liturgically necessary. It was realistic because, as Cranmer pointed out, the people did not understand Latin and were thus cut off from the priest and the liturgy, and yet "all the whole that is done should be the act of the people and pertain to the people, as well as to the priest."[13] Here was a liturgical principle to which Cranmer adhered tenaciously: the Holy Communion must not only be frequently attended; it must be understood and thus participated in by all those who hear God's Word and receive the "lively food" that sustains them in true godliness. People shun communion, reluctantly agree to receive once a year, insist that all be in Latin, in order that they may escape condemnation for their sins and renewal which changes lives.

The Holy Communion "is so holy a thing, and the threatenings of God be so sore against them that come thereto unworthy, that an ungodly man abhorreth it, and not without cause dare in no wise approach thereunto. But to them that live godly it is the greatest comfort that in this world can be imagined."[14]

Cranmer in his answer to the rebels points to that which in his Prayer Book I have called the rhythm of contrition and thanksgiving,[15] the bringing of the faithful sinners to contrition, repentance, and amendment of life that they may eat the "lively food," participate in Christ and he in them, and thereupon gives thanks in godly lives of mutual and charitable communion, in their homes and villages, being instrumental in the revival of the godly kingdom of England.

When discussing the rebels' insistence that "*every preacher in his sermon, and every priest at the mass, pray especially by name for the souls in purgatory, as our forefathers did,*"[16] Cranmer spoke to that which could be the supreme incentive to Christians to attend church, participate in the sacraments, repenting and giving thanks, and practicing godly virtues. But the concept of purgatory he found to be abhorrent, implying that those dead and beyond ability to repent can have their sins corrected and "that all have not full and perfect purgation by his [Christ's] blood, that die in his faith." The catholic faith, taught by Scripture and confirmed by the blood of prophets and martyrs, affirms that "all the faithful that die in the Lord be pardoned of all their offences by Christ, and their sins be clearly sponged away by his blood."[17]

In his answer to the rebels, Cranmer spoke of the Prayer Book for which he bore the greatest responsibility and defended it against the cavils of ordinary people in a distant part of the land. It is with his explanations in mind—together with the far more detailed and learned exegeses of Hooker—that we turn to the *Book of Common Prayer* itself, first to a summary view of its genesis as an official instrument for the reform of England and then to a more detailed consideration of its shape, language, style, and meaning.

The Genesis of the Book of Common Prayer

The first Prayer Book did not appear until the reign of King Edward VI. In all likelihood it was Henry VIII, the supreme head of the *Ecclesia Anglicana*, who prevented the appearance of such a thorough reform of traditional worship. He was undoubtedly conservative in his theological views, adhering "fervently to transubstantiation, clerical celibacy and Purgatory," taking "part in the procession of the Blessed Sacrament to the Altar of Repose on Maundy Thursday," and attending Mass several times a day, while chiding those who yearned for liturgical forms patterned after those of Luther's Germany.[1] Equally as important were the political interests and concerns of the 1530s and 40s. While ousting the pope and dissolving the monasteries, the English maintained the outward appearance of the old religion, in parishes as well as cathedrals and the Royal Chapel. Furthermore, it was evident that Cranmer himself, an immensely influential person as Archbishop of Canterbury, was moving slowly from the old religion—as regards liturgy and sacramental theology—toward the positions he was to take during the reign of Edward VI.[2] Before Henry's death, Cranmer was experimenting

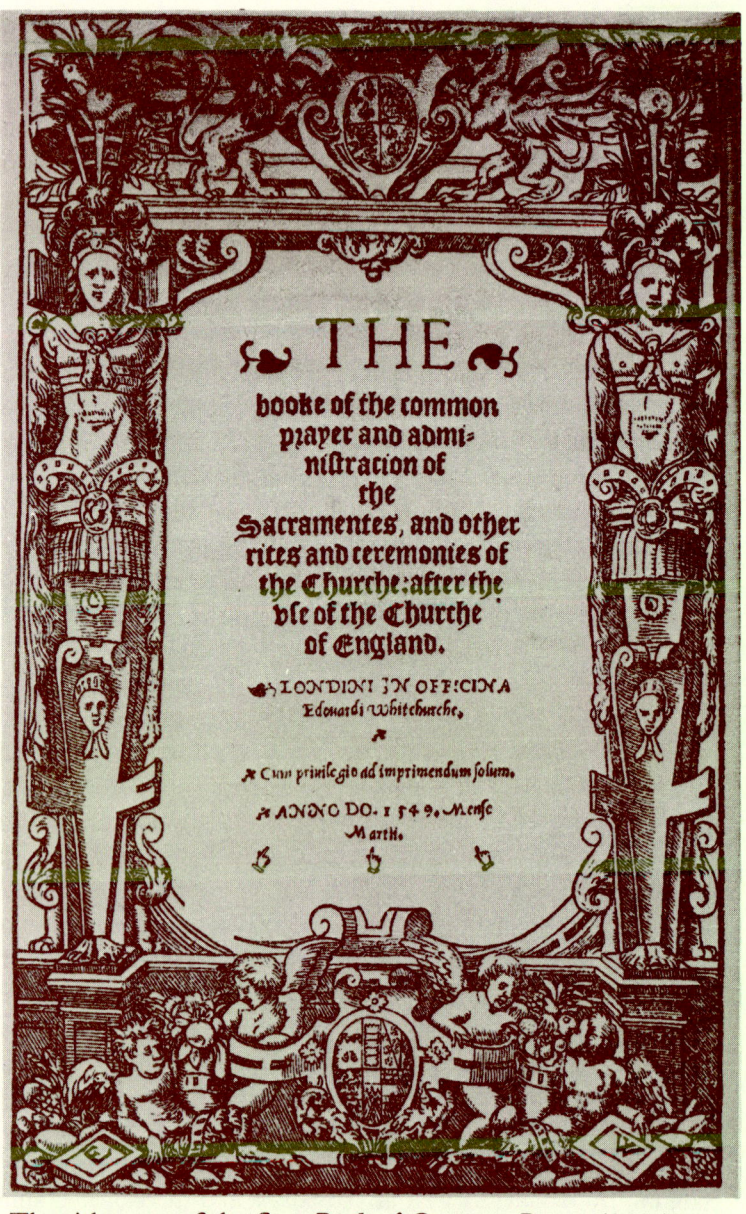

The title page of the first *Book of Common Prayer* (1549).

Communion and Commonweal 147

with the reform of processions and the daily offices. Yet, while there is some evidence that there was much talk and some action aimed at the radical reform of the church's worship, we have no evidence of Cranmer's drafting any revision of the Mass.

Although no Prayer Book was constructed during Henry's reign, the stage was being set for that which was to emerge in the next reign. The English Bible (1539) was more than a translation of the Scripture into the vulgar tongue and thus made more accessible to the people. It was a liturgical resource, providing lections in English for use in the daily offices and the Mass. The *Primer* in English, appearing in various versions from 1534 to the King's *Primer* of 1545, provided liturgical elements in the native language, such as the litany in 1535, largely a reproduction of Luther's 1529 litany, as well as Epistles and Gospels for the Sundays and holydays, and prayers, creed, commandments, Lord's Prayer, the hours, and psalms in English.[3] There is no indication that these items, which were to appear in the Prayer Book, were used in public worship, but the English were experimenting, learning, and working toward that which would appear in 1549. Both Bible and *Primer* appeared by public authority, duly licensed and promulgated as official instruments of reform.

In 1536 the observance of traditional feasts was adjusted by "King and Convocation," so that there was a marked reduction in the number of feasts kept as holydays, that is days without ordinary work.[4] At the same time efforts were begun to define the bounds of acceptable doctrine and practice for the church. The 10 Articles dealt with baptism, penance, and the Eucharist in moderate, although traditional fashion, and the ninth article spoke of lesser ceremonies such as ashes and holy bread as laudable but without power to remit sins.[5] The Bishops' Book (1537), the King's Book (1543), the 13 Articles (1538), and the 6 Articles (1539), all dealt similarly with doctrine and ceremony, although with sufficient variance to cause some dispute and arouse the king's concern.[6] In 1541, as a result of the work done by a commission of bishops appointed by Thomas Cromwell as the king's vicegerent in religious affairs, there appeared a book called *Ceremonies to be used in the Churche*, popularly known as the *Rationale of Ceremonies*. It provides detailed explanations of the ceremonies of baptism and the Mass, adopts the ninth article of the 10 Articles, and shows evidence of the influence of the reform of Hermann of Cologne.[7]

In 1542 Cranmer proposed to the Convocation of Canterbury that service books be amended and that the dressing of images and setting of candles before them be stopped. A new edition of the Sarum Breviary was imposed on all clergy, beginning the movement toward strict uniformity in liturgical matters. In 1543 Convocation responded to the king's wish that the service books be further reformed by setting up a committee to that purpose. The statement registered concerning this action is of importance, indicating that at an early stage permission was being given to proceed with that liturgical revision which eventuated in the *Book of Common Prayer:*

> Sequenti 21. Februarii (sess. xix.) 'reverendissimus significabat regiam majestatem velle; that all mass books, antiphoners, portuises in the church of England should be newly examined, corrected, reformed, and castigated from all manner of mention of the bishop of Rome's name, from all apocryphas, feigned legends, superstitious orations, collects, versicles, and responses; that the names and memories of all saints, which be not mentioned in the Scripture, or authentical doctors, should be abolished and put out of the same books and calendars; and that the services should be made out of the Scriptures, and other authentic doctors.'[8]

At this same Convocation it was ordered that "every Sunday and holyday throughout the year, the curate of every parish church after the Te Deum, and Magnificat, should openly read unto the people one chapter of the New Testament in English, without exposition; and when the New Testament was read over, then to begin the Old."[9]

In 1544 England was at war with France and Scotland and the king was about to go to France himself. He requested that a litany be provided for the occasion and Cranmer responded with the Litany in English which was to become a part of the Prayer Book. Called *An Exhortation unto prayer, thoughte mete by the kinges majestie, and his clergy, to be read to the people in every church afore processyons. Also a Letanie with suffrages to be said or song in the tyme of the said processyons,* it deals with petitionary prayer in ways which buttress the view of the Prayer Book as the instrument for the bringing in of Christ's kingdom in Tudor England. The *Exhortation* explains petitionary prayer in terms of the Lord's Prayer, concluding:

> let us make our prayers and supplications, rendering and giving of thanks for all men; and namely, for kings, princes and all other set in chief dignity and high rooms, that by their godly governance, their true, faithful, and diligent execution of justice and equity unto all their subjects, our heavenly Father may be glorified, the commonwealth may be daily promoted and increased, and that we all, that are their subjects, may live in peace and quietness, with all godliness and virtue....[10]

Discussing how to pray, the *Exhortation* argues the necessity of faith but also of "charity and brotherly love betwixt neighbour and neighbour."[11] Hypocrisy must be avoided. The English tongue is to be used: "to the intent...your hearts and lips may go together in prayer."[12] The *Exhortation* ends:

> Let us also furnish and beautify this our prayer, that it may please God the better, and delight the ears of our heavenly Father, with fasting and wholesome abstinence, not only from all delicious living in voluptuous fare, and from all excesses of meat and drink, but also to chastise and kill the sinful lusts of the body, to make it bow, and ready to obey, unto the spiritual motions of the Holy Ghost. Let us also furnish it with almsdeeds, and with the works of mercy and charity: for prayer is good and acceptable unto God, when it is accompanied with almosedeeds, and with the works of mercy....[13]

Thus was the asceticism of the monastery to be cultivated, day by day, by kings and commoners, landlords and yeomanry.

Cranmer was now busily engaged in liturgical revision. On June 11, 1544, he wrote a letter to King Henry which indicates that he had translated "into the English tongue, so well as I could in so short time, certain processions, to be used upon festival days."[14] We have no further knowledge of these translations beyond this letter. Cranmer had produced one scheme for a revision of the

Sarum Breviary in 1538 when negotiations for an alliance were under way between the Lutherans and the English. This scheme, not surprisingly, shows Lutheran influence. A second scheme, patterned after the reforms instigated by Cardinal Quinones in Spain, was devised by Cranmer sometime between 1545 and 1546.[15] The surviving manuscripts, along with the Litany he produced for the king, provide ample evidence of Cranmer's liturgical genius and support the contention that it was he who was chiefly responsible for the Prayer Books of 1549 and 1552.

By 1547 Henry VIII was dead. There is some evidence in Foxe's *Actes and Monumentes* and in a letter from Cranmer to the king, that toward the end Henry was prepared to remove by force if necessary certain superstitious practices as "the ringing of bells upon Alhallow-day at night, and covering of images in Lent, and creeping to the cross," as well as the crucifixes or roods in the churches.[16] Letters of authorization from the king were prepared but suppressed at the instigation of Cranmer's enemy, Stephen Gardiner, bishop of Winchester.[17] Further reform was to be postponed to the next reign.

Upon Edward VI's accession to the throne there was a flurry of activity. In 1547 the first *Book of Homilies* appeared, having been in the making since the Convocation of 1543. The Injunctions provided for the first Edwardian Visitation of all the churches of the land ordered that the Epistle and Gospel at high Mass be read in English so that the people could hear them, that an English lesson be read at Matins and Evensong, that the Litany be said kneeling and not in procession before the high Mass, that one of the homilies be read to the congregation each Sunday, that Prime and Hours be omitted when there was no sermon, and that a strong box be provided near the high altar to receive alms and oblations for the use of the poor.[18] There seemed to be a concerted effort by the Privy Council and Convocation, while restraining the most radical reformers, to extend the use of English and to abolish superstition. The Privy Council itself in January, 1548, ordered the omission of candles, ashes and palms at Candlemas, Ash Wednesday, and Palm Sunday. Subsequently it prohibited veneration of the Cross on Good Friday and the use of holy bread and holy water at any time.[19]

At Easter in 1547, in the Chapel Royal, compline was said in English, an early indication of the trend towards more and more services in the native tongue. In May, 1548, Matins, Mass, and Evensong were sung in English at Westminster Abbey. In June of the same year translations of these three services were sent to Oxford and in September to Cambridge.[20] This may have involved experimentation with liturgical forms in English, it may have been a signal to reformers and others of what was to come, but whatever the intent such actions in such high places would command attention and be taken seriously by friends and foes alike.

On November 4, 1547, Parliament met. At its opening Mass, the *Gloria in excelsis*, the Creed, and the Agnus Dei were sung in English.[21] The next day Convocation met to consider various articles, among which was one ordering that "'certain books' already believed prepared by learned men and certain prelates for the worship of the church be laid before the lower clergy 'for a better expedition of divine service.'"[22] This suggests that the work begun in the latter years of Henry's reign had proceeded to the point that there were drafts of services in English, seen, or rumored to be seen, which ought to be made public. If anything was produced for Convocation to view and discuss we do not know it. What can be believed is that such discussion in Convocation, especially in the upper house where the bishops sat, led to a request made to Parliament for relief from the repressive legislation of Henry's reign, in particular from the Six Articles Act of 1539, and that communion in both kinds, bread and wine, be allowed. A bill was drawn up, debated, and revised, between November 12 and December 17, when it was enacted.[23] This Act (1 Edw. VI, c.1) is entitled, "Against Revilers, and for Receiving in Both Kinds."

The Act reflects the views of the Commonwealth Men,[24] the concern for unity and concord in that true religion so essential to the commonwealth, desiring that the people should fulfill their duties to God and the king out of love rather than fear, "nourishing concord and love amongst themselves." The government is said to be most disturbed by the way people have reviled the Sacrament of the Altar, "the supper and table of the Lord, the communion and partaking of the body and blood of Christ." The emphasis is on communion, the main theme of the liturgical reform in England. The reviling of the Sacrament, the Act suggests, proceeds from wickedness or else from "ignorance and want of learning." Morality and learning were precious to Christian humanists and to reformers alike. They are important in this Act. Penalties are levied and inquiries instituted. In the second half of the Act we read:

> And forasmuch as it is more agreeable, both to the first institution of the said Sacrament of the most precious body and blood of our Saviour Jesus Christ, and also more conformable to the common use and practice both of the Apostles and of the primitive Church, by the space of 500 years and more after Christ's ascension, that the said blessed Sacrament should be ministered to all Christian people under both the kinds of bread and wine, than under the form of bread only, and also it is more agreeable to the first institution of Christ, and to the usage of the Apostles and the primitive Church, that the people being present should receive the same with the priest....[25]

the same is ordered by king and Parliament. The priest is to exhort all people to prepare to receive and none is to be denied the body and blood—"the benefit and comfort promised." Everyone is to "try and examine his own conscience before he shall receive."

To a limited extent, the very basis of Prayer Book worship is enunciated in this Act. The communion of all in the Sacrament of the body and blood of Christ is the basis of unity and concord in the commonwealth. That is to say that through contrition aroused by exhortation and participation the people composing the commonwealth are made participants in the Lord of life, receiving the benefit and power of divine grace, which nourishes love and concord in the land.

The ordering of communion in both kinds, together with the theological undergirding of such communion and the trend toward vernacular liturgy, necessitated the *Order of Communion*,

Communion and Commonweal 153

which was provided on March 8, 1548, in time for the Easter celebrations.[26] According to a letter of the Privy Council written on March 13, this liturgical form was prepared by "sundry of his majesty's most grave and well learned prelates, and other learned men in the scripture" who were brought together by the king and "after long conference" settled on such an order.[27] The *Order of Communion* was designed to be inserted into the Latin Mass. It consists of notice of the next time communion will be provided for the people, together with an exhortation, warning, and instruction concerning preparation for communion. The second part consists of a form of administration to be used after the celebrant's communion, with exhortation, warning, invitation, confession, absolution, and "comfortable words," a prayer before communion, words of administration, and a blessing. There are notes on the kind of bread used and on consecration of additional wine should the priest run out of that initially consecrated. Like the Litany, this *Order of Communion* was to become a part of the Prayer Book. That it was provided before 1549 in part indicates its importance as illuminating the meaning of the Prayer Book as a whole. The *Order* was not entirely new. It was customary to provide for the preparation of communicants with exhortation, confession, and absolution in the vulgar tongue.[28] There is evidence that the *Order* was influenced by the *Pia deliberatio* of Cologne.[29] In fact the precedents in English medieval practice are as important and suggest that here as in the Prayer Book to come continuity was sought after in the process of reform.

The committee which met to produce the *Order of Communion* may have been composed of those who subsequently met to draft the final form of the *Book of Common Prayer*. We first learn of this group in a statement enclosed within a Royal Proclamation issued from Windsor Castle on September 23, 1548. Here we read that the government wished "to see very shortly one uniform order" of worship, "for which cause at this time certain bishops and notable learned men, by his highness' commandment are congregate."[30] This was the so-called Windsor Committee which met at Chertsey Abbey, where Robert Ferrar was consecrated bishop of St. David's, "the holy Eucharist being then consecrated," and not only administered, "in the vulgar tongue."[31]

Parliament began the second session of the reign on November 24 and Convocation a day later. By that time it is reasonable to suppose that a book was ready. How like or unlike that which we know as the first *Book of Common Prayer* we cannot tell. We do know that whatever was ready was discussed. Sometime after December 14 and before Christmas adjournment on December 21, the Prayer Book was debated in the House of Lords.[32] There the debate centered on the presence of Christ in the Eucharist—bishops Tunstal, Thirlby, and Heath arguing that the book was objectionable for its language opposing transubstantiation; Cranmer, Ridley, Holbeach, and Goodrich defending its language and doctrine. The debate, as recorded, was moderate, but the contenders were firm in their positions. It was on the fourth and last day that Cranmer sounded the keynote of his reform, quoting 1 Corinthians 10:16: "*Panis quem frangimus est communicatio corporis*. Even so Christ when he said: *This is my body* he meant *communionem corporis*... To eat his flesh and drink his blood is to be partaker of his passion...." Nicholas Ridley, then bishop of Rochester, added: "In that bread is *communio Corporis Christi* in the good. But the ill do receive *mortem et judicium*."[33] The debate would seem to have ended without the views of either party being altered. The bill (with the book) was then (probably December 19) taken to the House of Commons. After Christmas it had its first formal reading in the House of Lords (January 7) and after a second reading on the tenth was put to a vote on the fifteenth of January. It was opposed by only two lay lords. Ten bishops voted for it while eight voted against, including Thirlby, who admitted that he had subscribed to the book earlier for the sake of unity, although he objected to its doctrinal statements. The statute (2 & 3 Edw. VI, c.1) argued the need for the *Book of Common Prayer* on the basis of the necessity for uniformity, for one order of worship in place of a variety of rites and ceremonies represented by various "uses" such as that of Sarum and by local "forms and fashions" of more recent times. The book was to stand alone as the sole order of worship in England after the feast of Pentecost. Penalties for non use or abuse were prescribed.[34]

Regarded from the vantage point of the medieval use of Sarum which preceded it, the *Book of Common Prayer* represented radical and innovative reform. It was entirely in English, it encompassed a library of liturgical books in one book, it greatly simplified medieval liturgy, and it contained doctrinal emphases which were considered offensive by traditionalists. For instance, in place of the *Hanc igitur oblationem* of the Sarum consecration in the Mass, the first Prayer Book has:

> O God heavenly father, which of thy tender mercie diddest geve thine only sonne Jesu Christ to suffre death upon the crosse for our redempcion, who made there (by his one oblacion once offered) a full, perfect, and sufficient sacrifyce, oblacion, and satysfaccyon, for the sinnes of the whole worlde, and did institute, and in his holy Gospell commaund us, to celebrate a perpetuall memory of that his precious death, untyll his coming again....[35]

The Sarum prayer simply refers to "This oblation" or sacrifice. It can be understood to refer to the Eucharistic sacrifice as a repetition of the sacrifice of Christ on the cross. The Prayer Book disallows any such interpretation. The one and only effective sacrifice was that of Christ on the Cross, which is now remembered. The Prayer Book strove to alter the popular understanding of the Mass, redefining "sacrifice" as "our Sacrifice of praise and thankes geving."[36]

On the other hand the Prayer Book seemed to be very traditional. Unlike Lutheran and Reformed Eucharists, the Prayer Book sacrament contained a canon, or prayer of consecration, remarkably similar to that of the Roman Missal, including a Communio Sanctorum, or Commemoration of the Saints, with its reference to the "most blessed virgin Mary, mother of thy sonne Jesu Christe."[37] Roman Catholics such as the rebels of Devon and Cornwall might refer to the Prayer Book Eucharist in derogatory fashion as "a Christmas game,"[38] but there were others, more Protestant or Reformed than Cranmer, who would feel that it was too popish. John Hooper wrote to Henry Bullinger:

> It is no small hindrance to our exertions, that the form [of the Mass] which our senate or parliament, as we commonly call it, has prescribed for the whole realm, is so very defective and of doubtful construction, and in some respects indeed manifestly impious...I am so much offended with that book, and that not without abundant reason, that if it be not corrected, I neither can nor will communicate with the church in the administration of the [Lord's] supper.[39]

In the middle were those who saw some faults and some strengths in the book, including the reformer Martin Bucer and the English bishop Stephen Gardiner, the latter believing that the Prayer Book Eucharist still contained basic dogmas concerning the Mass.[40]

We shall shortly have cause to deal more at length with this first Prayer Book, its design and contents. Now it is sufficient to observe that there was dissatisfaction over it, ranging from a desire for moderate amendment to an insistence upon outright rejection. Among those considering further reform was Cranmer himself, the chief architect of the book. He was clearly disturbed by Gardiner's locating in the book such doctrine as he had earnestly sought to correct or expell. Cranmer was also concerned to clarify its basic character and in particular its biblical content, its directness and simplicity, and its strong emphasis on communion and community.

A second Prayer Book was produced in King Edward's reign. It was seemingly ready in some form at the beginning of 1551 but did not make it through Parliament and onto the statute books until April 14, 1552. Little is known of the process by which the book took shape. It seems most likely that Cranmer was in charge, although not altogether, and that he consulted a number of people, gathering advice from various quarters. Nicholas Ridley, who became bishop of London, was in regular contact with the archbishop. Hugh Latimer, the preacher of the Commonwealth party, was a house guest at Lambeth Palace.

Cranmer was also busily engaged on the reform of canon law and thus had ample opportunity to consult with others on the committee which produced the *Reformatio Legum Ecclesiasticarum*, including Goodrich, bishop of Ely, Cox, the king's almoner, Taylor of Hadleigh, May, Dean of St. Paul's, Lucas, Master of Requests, and Peter Martyr Vermigli, the Italian monk turned reformer, resident in England at the time.[41] But in a letter to Martin Bucer, who in his *Censura* wrote a detailed critique of the first Prayer Book and was evidently taken quite seriously by Cranmer, Peter Martyr, on January 7, 1551, speaks of bishops meeting, having in hand their criticisms of the book.

> It has now been decided in their conference, as the Most Reverend [Cranmer] informs me, that many things shall be changed; but what corrections they have decided upon, he did not explain to me, nor was I so bold as to ask him. But I have been not a little gratified by what Mr. Cheke has told me; he says, that if they will not make the changes which have been considered necessary, the King himself will do this; and that, when Parliament meets, he will interpose his Royal authority.[42]

It cannot reasonably be argued that Cranmer managed the revision alone. There was evidently much work being done, persons like Bucer and Peter Martyr providing expert advice, bishops meeting in committee to draw up lists of necessary changes, arguments taking place between differing groups of bishops, with the government watching over all that was done and at the last moment acquiescing to pressures brought to bear by the most radical group under the leadership of John Hooper to interpose by authority of the Privy Council a rubric printed in black explaining that by kneeling to receive communion no adoration of the sacrament was intended. Such, seemingly, was the rather complex situation leading to the appearance of the second Prayer Book. That the book emerged as coherent and effective as it was suggests that Cranmer was not simply passive in the process, but that gathering in all suggestions and dealing with various contending groups he exercised the control of an arbiter and editor with considerable authority. He was defeated where the Black

Rubric was concerned, but there would not be many instances of such open flaunting of the archbishop's power, even though the government of the Duke of Northumberland favored the more radical reformers.[43]

The second *Book of Common Prayer* was incorporated in a second Act of Uniformity (5 & 6 Edw. VI, c.1). In this Act it was argued that although a godly order had been produced, "agreeable to the word of God and the primitive Church, very comfortable to all good people desiring to live in Christian conversation, and most profitable to the estate of this realm," yet

> because there has arisen in the use and exercise of the aforesaid common service in the church, heretofore set forth, divers doubts for the fashion and manner of the ministration of the same, rather by the curiosity of the minister, and mistakers, than of any other worthy cause:
>
> Therefore, as well for the more plain and manifest explanation hereof, as for the more perfection of the said order of common service, in some places where it is necessary to make the same prayers and fashion of service more earnest and fit to stir Christian people to the true honouring of Almighty God....[44]

the king and Parliament have attached the new book to this statute, together with the Ordinal produced in 1550.

Consequently, many of Bucer's suggestions were heeded, moving the Prayer Book further towards the orders of Strasbourg and Geneva. Considerable effort was made to clarify the Prayer Book's rejection of the doctrines of Real Presence and of the Sacrifice of the Mass. The Prayer of Consecration was divided with the communion inserted after the Words of Institution. To avoid adoration of the consecrated elements, they were to be consumed as quickly as possible. The Oblation and the Prayer of Humble Access were moved so that they could have no reference to the elements. Much was omitted, including terms such as "altar" and "Mass," the mass vestments, anointing, exorcism, communion at funerals, and much else. New sentences of administration were substituted for the old ones. For instance, where in the first book the priest said, upon giving the bread to the communicant: "The body of our Lorde Jesus Christe whiche was geven for thee, preserve thy bodye and soule unto everlastynge lyfe." In the second he said: "Take and eate this, in remembraunce that Christ dyed for thee, and feede on him in thy hearte by faythe, with thankesgeving."[45] There could hardly be found clearer proof of the fact that the second book wholeheartedly espoused the Reformation doctrine of justification by faith without benefit of works, by the power of Christ's death on the Cross, the sacrifice made once for all, which, remembered, enables the faithful to feed on him in their hearts, spiritually and not carnally. The second Prayer Book was unquestionably a further reform of the worship of the church and not merely a revision of the *Book of Common Prayer*. Viewed thus it constitutes a radical change, reforming by destroying, its language often didactic and argumentative.

There is another way of looking at the second Prayer Book, however, a way which takes account of the basic intent of the first book and sees the second as the logical development of that intent. That basic intent, as has been indicated, was the cultivation of communion with God, through Christ and the Holy Spirit, for the sake not only of the individual involved, but of the commonwealth as a whole. In the first book this sense of worship as communion was emphasized by the use of the common tongue, the care taken that people should hear and understand, the provision of greater participation by the laity, and especially by insistence upon communion as the heart of every Mass. The increased use of Scripture in substantial portions, the simplification of ceremonies, the eradication of much considered to be superstitious—all this served the basic intent and helped the Prayer Book become a chief and powerful instrument in the idealistic program of the Commonwealth party, which was more than the program of a party, as Bucer indicated in his *De Regno Christi*. The *Communio Christiana* is in process of being realized in and through the church and its worship, through the preaching of the Word and the administration of the sacraments, so that the commonwealth becomes ever more fully the *Societas Christiana*. This is no passive "Erastianism." Rather, here we find the church influencing and molding the state that it may become that which it is meant to be:

> all true kings and princes humbly hear the voice of Christ from the ministers and respect in them the majesty of the Son of God, as they administer not their own but only the words and mysteries of Christ, the words and mysteries (*verba et mysteria*) of eternal life.[46]

In the following sections of this chapter we shall be looking at these two books in detail, both as to over-all design, language, and style and as to meaning, especially in the sequence from Morning Prayer through Holy Communion which constituted the intended regular Sunday morning fare in parish churches and cathedrals alike. Now we note the fact that the second Prayer Book was in use from November, 1552, to sometime after July 6, 1553, when Mary, the Roman Catholic half-sister of King Edward, came to the throne. In the autumn her first Parliament met and by a statute (1 Mary, Statute 2, c.2) swept away both Prayer Books and ordered worship to be as it was in the last year of Henry VIII.[47] The Prayer Book did not pass entirely away. At home and abroad there were those who remained loyal to the Reformation in England, continuing to use the second book. At Frankfort-on-Main a struggle took place between those led by John Knox who wished to use a Genevan order of worship and those who insisted on the *Book of Common Prayer,* revised to meet contingencies, including the demands of their host church. These Prayer Book loyalists at Frankfort were led by Richard Cox, the king's almoner and one of those whom Cranmer may have consulted while revising the Prayer Book. The events at Frankfort contributed to the maintenance of Prayer Book worship and to the struggle to come between the Puritans who shared the convictions of the Knoxians and the Prayer Book loyalists who like the Coxians may have been willing to modify the Prayer Book but stubbornly refused to throw it out in favor of some foreign order of worship.

When Mary died and her half-sister Elizabeth came to the throne on November 17, 1558, there were high hopes expressed by some that she would retain the Mass. Others, such as those returning from exile on the continent, hoped that she would reinstitute the second Edwardian book, perhaps modifying it in a Genevan direction. A moderate such as Edmund Guest believed that the queen was inclined toward the first Prayer Book.[48] In reality, Queen Elizabeth I saw to the enactment of an uniformity bill which restored the 1552 book with certain, conservative modifications. These changes were specified in the Act as consisting of the "addition of certain lessons to be used on every Sunday in the year," the Litany altered so as to exclude the blatantly anti-Roman prayer for deliverance "from the tyranny of the Bishopp of Rome and al hys detestable enormities," and the sentences of the first and second Prayer Books combined, bringing together the contrasting (although not necessarily opposed) theologies of Real Presence and Memorialism.[49] Not mentioned, but of importance, was the dropping of the so-called Black Rubric. The Ornaments Rubric requiring the retention of mass vestments was inserted by the authority of a separate clause of the Act.[50] Nor can we ignore the queen's example in retaining cross, or crucifix, and candles in her chapel, thus openly defying the wishes of those who clamored for a further reform of worship after the example of the continental reformed churches.[51] While the Mass was once more abolished, the trend toward further reform was halted, the necessary liturgical compromise achieved, providing for England a liturgy both Catholic and reformed, one designed to influence the course of events in such a way that the nation should become the Kingdom of Christ in earth.

The Design of the Prayer Book

The *Book of Common Prayer,* its design and content, was influenced by the early church fathers, Eastern liturgies, continental Roman Catholic and Protestant liturgical revisions, English devotional literature in the vernacular, the English Primers, and much more. It is of interest, but not altogether surprising to discover that a Primer dated about 1400 should sound so much like the beginning of the Prayer Book office of Matins.

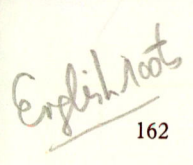

The "Lay Folks Prayer Book" began this way:

Domine labia
    Lord thou schalt opene my lyppes.
    And my mouth shal schewe thi preisynge.
    God tak hede to myn help.
    Lord hige the to helpe me.
    Joyge be to the fadir. and to the sone.
        and to the holygoost.
    As it was in the begynnynge and now and ever:
        in the werldis
        of werdlis.[1]

Of greater interest is the prayer in the *Cloud of Unknowing,* clearly an earlier form of the Prayer Book Collect for Purity:

God, unto whom all hertes ben open, and unto whom alle wille spekith, and unto whom no prive [privy] thing is hid: I beseche thee so for to clense the entent of myn hert with the unspekable gift of thi grace, that I may parfiteliche love thee and worthilich preise thee.[2]

The fact is that the versicles as found in the Primer and the Prayer Book are translations of those in the Sarum Breviary. The Collect for Purity is found in its Latin original in the Sarum Missal.

Without denying the contributions made by the church fathers, the Eastern liturgies, continental Roman Catholic and Protestant liturgical revisions, English Primers and devotional literature, it seems obvious that the Prayer Book is chiefly a revision of the Latin liturgy of the Western church and in particular that version of it in use at Salisbury known as the Sarum Use. Five "books" of the late medieval church are involved.

The Breviary is the book of daily offices which was supplanted by the Prayer Book Matins and Evensong, as well as the lectionary and other materials preceeding Morning Prayer. The Missal, containing the Mass and those things pertaining to it, was supplanted by the Prayer Book propers (Introits of 1549, Collects, Epistles, and Gospels of 1549 and 1552) and the Holy

Communion. The Processional, containing words and music for use in processions on Sundays, Rogation Days, and other special days, was supplanted by the Litany, which in 1549 follows Holy Communion and in 1552 follows Morning and Evening Prayer, the more logical place for it in terms of use. The Manual, containing those offices which are properly performed by a priest, was supplanted by the Prayer Book Baptism, Matrimony, Visitation and Communion of the Sick, Burial, Purification (1549) or Thanksgiving after Childbirth (1552), and Commination. The Pontifical, or book containing the services performed by a bishop, was supplanted in the Prayer Book of Confirmation and in 1550 by the Ordinal. In other words, the Prayer Book supplanted a veritable library of liturgical books. Its outline or overall form was not to change in any serious way from 1549 to the revisions of the twentieth century.

It would be misleading, however, to say that all worship was reduced to fit into one book. The Bible would be needed, as would the Psalter, until the Psalms were included in the Prayer Book. If no sermon was preached, the minister would need the *Book of Homilies* from which to read at sermon time. The Ordinal was not at first bound with the Prayer Book. *The Clerk's Book* was published in August of 1549 containing those things to be said or sung by the parish clerk, along with the necessary cues to guide him.[3] Finally, there was John Merbecke's *The Book of Common Prayer Noted*, published in 1550, providing the musical settings required at a time when the services were mostly sung.[4] We also note that from time to time officially authorized orders of worship, prayers, and thanksgiving, and the like were published for use in relation to particular needs and special occasions.[5]

There are two essays included in the Prayer Book which help to explain the bases on which the reform and consolidation of the church's worship were carried out: (1) the Preface, a translation of the preface to Cranmer's first revision of the Breviary, heavily influenced by Cardinal Quinones, and (2) "Of Ceremonies," which is an expansion of two of the 13 Articles (1538). Neither essay was devised as an introduction to the Prayer Book as a whole. The first pertains specifically to the use of Scripture in the offices and the second is a defense of the general procedure of revision which resulted in the deletion of some ceremonies and the retention of others in the Western liturgical tradition. And yet they clearly note principles which do in fact govern the whole.

The essays serve to emphasize that the over-all intent was to devise an order of worship which could be owned by all of the people and not be the private preserve of the clerical estate whom the commons were expected to acknowledge as acting on their behalf. Such a statement is pejorative, and indeed the entire process was colored by such opinions. The Bible and the order of worship as a whole were to be understood by the people that they might be edified—"influenced with the love of his [God's] true religion." The worship of the church was to be in the vernacular, simplified, clear, and uniform through the entire land. The Preface put it this way:

> here you have an order of prayer (as touching the reading of holy scripture) much agreeable to the mind and purpose of the old fathers, and a great deal more profitable and commodious, then that which of late was used. It is more profitable, because there are left out many things, whereof some be untrue, some uncertain, some vain and superstitious: and is ordained nothing to be read, but the very pure word of God, the holy scriptures, or that which is evidently grounded upon the same; and that in such a language and order, as is most easy and plain for the understanding, both of the readers and hearers. It is also more commodious, both for the shortness thereof, and for the plainness of the order, and for that the rules be few and easy. Furthermore by this order, the curates shall need none other books for their public service, but this book and the Bible: by means whereof, the people shall not be at so great charge for books, as in time past they have been.

The essay "Of Ceremonies" seeks a *via media*. Some ceremonies are put away because of excess, there were far too many, and some because they fostered superstition. Some have been retained because they are good, serving the need for decency and order, and because they edify the people. This essay acknowledges that some people will be offended because familiar things are discarded, some because not everything has been discarded. There is no allowance for diversity in England—uniformity is the rule—but in the end the essay makes it clear that uniformity is a matter for national churches to decide. Such churches may very well differ one from another.

The purpose then is that the people of the nation may be directed away from error and superstition, and that the pure Word of God may reach through all resistance to pierce them, enflaming them to love true religion and to live by that religion in their daily lives. This intent springs from both humanist and Protestant roots. Christian humanists and Protestants alike wished to see the Word of God freed from obscurity, from bondage in an unknown language, and from falsifying superstition. Thomas More may have disagreed with William Tyndale's translation and may have agreed with Tunstal that it was dangerous to put the Bible in the hands of mere commoners without instruction and guidance, but he had never heard any convincing reason given for not translating Scripture into English.[6] As for the Protestants, the case was put succinctly in the two propositions offered for debate at the Westminster Conference in 1559:

> First, That the use of a tongue not understood of the people, in common prayers of the church, or in the administration of the sacraments, is against God's word.
> The second, That the same is against the use of the primitive church[7].

Later on, the draft statement of those speaking in favor of these assertions reads, that the "definition of public prayer" as found in St. Paul is this: "Common-prayer is, to lift up our common desires to God with our minds and to testify the same outwardly with our tongues."[8] Thus it is clear that the use of the vernacular (as well as emphases on simplicity, clarity, and on edification) is in part sought so that prayer might be common in order that the people of any given place might make their common desires known to God. The purpose in view concerns the social dimensions of life as well as the personal.

The Structure of the Prayer Book in Relation to Time

Central to the purpose and design of the Prayer Book was the way in which it encompassed the whole of a person's life. Given the facts of strict uniformity and legally enforced church attendance, together with the essentially religious character of the sixteenth century, no one escaped from the all-pervasive influence of the Prayer Book. Shortly after birth the Christian was baptized (dipped into the water) in a rite which involved spiritual regeneration. From 1552 on the child was signed "with the signe of the crosse, in token that hereafter he shal not be ashamed to confesse the fayth of Christ crucified, and manfully to fight under his banner against synne, the world, and the devyll, and to continue Christ's faythfull souldier and servant unto his lifes end." The promise was there made which would find fulfillment in the ordinary occupations of Christian citizenship.

The Prayer Book Catechism, attached to the service of Confirmation, was the instrument used for the education of the child, which education was focused on the fulfillment of the promise made in baptism. This catechism was used every Sunday, in accordance with law,[1] the parish priest instructing the members of his parish in the Creed, the Ten Commandments, and the Lord's Prayer, and their meaning. When asked, "What is thy duetie towardes thy neighbour?" the children were expected to repeat, time and time again by rote, this answer:

> My duetie towards my neighboure is, to love hym as myself. And to doe to al men as I would they should do unto me. To love, honor, and succour my father and mother. To honour and obey the kyng and his ministers. To submit my self to all my governours, teachers, spiritual Pastors, and maisters. To order myself lowly and reverently to al my betters. To hurte no body by worde nor dede. To be true and juste in al my dealinge. To beare no malice nor hatred in my heart. To kepe my handes from pickyng and stealing, and my tongue from evil speaking, lying, and slandering. To kepe my body in temperaunce, soberness, and chastitie. Not to covet nor desyre other mens goodes. But learne and labour truly to geat myne owne living, and to do my duetie in that state of lyfe, unto which it shall please god to call me.[2]

It is of interest to consider the list of vices and virtues given in this response in relation to the civil and ecclesiastical records of the times, and especially in relation to the records of the church courts.[3] Not only did the church educate the young for Christian citizenship: it, along with the state, watched over their morals, punishing those who were guilty of sin against God and their neighbors.

To be confirmed was to have the bishop place his hands on the child's head, praying that this child may be defended by divine grace, continue God's forever, "and daily encrease in thy holy spirite more and more, until he come unto they everlastyng kyngdom." The primary instruments for this continuing growth in grace toward the fuller realization of the Christian life were the Holy Communion, together with the daily offices, through which the Word of God and the Sacrament of Christ's body and blood were administered to the people. The Holy Communion and the office of Morning Prayer will be subjected to careful consideration further on in this chapter.

At this point it is important to realize that the Prayer Book intended that the Christian community should gather daily for the offices and on Sundays and holy days for the offices and the Holy Communion. As the services derived from the medieval Manual encompassed the whole of a person's life, strengthening it at crucial junctures with the means of grace, so the Prayer Book also encompassed each day, each week and, through lectionary and propers and sundry special services, each season and the entire year. Time was sanctified by the church's liturgy: personal time, social and community time, all of time. From day to day the offices infused the Word, read and preached, into the lives of people and into the life of the community. Week by week the Holy Communion provided the grace necessary for continual growth in the Christian life, and for the growth of Christian community. From Advent to Advent the Prayer Book provided for the remembrance of God's mighty acts in Christ Jesus for the world's salvation. And through the year there were the holy days, greatly reduced in number but in 1561 increased again.[4] Holy days, including saints days, were related to the church year, but stretched beyond, encouraging and exhorting the saints of the sixteenth-century English church to follow the examples of Christian living provided by Apostles, Martyrs, the Virgin Mary, and All Saints. Thus, through Prayer Book worship, the baptized Christians lived under the daily influence of the Christian tradition.

As the Christian grew in years, the Prayer Book provided the liturgies marking the great turning points in life. "The Fourme of Solemnyzaccyon of Matrymonye" sanctified the bond which is the foundation of community, that between man and woman, constituting the family, the priest blessing them and praying that they may "lyve together in holy love." In sixteenth-century England the primary reason for marriage was procreation, the creation of a new family unit and additional citizens and saints. This was the message of the preface to the service, reiterated in the prayer which was omitted only when the woman was past the age of child-bearing:

> O Merciful Lord and heavenly father, by whose gracious gift mankind is encreased: we beseche thee, assist with thy blessing these two persons, that they may both be fruteful in procreacion of chyldren, and also lyve together so long in godly love and honestie, that they may see their childrens children, unto the third and fourth generacion, unto thy prayse and honour....

The other reasons given in the Prayer Book for marriage were clearly subordinate, although not unimportant. As the preface tells us, matrimony was also intended as "a remedye againste synne, and to avoide fornicacion," clearly great dangers to any community based on the close-knit family structure. The third purpose is of particular interest here: "for the naturall societie, helpe, and coumforte, that one ought to have of the other, both in prosperitie and adversitie."[5] Such language points to the persistent concern of the Prayer Book and the society for communion and community.

The two services of Visitation and the Communion of the Sick are provided to minister to people afflicted so that, like John Donne, they hear the church bell tolling, signifying the death of some one, and hear it tolling for them. The Visitation of the Sick refers to sickness not as a result of accidents but as allowed, if not provoked, by God "to trie your pacience for the example of other and that your fayth may be found in the day of the lord laudable ... Or els it be sent unto you to correct and amend you, whatsoever doeth offend the eyes of our heavenly father."[6] Steadfastness and repentance are called for, along with constant prayer for divine mercy. The 1549 rite included unction, or anointing with oil, indicating by the gift of the Holy Spirit, "who is the spirite of al strength, coumforte, reliefe, and gladnesse," that sickness is at least partially the doing of external and evil powers. However, both books emphasize the need for repentance and amendment of life if the sick person is to be cured.

The Communion of the Sick was not a casual, private affair. The priest, together with members of the community, gathered at the sick-bed to communicate together. But the collect provided for the celebration reiterates the main thrust of the service of Visitation:

> Almightie everlyvinge God, maker of mankinde, which doest correcte those whom thou doest love, and chastisest every one whom thou dost receyve: we beseche thee to have mercy upon this thy servant visited with thy hande, and to graunte that he may take his syckenesse paciently, and recover his bodelye health (yf it bee thy gracious wyll), and whensoever his soule shall departe from the bodye, it maye bee without spotte presented unto thee....[7]

Sickness constituted a threat to the community and the nation not only because disease—such as the dreaded and recurrent plague—worked havoc, making cities virtually death camps at times and bringing whole armies to their knees, but also because sickness reflected the conditions of people's souls and was a sign of God's displeasure with his people.[8]

If the Visitation provided for the person in danger by virtue of sickness, the Churching of Women, which the 1552 book preferred to call Thanksgiving of Women after Childbirth, provided a means of thanking God for having "delivered this woman ... from the great paine and peryl of childe birth." It was also, and just as importantly, the means for the new mother's re-dedication: "that she through thy helpe, maye both faythfully lyve, and walke in her vocacion, accordynge to thy wyl in thys life present."[9] In conceiving and birthing, the woman was considered to be deep in sin. The Prayer Book provided for her reentrance into the community of the faithful.

Finally, the Prayer Book provided for the Burial of the Dead. The 1552 Book greatly reduced the rite from the much fuller one of 1549, which was combined with a provision for a requiem Mass.[10] The second Prayer Book reflects the Protestant suspicion of burial rites as involving superstitious practices and teaching objectionable doctrines such as those connected with purgatory and indulgences. For that reason their burial offices involved the respectful interment of the body and little else.[11] Whatever differences existed between the rites of 1549 and 1552, there was the common, solemn note sounded for all the living to hear that "Man that is borne of a womanne, hath but a shorte time to lyve, and is full of misery: he commeth up and is cut downe lyke a floure; he flieth as it were a shadowe, and never continueth in one staye" (Job 9). Nevertheless, for those who are enflamed with a love of true religion, serve the Lord, living according to his will and commandment, death is not the end: "whoever liveth and beleveth in hym, shall not dye eternally." The collect provided for the rite proceeds: "We mekely beseche thee (O father) to raise us from the death of sinne unto the life of righteousnes, that when we shal depart this lyfe, we may reste in him."[12] The death of the covetous and sinful person, doomed for eternity, is the spectre which haunts the Christian, providing impetus for repentance, amendment of life, and for Christian citizenship.

And so through all of life, the Prayer Book ministers to the holy community exhorting the people to live as followers of Christ, providing through Word and Sacraments instrumental means to that end.

There is another sense in which the Prayer Book concerns time and the Christian life. Thus far we have been mindful of horizontal time, *chronos*, but the Prayer Book also concerns vertical time, *kairos*. For in and through this book, in the reading and preaching of the Word and in the administration of the sacraments, the holy community is forcefully made to remember God's mighty acts in history, and especially God's revelation through the cross of Christ, in order that the faithful may not forget what God has done, but remember, and in remembering participate in that which in terms of *chronos* is past. The eternal is present with power as the people remember Christ's birth, ministry, death, resurrection and (for the future) his coming again. As they remember they are indeed changed, their lives reformed and refashioned after the example of the Lord and all his servants. The *anamnesis* (or remembering, memorial) is central to the Eucharist. It is identified with a specific moment in the consecration of the 1549 book,[13] but it pervades the Prayer Book as a whole, for what is this order of worship but the communal remembering of God's mighty acts in the context of the present that the community may become the Kingdom of Christ and thus advance toward the fulfillment of mankind and history in the future?

The Language and Style of the Prayer Book

The language and style of the Prayer Book were devised in order that the common prayer of the church might exercise a reforming influence on the community. Stella Brook rightly points out that: "Liturgical writing calls for a simultaneous and balanced use of the physical and intellectual aspects of language which has something in common with the use of language in verse drama."[1] This language is, first of all, aural, meant to be spoken and heard rather than read. But then English poetry and prose in the sixteenth century were generally intended to be spoken aloud and one must imagine a literate individual reading a book aloud rather than reading silently. This is no trivial point and must be kept in mind. The Prayer Book was written to be spoken and heard. Secondly, it was written to be combined with certain actions. The rubrics are stage directions indicating what the actors—priest and people—are to *do* in relation to the words. The student of the Prayer Book must thus imagine what is done as well as reading what is said. Admittedly, this is not always easily achieved. At crucial points rubrical directions are wanting. For instance, in the Holy Communion the rubric directs that the people are to receive "the Communion in both kyndes...in their handes kneling," but nothing is said about where they are or how they got to be where they are. Thirdly, the language is poetic, compressed, allusive and sometimes obscure in contrast to homiletical style which is in prose and is clear and more explanatory and wordy.[2]

The fact that liturgical language is poetic, aural, and akin to verse drama does not mean, however, that it is strange or distant from the people towards whom it is directed. In the sixteenth century the language of the people differed by regions and locales; the rebels in Cornwall and Devonshire in 1549 must have found the language of the Prayer Book strange to their ears. Nevertheless, given the realities of dialect and developing style in the sixteenth century, the language of the Prayer Book was unique in the way it adhered to the "natural, native resources instead of trying to force English into an inevitably unsatisfactory mutation of the quite different resources of Latin."[3] Developed out of a process beginning with Anglo-Saxon, incorporating French and Latin loan words, the ordinary, common English spoken in the first half of the sixteenth century was flexible, rich in variations, and expansive. Liturgical writers of the time were confronted, for instance, by three words which were different but shared the same meaning: the Old English *hālig*, the Latin *sanctus*, and the French *saint*. All three possibilities were available for use in the *Sanctus*, but the old English *hālig* won out, issuing in the powerfully incantatory, "Holy, holy, holy...."

The language of the Prayer Book is effective language. Its speech is often simple and direct, as in the Litany, where a prayer for fair weather (1552) begins: "O Lorde God, which for the sinne of man diddest once drowne al the world, excepte eight persons...."[4] Doubling, which is so prevalent in the book, is often glossatory, as in the second exhortation of the Holy Communion where the two words ("love and charitie") with the same meaning explaine one another. The same is true of "serche and examine," and "confesse and open his sinne." Doubling is usually emphatic. Where one word might slip too easily by, two are better suited to make the desired impact. For instance, in the invitation to the General Confession in Morning Prayer (1552), we find "synnes and wychednesse," "dissemble nor cloke," "goodness and mercie," "assemble and mete," "requisite and necessarye." Alliteration is also used to good effect, howbeit with restraint, as in the Litany: "Remember not Lorde, our offences, nor the offences of our forefathers...of our synnes, spare us good Lorde, spare thy people." Alliteration and stress make this excerpt from the second exhortation of Holy Communion notable: "ghostly counsayle, advice and comfort, that his conscience may be releved...." Doubling and alliteration at times assist not only by means of emphasis but also by rhythm, reinforcing the poetic intent. This is true of the Prayer for the Whole State of Christ's Church where we hear: "that they may truly and indifferently minister justice, to the punishment of wickedness and vice, and to the maintenance of goddes true religion and vertue." This simply would not be as effective stylistically or emphatically without the doubling.

There are times when the rhythmic structure itself makes a prayer memorable. Examples abound. In the Litany we read: "That it may please thee to succoure, helpe and comforte all that be in daunger, necessitie, and tribulation," and in the prayer at the end in 1552 we have: "O God heavenly father, whose gyft it is that the rayn doeth fall, the yearthe is fruitfull, beasts increase, and fishes doe multiplye...."[5] See also the Prayer for the Whole State of Christ's Church for its rhythmic shifts, the General Confession in Holy Communion with its "you...you ...you," the rhythm of the sequence from the Sursum Corda, to the Proper Preface, Preface, and Sanctus, and the Prayer of Humble Access with the rhythmic "eat the flesh...drink the blood," "we in him...he in us," "bodies cleansed...souls washed." Concerning rhythmic structure there are signs of improvement in the 1552 book, as, for instance, in the prayer in Baptism which in 1549 said: "Almightie and everlasting God, heavenly father, wee give thee humble thanks, that thou haste vouchsaved to call us to knowledge of thy grace, and fayth in thee: Increase and confirme this fayth in us evermore...." In 1552 two words were added to the petition, changing it to read: "Increase *this knowledge* and confirm this faythe," improving the symmetry and rhythm of the prayer.[6]

Related to rhythmic structure are the rises and falls, as in the General Confession of Morning Prayer (1552): "and there is no health in us: but thou, O Lorde have mercy...." The depths of self-abnegation and contrition are reached with "no health in us." Indeed, the sound descends, taking the speaker with it. But from that point on the ascent begins, both in meaning and in sound, with: "but thou, O Lorde have mercy...." There is an aural descent followed by a rising up in the response to the 10 Commandments, "Lord have mercy upon us, and encline our hearts to keep thys lawe," although very often the officiant seems not to understand that this is so. The *Gloria in excelsis* is marked by a high note sustained in the first paragraph, a low note in the second, and a rising note in the third, which the best musical settings convey and thus assist with the transmission of the meaning. The Prayer of Humble Access provides another example. But the most impressive is that found in the consecration prayer of the Holy Communion, and in particular in the People's Oblation. The level plane of the oblation proper yields to a sharp drop with "And althoughe we be unworthy," passing over to a rising note ending on a high plane. This sort of phenomenon is not surprising in liturgical compositions, for liturgy is not only poetic, it is a kind of music. Customarily in the sixteenth century the liturgy was sung.

There are many other examples of the way meaning was conveyed by sound. In the Litany, for instance, we hear: "that these evylles be brought to nought...be dispersed." "Be brought to nought" indicates a sharp stop or cessation through sound as well as through the meaning of the words. "Be dispersed" suggests distribution by its very sound. In the Collect for Purity, "inspiration of thy holye spirite" is noteworthy, for "inspiration" has the sound of breathing in it suggesting the activity and influence of the Holy Spirit. In the 10 Commandments "bow downe to them, nor worship them" conveys prohibition in the very sound of the words. Other examples are found in the Prayer for the Whole State of Christ's Church, the Invitation to Confession ("Draw near with faith...take this holy Sacrament ...make your humble confession...mekely knelynge upon your knees"), in the General Confession itself ("we knowledge and bewayle...grievously have committed"), and supremely in the sequence from the Sursum Corda through the Sanctus, beginning with "Lift up your hearts" which virtually raises one up off the knees to stand up praising God.

Finally, there is repetition, particularly the repetition of the Lord's Prayer as it is said again and again on Sunday morning as the parish congregates to worship.[7] There is also the repetition of the basic rhythm of contrition and thanksgiving, already noted. The Puritans objected to the repeated use of the Lord's Prayer, while Hooker defended it.[8] Repetition was not a result of sloppiness, forgetfullness, or superstition. It was something inherited from the past and retained, quite deliberately, with the conviction that repetition serves a purpose and that where the Lord's Prayer is concerned it is abundantly clear that its purpose is to perfect the prayers and praises of the people which cannot help but be defective.

The Puritans objected to a number of things concerning the language and style of the Prayer Book. The to and fro exchanges between minister and people (or minister and clerk), in versicles, Commandments, Litany, and Commination, were objected to and defended on the grounds not only of antiquity and usefulness. Hooker believed that the practice emphasized and promoted the unity and community of minister and people.[9]

The Puritans objected to the use of short prayers called Collects.[10] A form of prayer reaching back to the Gallican rites, collects were so called originally because they gathered up the silent petitions of the people at the conclusion of a litany. The Prayer Book Collects follow the traditional form of the old Latin Collects, with an address to God, accompanied by mention of some divine attribute, usually connected to that which follows. Then comes the petition, often followed by what might be expected if the petition is granted (the "that" clause). At the end there is an oblation or pleading "through Jesus Christ our Lord," by whose mediation the prayer is made effective. If the prayer is addressed to Christ, the ending is different. The English Collects are not as brief or as tightly controlled as the Latin, but most of them are short, clear, simple, and easily memorized, possessing "a pearcinge kinde of brevitie."[10]

There are the set Collects of Morning and Evening Prayer, Collects such as that for Purity in the Holy Communion, and Collects for the church year and for holy days. It is undoubtedly true that not all of Cranmer's translations are equally felicitous, or on a par with the Latin Collects.[11] But given the fact that English expands where Latin contracts, the Prayer Book Collects are effective translations. One example must suffice. It is the Collect for Grace in Matins. The Latin version is from the office of Prime, but originally it appeared in the Gregorian Sacramentary:

| Domine sancte pater omnipotens eterne deus qui nos ad principium huius diei pervenire fecisti, tua nos hodie salva virtute: et concede ut in hac die ad nullum declinemus peccatum: nec ullum incurramus periculum: sed semper ad tuam iustitiam faciendam omnis nostra actio tue moderamine dirigatur. Per. | O Lord our heavenly father, almighty and everlyvyng God, which haste safelye brought us to the beginning of this day: Defend us in the same with thy mighty power, and graunt that this day we fall into no sinne, neither runne into any kinde of daunger, but that all our doinges may be ordered by thy governaunce, to doe always that is rygtheous in thy sight: through Jesus Christe our Lorde. Amen.[12] |

The rhythm is impressive, the symmetry complete. It is as though the translation, while representing the Latin Collect, possesses a momentum of its own, perhaps based upon Cranmer's understanding of the mathematics of music, and especially of ratios, recreating in spoken words the music of the spheres.[13]

Communion and Commonweal

The care and skill expended on language and style were all to a purpose: that through Word and Sacrament the people—the holy community—might be reached, reformed, and perfected as the Kingdom of Christ. King Alfred the Great in his work of translation was aware of the affective power of the spoken word made more powerful when used with care and skill.[14] There were those in the sixteenth century, as there are in the twentieth, who wished liturgy to be contrived in the vernacular of the streets and the homes, the most common language. As such it is inclined to be an ineffective instrument of the Gospel, in large part because it ceases to be liturgy, utilizing the poetic language and music which relates the Eternal to the present. The most common language may be uncommunicative to most or if communicative it may convey the opposite of what was intended. It may be flat and dull, lacking "inspiration" in the deepest and fullest sense of that word. It may be too wordy, argumentative, and didactic. The Puritan Prayer Book of the 1580s has many felicitous and effective sentences and phrases, but too often it is didactic and uninspired, reading like a text book or a company report, in reality neither memorable nor effective.[15] The Puritan Prayer Book in fact presumed that the most able ministers would pray as inspired in their own words. The prayers set down were examples, or directions, to be used if necessary.

The *Book of Common Prayer* was a set liturgy, with prayers whose language was not to vary. The book was to be used day by day, week by week, year by year, until the words and phrases, the sounds and music, sank into the deep recesses of the mind and there effected the reformation of the individual in mind and will. This was the intent: to bring the sinful Christian to contrition that that person might receive grace to amend his or her life and contribute toward the building of the Kingdom of Christ in England.

Sunday Morning in a Tudor Parish Church

It is difficult at best to know what actually went on in a Tudor parish church on Sunday mornings. The Prayer Book represents

The Communion.

And when he had geuen thankes, he gaue it to them, saying: Drinke ye all of this, for this is my bloud of the new Testament, whiche is shed for you and for many, for remission of synnes: Doe this as ofte as ye shal drinke it in remembraunce of me.

¶ Then shal the minister first receyue the Communion in bothe kyndes him selfe, and next deliuer it to other ministers, yf any be there present (that they may help the (chief) minister) and after to the people (in their handes kneling.) And when he delyuereth the bread, he shall saye.

Take and eate this, in remembraunce that Christ dyed for thee, and feede on him in thy hearte by faythe, with thankes geuinge.

¶ And the minister that delyuereth the cup, shall saye.

Drinke this in remembraunce that Christes bloude was shed for thee, and be thankefull.

¶ Then shall the priest saye the Lordes prayer, the people repeating after him euery peticion.

¶ After shalbe sayde as foloweth.

Lorde and heauenly father, we thy humble seruauntes, entierly desyre thy fatherly goodnes, mercifully to accepte this our Sacrifice of prayse and thankes geuing: most humbly besechyng thee to graunt that by the merites & death of thy sonne Jesus Christ, and through faith in his bloud, we and al thy whole church, may obtaine remission of our synnes, & al other benefites of his Passion. And here we offre and present vnto thee, O lord, our selfes, our soules & bodies, to be a reasonable, holy, & liuely Sacrifice vnto thee: humbly beseching thee, that all we which be partakers of this holy Communion, may be fulfilled with thy grace & heauenly benediction. And althoughe

The communion within the consecration of the *Book of Common Prayer* (1552).

the ideal envisioned by its framers—principally Thomas Cranmer. According to the Prayer Book there would have been the regular sequence of Morning Prayer, Litany, and Holy Communion, with Baptism, when required, coming after "the last lesson at Morning Prayer."[1] We know for a certainty that the ideal was not always pursued, let alone realized. William Harrison in *The Description of England* (1577) points out that in the Elizabethan era, if there are not communicants to receive the Eucharist, "we read the Decalogue, Epistle, and Gospel, with the Nicene Creed (of some in derision called the 'dry communion'), and then proceed unto an homily or sermon...." Furthermore, he places Baptism at the end of the sequence, which was most likely not the rule.[2] What is certain is that the "dry communion," or Antecommunion, was the rule, save on three Sundays during the year when parishioners were forced by law to communicate, Easter being the chief day of obligation. Cranmer, like Calvin, envisioned the Holy Communion in its entirety as constituting the chief service of worship on Sundays. From his time on conscientious bishops were much concerned that the people refused to communicate except when forced to do so.[3] In that which follows we shall consider the ideal rather than actual practice, for our concern is chiefly to understand the Prayer Book itself. Nor shall we be able to take into account all of the differences between the 1549 book and those books that followed after it in the sixteenth century and later. We shall, however, consider such differences when they concern our main theme: the efforts made to bring into being the Kingdom of Christ in Tudor England.

The community gathered at the parish church on Sunday morning. All inhabitants of the geographical parish were expected to be there and those who absented themselves were liable to be cited in the church court. Once in the church building, the people were seated according to their rank and importance, the physical arrangement conforming to the structure of the community. Being seated they were expected to be attentive, or at least quiet, and thus accessible to the Word of God. Facing them as they awaited the beginning of morning prayer, dominating the east wall, were the Creed, the Ten Commandments, and the Lord's Prayer. Such details are known to us largely due to articles and injunctions of visitation and church court records. From the latter we learn of Margery Hopkins and Barbara Nichols fighting over a seat in St. Ebbe's, Oxford, John Kevill victualling and playing cards and Thomas Cutt bowling during service time, the wife of Alexander Dence talking during service, dogs and children causing disturbances, and Robert Homes hurling a pot at a sidesman who admonished him for not attending church.[4]

Morning Prayer began with the priest situated in the choir or in some other place where he could be easily heard. In the 1549 book the service began with the priest reciting the Lord's Prayer, "with a loude voyce." In 1552 there was a penitential opening comprised of sentences, invitation, General Confession, and absolution. This addition to the office provided the necessary preparation for worship, which in the old religion was provided by the sacrament of penance. As the invitation explains, confession is preparation for that rendering of thanks in Canticles and Psalms which is to follow, for hearing God's Word through the lessons from the Old and New Testaments, and for asking "those things which be requisite and necessarye, as well for the body as the soule." In the confession, perhaps led by the parish clerk, the kneeling parishioners confess: "We have followed too much the devices and desyres of oure own heartes. We have offended against thy holy lawes." The sin to which reference is made is selfishness, covetousness, and the violation of divine law prescribing love of God and love of neighbor. At the end of this community confession the prayer is made: "graunt, O most mercyful father, for his sake [Christ's], that we may hereafter lyve a godly, righteous, and sobre lyfe, to the glory of thy holy name." The absolution pronounced by the priest begins the upward movement out of contrition toward praise. It is followed by the Lord's Prayer, marking the conclusion of the penitential sequence and the final collection of the prayers of all, priest and people, as they approach the throne of God.

From the Lord's Prayer on the 1549 and subsequent books

agree. The dominant note struck now is that of praise. The Priest speaks: "O Lorde open thou our lyppes." The people respond, "And our mouth shal shewe forth thy prayse." The 1552 book has changed the singular to plural, "my" to "our", emphasizing the communal character of the office. There is, however, still penitence mixed with the praise in that which follows. The Venite begins with rejoicing but ends with God speaking: "it is a people that do erre in their heartes, for they have not knowen my wayes." Psalms and Canticles and Lessons may also alternate between penitence and praise. But praise is the most prominent characteristic of this sequence from the Venite through the Creed. The rubrics direct once more that the minister be heard, turn to the people when reading the lessons, and if the lessons are sung they are "to be sung in a plain tune, after the maner of distincte reading." Furthermore, we know from injunctions of visitation and from church court records that to further assist the people in hearing and understanding what is read or sung from the New Testament an appropriate portion of Erasmus' *Paraphrases* may be read.[5]

It is of interest to note the relation between the Lukan Benedictus and the Apostles' Creed which follows. The Benedictus is praise to the God of Israel who saved his people from bondage and covenanted with them, whose steadfast love and mercy is acknowledged. This is the God who does not forget but remembers "his holy covenant," speaks to his people through the prophets, that his people "might serve him without feare," and thus serve him with holiness and righteousness "all the days of our lyfe." It is this God who has sent his child, the prophet of prophets, to "goe before the face of the Lorde, to prepare his wayes./ To geve knowledge of salvacion unto his people: for the remission of their sinnes." This is the last Canticle in 1549; an alternate is simply listed without being written out in the 1552 book, indicating that the Benedictus rather than Psalm 100 (the Jubilate) was the rule. And it was right that the Benedictus be used here, for it is a fitting introduction to or companion of the Apostles' Creed, which is the common profession of faith in God, the God of Israel, in Jesus Christ the mediator and redeemer, and in the Holy Spirit working in the church, wherein there is "The forgevenesse of synnes." Both Benedictus and Creed, thus, provide the appropriate response to the Word heard in and through the lessons and canticles, and the appropriate preparation for that which follows most immediately with the petitions of the people.

The final movement of Morning Prayer begins with "The Lorde be wyth you," pronounced with a "loude voyce," to which the people respond, led by the clerk, "And wyth thy spyryte." In the 1549 book the Canticle is simply followed by the Kyrie, but in 1552 the Kyrie comes after the Creed and Versicles. 1552 is in fact improving the liturgical drama here by providing the sequence of Creed (closely related to the preceding Benedictus), Versicles, Kyrie, and then once more at a critical turning point the Lord's Prayer. In the versicles which follow the people once more descend to penitence, asking for mercy and for salvation, for the welfare of the king, the righteousness of ministers, and the joy of the people. The "O God make cleane our heartes within us./ And take not thyne holy spyryte from us" anticipates the Collect for Purity which is to come when the Holy Communion begins.

Three Collects conclude the service. The Collect for the Day comes first, bringing to the consciousness of the people the church year and the petition appropriate to the particular day or time in the church year now observed. It is heard here for the first time; it will be heard again in Holy Communion. The second Collect is for Peace and is related to the Benedictus. It is in reality a prayer for defense against our enemies. In it God is addressed as "author of peace, and lover of concorde, in knowledge of whom standeth our eternall lyfe, whose service is perfecte fredome (*cui servire regnare est*)." The third Collect, as we have seen,[6] is for Grace and is a prayer "to lyve well," "to doe alwayes that is righteous in thy sight." These latter two Collects, which "shal never altre, but dayly be sayd at *Morninge Prayer*," must have been known by all in a short time, by clergy and people alike, so well known that they were inscribed in the mind and on the heart. God who gives eternal life, whom to serve is to reign and to enjoy perfect freedom, is the defense of his servants against "all assaults of our enemies," against plague and highwaymen, against sinners and foreign powers, so that trusting in God's defense, his people may live as becomes those who have been freed from paralysing anxiety. Furthermore, the God who brings his people to each new day, defends them, when they pray for grace, from sin and danger, in order that all they do may be done according to the divine will, that they may "doe alwayes that is righteous in thy sight." God is ever present, always watching, ready to judge, but always ready to forgive. Here in these prayers there is the impetus, the motivating force, to newness of life. To those who approach God with penitence, hearing God's Word and responding in a profession of faith, these prayers lend strength to go forth, living the Christian life, surrounded, watched over, guided by God, Father, Son, and Holy Spirit.

This is not, however, the end of the community's worship on Sundays. The people are not now to go forth. Instead, as we learn from the 24th Injunction of Edward VI, immediately before Holy Communion the Litany is said. It is said or sung, not in procession but with the people in their places and the priests and others of the choir kneeling "in the midst of the Church." Saying the Litany in procession has been done away with to "avoid all contention and strife, which heretofor hath risen...by reason of fond courtesy, and challenging of places in procession." It shall be read or sung "plainly and distinctly...to the intent the people may hear and answer."[7] The Elizabethan Injunctions allow that it may be said in procession on Rogation day when "the Curate and substantial men of the parish, walk about their parishes, as they were accustomed, and at their return to the church make their common prayers."[8] Once more emphasis is placed on edification, to which end the people must not be distracted by the confusion of an actual procession from hearing and responding to the priest who leads them in their prayers, prayers patterned after the ancient prayers of the church. The rubric at the beginning of the Prayer Book service indicates that the Litany is to be used on Sundays, Wednesdays, Fridays, and other days as "commanded by the Ordinary."

The Litany opens with the Invocation of Father, Son, and Holy Spirit—the glorious Trinity—and with the penitential response: "have mercie upon us miserable sinners." Here the English takes the "Miserere nobis" and expands it, greatly heightening the penitential emphasis. This is the only proper approach to prayer. Omitting 1549's requests that the Virgin Mary, the angels and archangels, and the Patriarchs, Prophets, Apostles, Martyrs, Confessors, and Virgins, "and all the blessed company of heaven," "Praye for us," the 1552 Litany proceeds from the Invocation to the Deprecations, or prayers for protection from various personal evils, natural disasters, and from "sedicion and privy conspiracie." The 1549 and 1552 books both ask for deliverance "from the tyrannye of the bishoppe of Rome and all his detestable enormities," a prayer which Queen Elizabeth I wisely deleted. The Deprecations end with prayer for deliverance "from all false doctrine and heresy, from hardnes of hearte, and contempt of thy worde and commandemente," thus returning to the personal emphasis with which they began. Those opening Deprecations pertain to the ethic of the Kingdom of Christ and are worth citing in their entirety:

> From all evill and mischiefe, from synne, from the craftes and assaultes of the devil, from thy wrathe, and from everlastyng damnacion:
> *Good Lorde deliver us.*
>
> From blindnes of heart, from pryde, vainglory, and Hypocrisy, from envy, hatred and malice, and all uncharitablenesse:
> *Good Lorde deliver us.*
>
> From fornicacion, and all other deadly synne, and from all the deceytes of the worlde, the flesh, and the devill:
> *Good Lorde deliver us.*[9]

Deprecations are followed by Obsecrations or entreaties whereby we call upon the Lord for his help, by virtue of all that he has done for us in his incarnate life, his death, resurrection, and ascension, and in the sending of the Holy Spirit. The Obsecrations constitute a remembering or *anamnesis* on the part of the holy community, a fact which must not be forgotten as we proceed to discover that the *anamnesis* in the 1549 prayer of consecration is dropped from that of 1552.[10] Here the Obsecrations serve to remind the worshippers that their help comes from One who in life and death, by his obedience, overcame sin and death for them.

Deprecations and Obsecrations are the prelude to the Suffrages or intercessions which account for the main body of the Litany. The Suffrages include prayers for the universal church, for the king, for the clergy and specifically for a devout and learned ministry,[11] for the Privy Council and the nobility of the realm, for magistrates, for all people and for all nations. There is a dramatic shift, then, to the personal, howbeit the personal in the context of the wider community, for there are these prayers:

> That it may please thee to geve us an hearte to love and dreade thee, and diligently to live after thy commaundementes:
> *We beseeche thee to heare us good lorde.*
>
> That it may please thee to geve all thy people increase of grace to heare mekely thy worde, and to receyve it with pure affeccion, and to bryng furth the fruites of the spirite:
> *We beseeche thee to heare us good lorde.*

However, the emphasis then shifts again, now to petitions for those in need, those who err and are deceived, those in "daunger necessitie and tribulacion," those who travel by land or sea, "all weomen labouring of childe, all sycke persons and young chyldren," all prisoners and captives, fatherless children and widows, and "all men," that they may all receive mercy. The attention is here focused on the community and its needs.

As the Litany proceeds, suffrage by suffrage, one can imagine the parishioners thinking of particular persons whom they might assist as instruments of the Lord. The intercessions shift again, approaching their climax. Now there are prayers for our "enemies, persecutors and sclaunderers," for the prosperity and fruitfulness of the earth, and, in the end, for repentance. Looking backward over all the Suffrages, the members of the congregation would have no basis on which to be proud of their lives or smug in the assurance that they have demonstrated by word and deed love of God and love of neighbor. The prayer they were directed in making then seems most appropriate:

> That it may please thee to geve us true repentance, to forgeve us all oure synnes, neglygences and ignoraunces, and to endue us with the grace of thy holy spirite, to amend our lyves according to thy holy woorde:
> *We beseche thee to heare us good lorde.*

The dramatic impact of the Litany is assured by this prayer and by the terse, pleading versicles that follow, together with the Agnus Dei, the Kyrie, and concluding with the Lord's Prayer and some final versicles. This is without doubt one of the most impressive and one would assume effective portions of the Prayer Book and, indeed, of all known liturgical drama. The Litany was designed to produce that conversion in the deepest roots of the heart—that *metanoia*—capable of changing society and the world.[12]

The Litany proceeds, perhaps anticlimactically, to a final sequence of prayers and versicles, now in a quiet mood, yet influenced by that which has gone before, so that there is a calm earnestness and zeal expressed, as the people are led to pray that God will hear them, assist their prayers, defeat all evil, that they "maye evermore geve thankes" to God in his holy church. There is a quiet, controlled emotion in the exchange: "Pitifully beholde the sorowes of our hearte./ Mercifullye forgeve the sinnes of thy people...O Lorde, let thy mercie be shewed upon us./ As we doe put our trust in thee." The final prayers of the 1549 and 1552 books differ markedly but both begin with "We humbly beseche thee, O father, mercifully looke upon our infirmities..." and both end with the prayer of St. John Chrysostom. The 1544 Litany has a prayer for grace which anticipates the sacrament which follows:

> Almyghtye and everlyvynge God, whyche onely workest great marvayles, send downe upon our byshoppes, and curates, and all congregacyons, commyetted to theyr charge, the healthful spirite of thy grace, and that they maye trulye please the: poure upon them the contynuall dewe of thy blessynge. Grante this (O Lorde)

for the honoure of oure advocate and mediatour Jesu Christe.[13]

The Holy Communion followed the Litany. Here there is considerable difference between the 1549 and the 1552 books. For one thing, the Holy Communion in 1549 was begun by the priest standing "humbly afore the middes of the Altar" dressed in a plain alb with chasuble or cope. In 1552 it was begun by the priest standing at the north side of the Table which was to be set in the body of the church, or wherever the congregation had gathered for the office. In addition, the 1549 celebration opened with the Lord's Prayer, the Collect for Purity, the Nine-Fold Kyries, and the Gloria in Excelsis, while in 1552 the opening was far more penitential with the Lord's Prayer, Collect for Purity, the Ten Commandments with kyrie responses, and no Gloria in Excelsis. Yet the most striking difference is found following the Offertory. In 1549 the sacrament proceeds directly to the Sursum Corda, Preface, Proper Preface, and Sanctus. Then comes the Canon, or Consecration Prayer, beginning with intercession for the Whole State of Christ's Church, and proceeding to an epiclesis or invocation of the Holy Spirit, the Words of Institution, an *anamnesis,* and the people's Oblation. The Lord's Prayer follows and the communion begins with the Peace, the "Christ our Paschal Lambe," invitation to confession, confession and absolution, Comfortable Words, Prayer of Humble Access, and the reception of "body" and "blood" while the clerks sing the Agnus Dei. After the Communion there was sung the Post Communion anthem, one of many provided from verses of Scripture, then the Thanksgiving, and, finally, the blessing.[14] In the 1552 book all was drastically reordered. Some things were dropped, but the intent was not only to exclude material considered to be superstitious or unnecessary. More basically, the intent was to clarify the sacrament as the Holy Communion, the sacrament of the holy community building the Kingdom of Christ in England.

In the 1552 book, after the Offertory, there came the "Prayer for the Whole State of Christ's Church Militant here in Earth." This was followed by the exhortations, which in 1549 preceded the Offertory. Next were the Invitation to Confession, the General Confession, Absolution and Comfortable Words. The Sursum Corda, Preface, Proper Preface and Sanctus followed. Then came the Prayer of Humble Access and the Consecratory Prayer with communion of the priest and the people set in its midst and concluding with the Lord's Prayer and with either the People's Oblation or the Thanksgiving. The sacrament ended with the Gloria in Excelsis and the Blessing.

It has been said[15] that the 1552 version of the sacrament was a perfecting of the Lord's Supper as the Holy Communion. The greatest proof of this exists in the way the communion of priest and people is set in the midst of the Consecration Prayer, between the words of institution and the oblation or thanksgiving. The purpose of consecration as Richard Hooker understood it[16] was not the change in the elements of bread and wine but the change in the faithful for which the bread and wine as the body and blood of Christ are instrumental. The consecration is not complete until the people have communicated. Having communicated they are then ready to offer themselves as a reasonable sacrifice. They are, indeed, the body and blood of Christ. The critical readjustment of the consecration prayer in the 1552 book is the basic change in the Holy Communion necessitating the moving of other things to new places. It is because of this understanding but also because of the fact that this rite was the one which became the norm in England for generations to come that we shall concentrate on it, although from time to time we shall need to consider the 1549 rite as well.

The sacrament in both 1549 and 1552 begins with a series of rubrics pertaining to the discipline of the members of the holy community. Those who intend to communicate are to make their intention known "to the Curate over nyghte, or els in the morninge, afore the begynninge of morninge prayer, or immediatly after."[17] If any parishioner thus signifying his intention is known to be "an open and notorious evyll lyver... or have done anye wronge to hys neyghbours...," he shall be told that he cannot communicate until he has repented, amended his ways, and recompensed any whom he has harmed, "or at the least declare hym selfe to be in full purpose so to doe, as soone as he conveniently maye." Turning from the individual to the community, the rubrics order that the curate shall follow the same procedure in regard to persons "betwyxte whome he perceyveth malyce and hatred to rayne." Thus the Holy Communion, which must be received at least three times a year according to law, is viewed not only as so sacred that it must be guarded, but also as a prime instrument for securing correction of faults in individuals and between individuals in the holy community. We shall see how this emphasis recurs as the sacrament proceeds.

We must now envision, as the 1552 rite is reviewed, the Table covered with fair linen set in the midst of the people, the priest stationed at the north side. Here the community is gathered around the Table for the Lord's Supper, participants in the rite and partakers of the wholesome food, engaged in the intimate act of eating together. The Lord's Prayer is said, marking the major transition now from the Litany to the Holy Communion. Then comes the Collect for Purity, picking up a theme already introduced in the versicles of Morning Prayer. Standing before God the parishioners acknowledge that their inmost thoughts and desires are known to Almighty God, therefore they pray that the thoughts of their hearts may be cleansed: "by the inspiration of thy holy spirit, that we may perfectly love thee, and worthilye magnifye thy holye name." Thus is the penitential approach to the sacrament begun. There follows self-examination by means of a recital of the Ten Commandments with kyrie responses. The Commandments touch upon most of human experience in one way or another, the spiritual and social relationships which impinge on everyone. The cleansing of the thoughts of our hearts in part at least involves remembering God's law with penitence: "Lord have mercye upon us, and write all these thy lawes in our heartes we besech thee." With this act of penitence the stage is set for the hearing of God's Word and for response to that Word in the recital of the Nicene Creed. The ministry of the Word begins with the Collect for the Day which is related to the Epistle and Gospel appointed to be read, usually stating the main theme in the Scripture readings. Thus, for instance, on the Sixth Sunday after Trinity the collect asks that God will "Pour into our hearts such love toward thee, that we, loving thee in all things, may obtain thy promises." The Epistle from Romans 6 states emphatically that being dead to sin with Christ we are alive to God through Jesus Christ. God pours into our hearts abundant love towards himself in and through his Son. The Gospel from Matthew 5 then places emphasis on loving God in all things, but in particular through reconciliation with those whom we have harmed by our anger or otherwise: "if thou offerest thy gift at the altar, and there rememberest that thy brother hath ought against thee, leave there thine offering before the altar, and go thy way first and be reconciled to thy brother, and then come and offer thy gift."[18] The Creed provides the appropriate response. Having heard God's Word, the parishioners respond: "I believe."

Before proceeding we must note that after the Collect for the Day and before the Epistle one of two collects for the king must be read. Both are written in relation to that which has gone before. They both reflect the Collect for Purity and the responses to the Ten Commandments, the first praying that God will "have mercye upon the whole congregacion, and so rule the heart of thy chosen servant Edward the sixth. . . ." Thus the nation at large, as well as the particular community at prayer, is brought to mind. It is as though we are being told that what is done in this rite pertains to the realization of the Kingdom of Christ in England. The king is the symbol of the nation, and more. As his heart is inspired so shall the hearts of all his people be influenced with the love of true religion and with love of all others constituting the community. So shall the people be preserved "in wealth,[19] peace, and Godlynes."

The Creed is followed by the Sermon, or, if the priest is not licensed to preach or for some reason does not choose to do so, a portion of one of the Homilies. We have noted the social and ethical importance of the Homilies in Chapter 2. Sermons in the sixteenth century were variously concerned with personal or social issues or with some controverted point of doctrine, or some other issue of importance at the time. Whatever the subject of the sermon was likely to be, it would begin with the reading of the text establishing the theme, an exordium based on some part of the main theme of the sermon, or there might be the reading of another text from Scripture allied to the main theme by one of its words or phrases. The opening might end with a bidding prayer. Then the theme was introduced by means of a narration, an analogy, or some quotation from a secular source explaining its meaning. The theme was divided next and in the bulk of the sermon the theme was discussed division by division.[20] The most famous preacher of King Edward's reign was Bishop Hugh Latimer whose sermons, for instance those on the Card, on the Lord's Prayer, and those given at Court, were noted for their orderly structure, simplicity and directness of language, and for the pastoral sense they exhibited along with courageous prophetic criticism of life and morals.[21] John Jewel, bishop of Salisbury and one of the most accomplished preachers of Queen Elizabeth's reign, preached sermons according to the style noted above on subjects such as reform, the ministry of the church, the nature of the Christian life, the challenges facing the commonwealth, as well as series of catechetical sermons on Scripture and the sacraments.[22] The brief rubrical reference to preaching after the Creed indicates a major element in the Prayer Book Holy Communion, major both in terms of time and emphasis given during the parish Sunday morning worship. The Prayer Book intended no brief and casual homily. The sermon or homily was intended to be substantial, solid meat rather than thin soup, after the example of the homilies contained in the *Book of Homilies,* or the sermons of preachers such as Latimer and Jewel.

After the Sermon the curate announced any holy days or fasting days in the coming week. The Ministry of the Word having been completed, the people were admonished "to remember the poore" with the reading of one of the offertory sentences. These sentences, one or more being read or sung while the churchwardens collected the alms of the people and placed them in the parish poor box, were all from Scripture. They exhorted the people not only to remember the poor, but to recognize that their earthly goods are perishable, to do good works to the glory of God, doing God's will in accordance with the Golden Rule, ending with recognition that those who serve the poor, serve the Lord. The parish church was the social service agency of England, charged with care for all of the poor within the parish bounds.[23] The emphasis on the offering for the poor here in the midst of the Holy Communion serves a practical administrative need, as well as reflecting a profound truth proceeding from the Gospel. In addition to alms for the poor, tithes and other offerings are mentioned. Tithes may have been paid at this point in the service on occasion as they were due, but much of the time this would be impracticable, especially when the tithes were in kind rather than in money. But however they were paid, they are related to the Eucharistic offerings by this rubric and are thus sanctified.[24] Tithes, like the alms for the poor, are a response to the ministry of the Word. At this time too, according to the 1549 book, bread and wine were offered, being placed on the altar in suitable vessels. No mention of this is made in the 1552 book. It is possible that the bread and wine were already on the Table, being placed there before the service began. If there was to be no communion, however, there would be no need for bread and wine.[25]

We must remember that in fact there was no communion in the parish church, except on certain specified days. There must have been variance in practice, but it would seem that in most places communion was received only when the law required. If there was no communion it is quite possible that the people stayed where they had been for Morning Prayer and Litany, that the Table was not moved out into their midst, and that the Sermon occupied the climactic position in morning worship, followed, as the rubric directs, by the "Prayer for the Whole State of Christ's Church" and one of the collects found at the end of the sacrament, these prayers constituting the "Post-Sermon Prayer" as it would have been called by the Puritans.[26] If the service did end this way, the Offertory, concentrated on the collection of alms for the poor, might be inserted between the Sermon and the prayer, or in some other appropriate place.

We are here confronted by the "Ante-Communion," or "dry communion" as William Harrison called it.[27] As a climax to the morning worship it resembles the medieval Prone, that vernacular insertion into the Mass consisting of a sermon preceeded or followed by the bidding of the bedes, notices, instructions in the Decalogue, the Lord's Prayer, and similar formularies.[28] In part the Ante-Communion provides the heart of Christian education. The sequence of Morning Prayer, Litany, and Ante-Communion emphasizes contrition and thanksgiving, enabled by God's Word, read and preached. The sequence furthermore stresses, as we have observed, the reform of individuals and of the community, thus furthering the growth of the Kingdom of Christ in England.

A rubric in the 1549 book seems to assume that this is a natural breaking point in the Holy Communion, for it says that after the Offertory

> so manye as shalbee partakers of the holy Communion, shall tarye still in the quire, the men on the one side, and the women on the other syde. All other (that mynde not to receive the said holy Communion) shall departe out of the quire....[29]

There is no such rubrical direction in 1552. We can imagine various possibilities for this omission: (1) that morning worship shall end with the end of Ante-Communion; (2) that there shall be communion, but that many or most of the people will leave after the Offertory and a few remain for communion; (3) that on Easter Day the service shall proceed to communion with none leaving, except for those prohibited from communion for some reason. Although 1549 has the rubric mentioned and 1552 refers to a complete service of Ante-Communion, the Prayer Book was here simply acknowledging common practice and practical necessities. The ideal called for the entire sequence, concluding with communion and thanksgiving.

Thus, after the Offertory in 1552 there came the general intercession called the prayer "for the whole state of Christes Churche militant here in earth." It involves prayer for the church as indicated, for the church's faith and life, that it may "live in unitie and godly love," but also prayer for the king, his council and all in authority that they may administer justice and defend the true religion, for bishops and other ministers, their life and doctrine, that they may set forth God's Word and rightly administer the sacraments, and for all the people, that they may with meek hearts and reverence hear and receive the Word of God and serve in holiness, as well as for those especially in need, the troubled, those who sorrow, the "needy," the sick, and any others in like circumstances. The prayer parallels the intercessions of the Litany and is not unlike the bidding prayer.[30] It involves the nation, all estates of the same, that the English people may hear God's Word and live accordingly, fostering the coming of the Kingdom of Christ.

The exhortations follow. The first, from Peter Martyr Vermigli and not found in the 1549 book, is to be read out at this juncture when the priest observes that the people are negligent in coming to the Holy Communion and partaking of it. Based on the Parable of the Great Feast (Luke 14:15ff.) it places emphasis on God's call to partake of the Lord's Supper. The exhortation deals briefly with the excuses often given for not heeding the call, namely business and a feeling of unworthiness, and it gives the reason for obeying the call despite all excuses:

> And as the sonne of god did vouchesafe to yelde up his soule by death upon the Cross for your helth: even so it is your duetie to receve the communion together in remembraunce of his death, as he hymselfe commaunded.

The second exhortation, taken from the *Order of Communion* (1548), in some ways resembles Cranmer's Homily on Salvation in the first *Book of Homilies*. The 1552 version modifies the Eucharistic theology of the original to make it conform more nearly to the theology of the revised consecratory prayer. The reason given for the sacrament is that it is our duty to give thanks to God "for that he hath geven his sonne oure saviour Jesus Christ, not only to die for us, but also to be our spiritual fode and sustenance, as it is declared unto us, as wel by goddes worde, as by the holy Sacramentes of his blessed body, and blood...." The people are then admonished to prepare themselves to receive this spiritual food through self-examination, confession, amendment of life (including reconciliation with their neighbors), and restitution or satisfaction. The sacrament of penance is very much in mind here as is the following advice that if persons are troubled in conscience they must seek out their priest, "or some other discrete and learned minister of gods word," to confess that which troubles them and receive "comfort and the benefyte of absolucion." There could hardly be more direct and forceful instruction given, revealing the Prayer Book's intent that people should not receive the sacrament casually or unworthily. They are to receive the sacrament in such a condition that it may be the means of strengthening them in the Christian life for the good of the community.

The third exhortation, which is also from the *Order of Communion*, and is meant to be recited whenever the Holy Communion occurs, is an exhortation to self-examination in the light of an understanding of the sacrament, which is in the 1549 book and preserved in the 1552: if we receive the sacrament with penitence and faith we will benefit greatly, "for then we spirituallye eate the flesh of Christe, and drinke hys bloude, then we dwell in Chryste and Chryste in us, wee bee one with Chryste, and Christe with us." This recurrent theme is that of participation in Christ or mutual indwelling, based on John 6:56. To receive unworthily is most dangerous. Therefore sinners are to repent, believe, amend their lives, and be reconciled one to another. Once more the theology of the sacrament is explained, for we read that above all the penitent partaker of Christ

> must geve most humble and hartie thankes to God the father, the sonne, and the holy ghost, for the redempcion of the worlde, by the death and passion of our saviour Christe, bothe God and man, who dyd humble hym selfe, even to the death upon the Crosse, for us myserable synners, which laye in darknesse, and shadowe of death, that he myghte make us the chyldren of God, and exalte us to everlastyng lyfe. And to thende that we should alwaye remembre the exceding greate love of oure maister, and onely Savioure Jesu Christ, thus dyinge for us, and the innumerable benefytes (whiche by his precious bloudshedinge) he hath obteyned to us, he hathe instituted and ordeyned holye misteries, as pledges of his love, and continuall remembrance of hys death, to our greate and endles comforte. To hym therefore with the fathe

> and the holy Ghoste, lette us geve (as we are most bounden) continual thankes: submittinge oure selves wholy to hys holy wyll and pleasure, and studying to serve him in true holynesse and ryghteousnesse all the dayes of our lyfe.[31]

The sacrifice of Christ on the Cross is verbally presented to the congregation here as it was visually presented to them on the rood screen. This is the sacrifice made for the sake of all those present, which when it is held up and understood arouses human wills to give thanks (the sacrifice of praise and thanksgiving) and to offer the sacrifice of souls and bodies to serve the Lord in true holiness and justice. This is the sacrifice which forms the basis for building the Kingdom of Christ in England.

There is then presented the penitential sequence from the Invitation to Confession to the Comfortable Words. The Invitation summons those who repent, are "in love and charitie wyth" their neighbors, and intend to lead new lives, to "Drawe nere and take this holy Sacrament" to their comfort, first confessing their sins on their knees. In the Confession, which is an example of the most effective prose/poetry in the Prayer Book, the parishioners together say (or hear read on their behalf):

> we do earnestly repent, and be hartely sory for these our misdoynges, the remembrance of them is grievous unto us, the burthen of them is intollerable, have mercy upon us, have mercye upon us mooste mercyfull father....

The mood and some of the rhythms of the Litany are reflected here and for the fourth time (the Confession in Morning Prayer was the first, the Litany the second, and the Kyries of the Ten Commandments the third) the people repent their sins and pray for the power to amend their lives. The Absolution and Comfortable Words are the assurance that God does forgive, that Christ's sacrifice was and continues to be effective, and that those who repent with faith can live as becomes the recipients of divine mercy. This sequence from the exhortations through the Comfortable Words, is a preparation for Communion. Such it was in 1548 and 1549. We now approach not only the Consecration but the Communion, the two formerly separate parts of the liturgy now viewed as one, concentrating on the Holy Communion wherewith the Consecration is finally complete.

The next sequence, to be seen as a whole, proceeds from the Sursum Corda through the Gloria in Excelsis. "Lyft up your heartes./ We lyft them up unto the Lord./ Let us give thankes unto our Lorde God./ It is mete and right so to do"—this is the beginning of the great thanksgiving which in Preface and Proper Preface is justified, and which finds expression in the Sanctus, "Holy, holy, holy...." The reasons given for giving thanks in the Proper Prefaces include the Incarnation, the death and resurrection of Christ, the Ascension, and the coming of the Holy Spirit. The Prayer of Humble Access which follows the Sanctus seems to interrupt the flow of thanksgiving, but it can be viewed as further explaining the reasons for giving thanks (that although we are unworthy, God in his mercy invites us to partake of Christ, our Savior) and focusing people's minds on what is now to occur, by praying that God will grant us "so to eate the fleshe of thy dere sonne Jesus Christ, and to drink his bloud, that our synful bodyes may be made cleane by his body, and our soules washed through his most precious bloude, and that we may evermore dwell in hym, and he in us." This is the fulfillment of the prayer made in the Collect for Purity.

The priest standing at the north side of the Table—the bread and wine before him, the people gathered around—addresses God, who gave his Son "to suffer death upon the crosse for oure redempcyon" making there that sacrifice which can not be repeated, which was wholly sufficient, making satisfaction for the sins of the whole world, present, past, and future. This Jesus Christ instituted and commanded a memorial of his sacrifice in this sacrament. With this divine action in mind the priest prays:

> Hear us O mercyfull father wee beseche thee: and Grante that wee, receyvyng these thy creatures of bread and wine, according to thy sonne our savior Jesus Christes holy institucion, in remembrance of his death and passion, may be partakers of his most blessed body and blood....

There follow the familiar words of institution without any directions as to manual acts, without any epiclesis or prayer for the blessing of the Holy Spirit, and without any prayer following, but rather with the Communion of priest and people, the people receiving "a piece of the beste and pureste wheat bread," drinking from the cup of wine, the priest and his assistants moving around to administer the sacrament to the people kneeling, hands outstretched to receive the bread. As the clergy circulate they say the words of administration: "Take and eate this, in rememberance that Christe died for thee [again the emphasis is on Christ's sacrifice], and fede on him in thy heart by faith with thankesgeving," "Drinke this in remembrance that Christes bloud was shed for thee, and be thankfull." The sentences seem opposed to those of 1549 which specified "The Body" and "The bloud," but in 1559 it was discovered that they belonged together, complementing each other. Immediately after the Lord's Prayer is said (the fifth recitation of it in the morning's worship) there follows the Oblation of the People, either in the form of the oblation contained in the 1549 Prayer of Consecration or in that of the post-Communion Thanksgiving. It is as though the communion of the people is the appropriate prelude to the people's response, the sacrificial response of praise and thanksgiving which is the sacrifice of ourselves, souls and bodies. If it is the Oblation it begins:

> O Lorde and heavenly father, we thy humble servauntes, entierly desire thy fatherly goodness, mercifully to accepte thys our Sacrifice of prayse and thankes gevyng: most humbly besechyng thee to graunte, that by the merites and death of thy sonne Jesus Christ, and through faith in his bloud, we and all thy whole church, may obtein remission of our sinnes, and al other benefytes of hys passion. And here we offer and present unto the, O lord, our selves....

If the priest chooses, instead, the post-Communion thanksgiving, he reads:

> Almightie and eveliving God, we most hartely thanke the, for that thou doest vouchsafe to fede us, whiche have duely received these

holy misteries, with the Spiritual fode of the most precious body and bloud of thy sonne, our saviour Jesus Christ, and doest assure us therby of thy favour and goodnesse towarde us, and that we be very membres incorporate in thy misticall body, whiche is the blessed companie of all faythfull people, and bee also heyres throughe hope, of thy everlastyng kingdome, by the merytes of the most precious death and Passion of thy deare sonne: we now most humbly beseche thee, O heavenly father, so to assist us with thy grace, that we may continue in that holy felowship, and do al such good workes as thou hast prepared for us to walke in. . . .

Both prayers aim towards the realization of the new life begun here in those who have partaken of Christ, and through that new life, characterized by sacrifice enabled by divine grace, the creation of the Kingdom of Christ in England. It must be remembered that the prayer for the church—"we and all thy whole church" and "be very membres incorporate in thy misticall body"—is a prayer for the commonwealth, the same person being both a citizen and a member of the Church of England.

The sequence closes with a great burst of praise and thanksgiving in the Gloria in Excelsis. Praise is offered to God on high with the prayer that there may be peace and good will on earth. The people praise God, their heavenly king, the father almighty, who through his Son Jesus Christ takes away the sins of the world. The people pray that he may ever have mercy and receive their prayers. This prayer for mercy—and that which follows, directed to the Son—is made here as a part of that praise due to the One who has forgiven and will forgive. But it is also a reminder that on the one hand Christians must ever pray for forgiveness and on the other hand that as the instruments of God they must ever be forgiving.

With the Peace and the Blessing the Sunday morning worship ends. The people are sent out of the church with the assurance that by the grace of God their hearts and minds have been in this sacrament rooted in the knowledge and love of God and of the Son in whom they participate. The earnest hope is that they may continue in this knowledge and love. Thus we end with a kind of exhortation to holiness based upon the realization that the grace to realize that holiness has been given.

Conclusion

In its central concerns, as well as in many that are subsidiary, the *Book of Common Prayer* enables the English citizenry to worship God, in deeds as well as with words, and to be worthy members of the commonwealth. The reading and preaching of the Word of God was acknowledged at the time as possessing the power to change lives. For Cranmer the Bible is that Word "inspired and used by the Holy Spirit, a living Word."[1] It "containeth fruitful instruction and erudition for every man; if any thing be necessary to be learned, of the Holy Spirit we may learn it. If falsehood shall be reproved, thereof we may gather wherewithal. If any thing be to be corrected and amended, if there need any exhortation or consolation, of the scripture we may well learn. In the scriptures be the fat pastures of the soul; therein is no venemous meat, no unwholesome thing; they be the very dainty and pure feeding." Thus Cranmer wrote in the Preface to the Great Bible (1540). He viewed the Bible as the handbook and the inspiration for Christian living.

> Herein may princes learn how to govern their subjects; subjects obedience, love and dread to their princes; husbands, how they should behave them unto their wives; how to educate their children and servants: and contrary the wives, children, and servants may know their duty to their husbands, parents, and masters. Here may all manner of persons, men, women, young, old, learned, unlearned, rich, poor, priests, laymen, lords, ladies, officers, tenants, and men, virgins, wives, widows, lawyers, merchants, artificers, husbandmen, and all manner of persons of what estate or condition soever they be, may in this book learn all things what they ought to believe, what they ought to do, and what they should not do, as well concerning Almighty God, as also concerning themselves and all other.[2]

The fact that Anglican apologists such as Richard Hooker found it necessary—in the face of Puritan claims—to argue that Scripture is not self-sufficient, that it presupposes the operation of right reason, does not detract from the intent of Cranmer and those who followed after to set forth by means of the orderly pattern of Prayer Book worship the Word of God for the transformation of individuals and the nation. Hooker believed the Scriptures to be sufficient for that for which they were intended, that is, to heal the wounds created in human reason by sin, revealing those supernatural truths which reason cannot of itself discover. In Book V of the *Laws*, Hooker states that the Word of God in Scripture is powerful "to *convert*, to *edifie*, and to *save* soules."[3] And this is so, to a large extent, because as the Scripture itself testifies (2 Chron. 34:21) the reading of Scripture is able to produce true repentance "in the hartes of such as feare God." Such repentance is the beginning for which regular reading of Scripture provides further degrees of "perfection in the feare of God." Scripture is powerful to produce that *metanoia* which engenders radical change in people, turning them from covetous sin to become instruments of God's unbounded love. It may be the inspiration by which the Word is preached in a sermon such as that of Hugh Latimer on Romans 15:4, delivered before King Edward VI in March, 1549;[4] it may be the basis on which Christ's saving death is recalled in the Prayer Book liturgy;[5] it may be the bulk and substance of the daily offices with their provision for reading through most of the Bible over and over again. For those who are prepared, the Word of God mediated to them in diverse ways is powerful to change and perfect persons and nations.

George Herbert, whose *Temple* and Latin poems reflect the powerful influence of the Prayer Book,[6] understood the effectiveness of Scripture when he wrote "In S. Scripturas":

> Heu, quid spiritus, igneusque turbo
> Regnat visceribus, measque versat
> Imo pectore cogitationes?
> Nunquid pro foribus sedendo nuper
> Stellam vespere suxerim volantem,
> Haec autem hospitio latere turpi
> Prorsus nescia, cogitat recessum?
> Nunquid mel comedens, apem comedi
> Ipsa cum domina domum vorando?

> Imo, me nec apes, nec astra pungunt:
> Sacratissima Charta, tu fuisti
> Quae cordis latebras sinusque caecos
> Atque omnes peragrata es angiportus
> Et flexus fugientis appetitus.
> Ah, quam docta perambulare calles
> Maeandrosque plicasque, quam perita es!
> Quae vis condidit, ipsa nouit aedes.[7]

This power to change lives is also vividly apparent in the Prayer Book sacraments, Baptism and the Holy Communion, which Peter Martyr Vermigli (who wrote the first Exhortation in the 1552 Book) called the "visible words of God,"[8] and which John Jewel in his *Apology* called "visible words, seals of righteousness, tokens of grace."[9]

By 1552 there could be no doubt that the *Book of Common Prayer* repudiated the doctrine of transubstantiation. The Articles of Religion reinforced this repudiation, the Thirty-Nine Articles emphasizing the "spiritual" eating of Christ's body.[10] What this meant has been referred to more than once in this chapter, but it deserves further emphasis in this conclusion.

In his *Answer* (1551) to Stephen Gardiner, Thomas Cranmer wrote that the papists "teach, that Christ is in the bread and wine; but we say (according to truth), that he is in them that worthily eat and drink the bread and wine."[11] He reiterated this, saying that

> the papists do teach, that Christ is in the visible signs, and whether they list to call them bread and wine, or the forms of bread and wine, all is one to me; for the truth is, that he is neither corporally in the bread and wine, nor in or under the forms and figures of them, but is corporally in heaven, and spiritually in his lively members, which be his temples where he inhabiteth.[12]

Richard Hooker, in his theology of participation, interpreting the Prayer Book Holy Communion, boldly and emphatically stated: "The real presence of Christes most blessed bodie and bloode is not... to be sought for in the sacrament, but in the worthie receiver of the sacrament."[13] Or, to put it another way,

Hooker interprets "*Hoc est corpus meum:* This is my body," by imagining Christ as saying:

> "This hallowed foode, through concurrence of divine power, is in veritie and truth, unto faithfull receivers, instrumentallie a cause of that mysticall participation, whereby as I make my selfe whollie theires, so I give them in hande an actuall possession of all such saving grace as my sacrificed body can yeeld, and as their soules do presentlie need, this is 'to them and in them' my bodie...."[14]

However we categorize Hooker's doctrine here; whether or not this is the "virtualism" of Bucer and Calvin, half-way between Luther and Zwingli, preserving the values of the doctrine of the Real Presence while avoiding the "metaphysical explanations that baffle the intelligence," and avoiding the "reductionism of the Zwinglian Memorialist views;"[15] Hooker's doctrine emphasized *participation,* we in him and he in us, as the means of transformation, the transformation of sinful, broken people and societies.

George Herbert, writing from experience gained in Prayer Book worship, explaining the Prayer Book doctrine of the Eucharist, spoke of his conviction that Christ endured the pains of his earthly existence "To abolish Sinn, not Wheat./ Creatures are good, & have their place;/ Sinn onely, which did all deface,/ Thou drivest from his seat."[16] But it is his poem "The H. Communion" in *The Temple* which puts it best:

> Not in rich furniture, or fine aray,
>   Nor in a wedge of gold,
>   Thou, who for me wast sold,
> To me dost now thy self convey;
> For so thou should'st without me still have been,
>   Leaving within me sinne:
>
> But by the way of nourishment and strength
>   Thou creep'st into my breast;
>   Making thy way my rest,
> And thy small quantities my length;
> Which spread their forces into every part,
>   Meeting sinnes force and art.

> Yes can these not get over to my soul,
>   Leaping the wall that parts
>   Our souls and fleshy hearts;
>   But as th' outworks, they may controll
> My rebel-flesh, and carrying thy name,
>   Affright both sinne and shame.
>
> Onely thy grace, which with these elements comes,
>   Knoweth the ready way,
>   And hath the private key,
>   Op'ning the souls most subtile rooms;
> While those to spirits refin'd, at doore attend
>   Dispatches from their friend.[17]

Hugh Latimer, preaching in Lincolnshire in 1552, spoke of the moral power of the sacrament, when eaten worthily, emphasizing as the Prayer Book does that at least contrition and the intention of making restitution to those one has harmed must be present before the benefits of the spiritual eating can be acquired. Latimer affirmed:

> they that be in Christ are partakers of all his merits and benefits; of everlasting life, and of all felicity. He that hath Christ hath all things that are Christ's. He is our preservation from damnation; he is our comfort; he is our help, our remedy. When we feed upon him, then we shall have remission of our sins: the same remission of sins is the greatest and most comfortable thing that can be in the world.[18]

For Hugh Latimer, preacher of the Commonwealth Men, such words had social implications for the common folk and for kings, for yeomanry and for landlords, for all the commonwealth in which disinterested love and justice were opposed by greed and injustice. Thomas Cooper, bishop of Lincoln, in a homily intended for wide distribution, published in 1580, asserted that:

> The scriptures teach, that in the use of the sacraments, through faith we be united unto Christ, and ingrafted into his mysticall bodie, so that we live now onely by him, and whatsoever is his, by the truth of his promise, is ours also. The word of God teacheth that the sacrament of the Lordes supper is a linke of unitie, that knitteth us together, as members of one mysticall bodie, and

therefore, that we ought to be joyned in mutuall love, and charitie among our selves, and that it is a foule reproch both to Christ our head, and to the whole bodie, if we hate, hurte, or hinder one another. For by the use thereof, we confesse that we are all members of one bodie, all servants of one Maister, all children of one Father, all subjectes under one Lord and king, and all partakers of one redemption, all heires of one heritage, and gifte of eternall life. And in so many linkes of unitie, to be at discorde among our selves, is in Gods judgement, an heavie testimonie against us, in the day of his wrath.[19]

Such an understanding agrees with the humanist and Christian views expressed in the *Discourse of the Common Weal* and shows that Cooper, writing thirty-odd years after the appearance of the first Prayer Book, would have been an able Commonwealth Man promoting the ideals of their "party" through the liturgy which was intended to be an instrument for the achievement of the *Societas Christiana*.

The Book of Common Prayer was such an instrument. Through it the Word of God was preached, the sacraments were administered, and discipline was meted out. Faithfully used, it affected the whole of a person's life, from birth to death, week to week, season to season, year to year, creating that mutual participation between Christ and the Christian which was powerful to change lives, turning penitent sinners from love of self to love of others. Furthermore, Prayer Book worship was communal, the worship of an actual community defined by parish bounds. In mid-sixteenth-century England little could be done to hide or obscure the activities of the inhabitants of a parish. One's sins and one's righteousness would be apparent to all. Taken seriously and used conscientiously, the Prayer Book would most certainly affect individual and communal existence. But even if it were not taken seriously or used conscientiously, as was often the case, the use of the Prayer Book in parishes all through the land, with the weekly repetition of its main themes, could not help but have its effects in time.[20] One of the most effective—as well as socially relevant—liturgical gems, a prominent element of daily Evening Prayer, retained in the consciousness, and the unconsciousness, of people generation after generation, may be regarded as the theme song of the Christian Commonwealth. The song is the Magnificat:

> My soule doth magnifie the Lord:
> And my spirite hath rejoyced in god my Saviour.
> For he hath regarded the lowelyness of hys handmayden.
> For beholde from henceforth all generacions shall call me blessed.
> For he that is mightie, hath magnified me: and holy is his name.
> And his mercy is on them that feare him: through all generacions.
> He hath shewed strength with hys arm: he hath scatered the proud, in the imaginacion of their hearts.
> He hath put down the mighty from their seate: and hath exalted the humble and meke.
> He hath filled the hungrye with good thyngs: and the riche he hath sent emptie away.
> He rememberynge hys mercy, hath holpen hys servaunt Israel: as he promised to our forefathers, Abraham and his sede, for ever.

NOTES

Communion and Commonwealth:
The Book of Common Prayer

[1] Book V is the longest of the eight, being 271 pages in the first edition (London: John Windet, 1597) compared to 209 pages for the first four books (London: John Windet, [1593]).

[2] W. H. Frere and C.E. Douglas, *Puritan Manifestoes* (London: S.P.C.K., 1954), p. 15. This is the judgment found in the Puritan first *Admonition to Parliament* (1572).

[3] *Of the Laws of Ecclesiastical Polity: Book V*, W. Speed Hill, ed., Folger Library Edition of the *Works* of Richard Hooker, Vol. 2 (Cambridge, Mass.: The Belknap Press of Harvard University Press, 1977), p. 15. This is in the title of the book.

[4] This and subsequent such citations refer to Hooker's *Laws*, book number (Roman), chapter (arabic), and section (arabic), as these are found in the Folger edition of Hooker's *Works* (see note above). This form of citation is also used in the Everyman's edition and in the 7th

Keble edition (1888), and elsewhere.

5. See *Laws*, V.25.3, concerning the priest and the liturgy.
6. See Hugh Latimer, *Sermons*, G. E.Corrie, ed., Parker Society (Cambridge: Cambridge University Press, 1844); John Jewel, *Works*, Parker Society, Vol. 2, John Ayre, ed. (Cambridge: Cambridge University Press, 1847), pp. 947-1139; and Thomas Cooper, *Certaine sermons* (London: Ralph Newberie, 1580), STC 13682.
7. Introduction, p. 38 above.
8. *Works*, Vol. 2: Miscellaneous Writings, John Edmond Cox, ed. (Cambridge: Cambridge University Press, 1846), p. 173.
9. *Ibid.*, p. 180.
10. *Ibid.*, p. 176; see *Works*, PS, 1:3.
11. *Ibid.*, p. 175.
12. *Ibid.*, p. 174.
13. *Ibid.*, p. 169.
14. *Ibid.*, p. 174; "comfort" here means "strengthening aid."
15. See John Booty, *Three Anglican Divines on Prayer: Jewel, Andrewes, and Hooker* (Cambridge, Mass.: Society of St. John the Evangelist, [1978]), espec. pp. 9-13.
16. Cranmer, *Works*, PS, 2:181.
17. *Ibid.*

The Genesis of the Book of Common Prayer

1. J. J. Scarisbrick, *Henry VIII* (London: Eyre & Spottiswoode, 1968), p. 409; but see pp. 419-20 for some modification of this assertion.
2. There is still room for disagreement concerning this process, but there is no denying that Cranmer's views changed gradually. For one view, see Peter Brooks, *Thomas Cranmer's Doctrine of the Eucharist: An Essay in Historical Development* (New York: Seabury Press, 1965).
3. On the *Primer*, see the following essay in this book. See also F. E. Brightman, *The English Rite*, 2 vols. (London: Rivingtons, 1914), pp. li-liii.
4. *Ibid.*, p. lvii.

[5] Found in Charles Hardwick, *A History of the Articles of Religion* (London: George Bell and Sons, 1895), Append. I.

[6] Brightman, *The English Rite*, pp. lvi-vii; Scarisbrick, *Henry VIII*, Ch. 12; and Hardwick, *History*, for discussion, but mainly for the articles.

[7] See *The Rationale of Ceremonial 1540-1543*, M. S. Cobb, ed., Alcuin Club Collections xviii (London, 1910).

[8] David Wilkins, ed., *Concilia Magnae Britanniae et Hiberniae*, 4 vols. (London, 1737), 3:863.

[9] *Ibid.*

[10] *Private Prayers put forth by Authority during the reign of Queen Elizabeth*, William Keatinge Clay, ed., Parker Society (Cambridge: At the University Press, 1851), pp. 566-67.

[11] *Ibid.*, p. 568.

[12] *Ibid.*, p. 569.

[13] *Ibid.*, p. 570.

[14] See *The Book of Common Prayer, 1559*, John E. Booty, ed. (Charlottesville, Va.: University Press of Virginia for The Folger Shakespeare Library, 1976), pp. 350-51; Cranmer, *Works*, PS, 2:412.

[15] *Ibid.*, pp. 349-50; *Cranmer's Liturgical Projects*, J. W. Legg, ed., Henry Bradshaw Society, 50 (London, 1915).

[16] See C. J. Cuming, *A History of Anglican Liturgy* (London: Macmillan, 1969), p. 59, and Cranmer, *Works*, PS, 2:415-16.

[17] See the report in the State Papers detailing Gardiner's efforts to inhibit the letters of authorization, in Cranmer's *Works*, PS, 2:415-16n.

[18] In *Visitation Articles and Injunctions*, W. H. Frere and W. M. Kennedy, eds., 3 vols. Alcuin Club Collections, xiv-xvi (London, 1910).

[19] Brightman, *The English Rite*, p. lxx.

[20] Cuming, *History of Anglican Liturgy*, p. 60.

[21] Francis Procter and W. H. Frere, *A New History of the Book of Common Prayer* (London: Macmillan, 1911), p. 37.

[22] W. K. Jordan, *Edward VI: The Young King* (Cambridge, Mass.: The Belknap Press of Harvard University Press, 1968), p. 171.

[23] For the details of the bill and its passage, see Francis Aidan Gasquet and Edmund Bishop, *Edward VI and the Book of Common Prayer* (London: Hodges, 1890), pp. 69-73.

[24] Concerning the Commonwealth Men, see the Introduction, above, p. 35.

[25] Quoted from the copy of the act in Henry Gee and William John Hardy, *Documents Illustrative of English Church History* (London: Macmillan, 1914), p. 327.

[26] See Henry A. Wilson, ed., *The Order of Communion, 1548*, Henry Bradshaw Society, 34 (London, 1908).

[27] Brightman, *The English Rite*, p. lxxi.

[28] See William Maskell, *Monumenta Ritualia Ecclesiae Anglicanae*, 2nd ed., 3 vols. (Oxford: At the Clarendon Press, 1882), 3:408-9.

[29] This was the Church Order of Cologne, anonymously translated into English in 1547 and published by John Daye, with a revised edition published in 1548 by Daye and Seres (STC 13213, 13214).

[30] In Paul L. Hughes and James F. Larkin, eds., *Tudor Proclamations*, 3 vols. (New Haven and London: Yale University Press, 1964-69), 1:432-3.

[31] Gasquet and Bishop, *Edward VI*, pp. 143-4. Cranmer was the consecrator, assisted by Bishops Ridley and Holbeach, with Bishops Thirlby and Goodrich present, along with Doctors May, Haynes, Robertson and Redman. These were all most likely members of the committee. Thomas Fuller also mentions Bishops Day and Skip, Taylor, dean of Lincoln, and Cox, the king's almoner. See Thomas Fuller, *The Church History of Great Britain* (Oxford: At the University Press, 1845), 4:27, and Procter and Frere, *A New History*, p. 46.

[32] Royal MS 17, B, xxxix, printed by Gasquet and Bishop, *Edward VI*, pp. 397-443.

[33] Gasquet and Bishop, p. 434.

[34] Gee and Hardy, *Documents*, pp. 358-66.

[35] *The First and Second Prayer Books of Edward VI*, Everyman's Library (London: J. M. Dent; New York: E. P. Dutton, 1910), p. 222.

[36] See F. C. Burkitt, *Eucharist and Sacrifice* (Cambridge: At the University Press, 1921), and *The Book of Common Prayer 1559*, p. 369.

[37] *Prayer Books,* Everyman's Library, p. 222.

[38] Cranmer, *Works,* PS, 2:179.

[39] Hastings Robinson, ed., *Original Letters Relative to the English Reformation.* The First Portion, Parker Society (Cambridge: At the University Press, 1846), p. 79. The letter is dated March 27, 1550.

[40] See Horton Davies, *Worship and Theology in England: From Cranmer to Hooker, 1534-1603* (Princeton: Princeton University Press, 1970), p. 94.

[41] *Acts of the Privy Council of England,* J. R. Dasent, ed., 32 vols. (London, 1890-1907), 3:382 (Oct. 6, 1551), and 410 (Nov. 9, 1551).

[42] In G. C. Gorham, *Gleanings* (London, 1857), pp. 231-2.

[43] This view of the process whereby the 1552 book appeared stands in marked contrast to that of C. W. Dugmore, who absolves Cranmer of responsibility for the new book and places it on Northumberland and Hooper. See "The First Ten Years, 1549-1559," in *The English Prayer Book, 1549-1662,* Alcuin Club (London: S.P.C.K., 1963), pp. 6-30.

[44] Gee and Hardy, *Documents,* pp. 370-1.

[45] *Prayer Books,* Everyman's Library, pp. 225, 389.

[46] *De Regno Christi,* 2; Bucer, *Opera,* Vol. 15, Francois Wendel, ed. (Paris: Presses Universitaires de France, 1955), p. 16; LCC 19, p. 188.

[48] Gee and Hardy, *Documents,* pp. 377-80.

[48] See Henry Gee, *The Elizabethan Prayer-Book and Ornaments* (London: Macmillan, 1902), for Guest's famous letter, pp. 215-224, which Gee assigns to 1552.

[49] Gee and Hardy, *Documents,* p. 459.

[50] *Ibid.,* p. 466.

[51] See Gee, *Elizabethan Prayer-Book,* pp. 150-151, and John E. Booty, *John Jewel as Apologist of the Church of England* (London: S.P.C.K., 1963), p. 24.

The Design of the Prayer Book

[1] *The Prymer or Prayer-Book of the Lay People in the Middle Ages,* Henry Littlehales, ed., Part I. Text (London: Longmans, Green,

and Co., 1891), p. 17. I have modified the orthography.

[2] From Stella Brook, *The Language of the Book of Common Prayer*, The Language Library (New York: Oxford University Press, 1965), p. 76.

[3] J. Wickham Legg, ed., *The Clerk's Book of 1549*, Henry Bradshaw Society, 25 (London, 1903). Contains a valuable introduction.

[4] See the facsimile in J. E. Hunt, ed., *Cranmer's First Litany, 1544, and Merbecke's Book of Common Prayer Noted, 1550* (London: Macmillan, 1939).

[5] See, for instance, *Liturgies and Occasional Forms of Prayer set forth in the Reign of Queen Elizabeth*, William Keatinge Clay, ed., Parker Society (Cambridge: At the University Press, 1847), pp. 457-695.

[6] See More's *Dialogue* in his English *Works*, William Rastell, ed. (London: John Cawood, John Waly, and Richard Tottell, 1557), STC 18075, p. 243.

[7] In Edward Cardwell, *A History of Conferences*, 3rd ed. (Oxford: At the University Press, 1849), p. 56.

[8] *Ibid.*, p. 59-60.

The Structure of the Book of Common Prayer in Relation to Time

[1] The Prayer Book Rubrics order that none shall be confirmed before being able to answer such questions as are put in the Catechism, and that the curate, or someone appointed by him "shall diligently upon Sundaies, and holy daies halfe an hour before Evensong, openly in the Churche instructe and examine" those children present in some part of the Prayer Book catechism (see *Prayer Books*, Everyman's Library, pp. 404, 409. These rubrics were reinforced by Edwardine (1547) and Elizabethan (1559) injunctions (see Injunction 44 in Gee and Hardy, *Documents*, p. 434).

[2] *Prayer Books*, Everyman's Library, p. 407.

[3] See, for instance, Arthur J. Willis, *Church Life in Kent, being Church Court Records of the Canterbury Diocese, 1559-1565* (London and Chichester: Phillimore, 1975), where cases are grouped under the following headings: "Teller of tales," "Railing," "Swearing," "Slander," "Blasphemy," "Drunkenness," "Incontinence," "Fornication," "Whoredom," and "Adultery."

[4] See *Liturgies...of Queen Elizabeth,* PS, pp. 435-55, where the revised Kalendar is printed.

[5] *Prayer Books,* Everyman's Library, p. 252. See the report of the Convocations of Canterbury and York, *The Church and Marriage* (London: S.P.C.K., 1935), which recognizes the importance of this third purpose (p. 5) but does not really acknowledge its social importance.

[6] *Prayer Books,* Everyman's Library, p. 418.

[7] *Ibid.,* p. 422.

[8] See, for instance, John Donne's plaintive question: "Lord, dost thou not accuse me, dost thou not reproach to me my former sins, when though layest me upon this bed?" *Devotions upon Emergent Occasions,* Expostulation III (Ann Arbor: University of Michigan Press, 1959), p. 19.

[9] *Prayer Books,* Everyman's Library, p. 429.

[10] *Ibid.,* pp. 276-7.

[11] See Horton Davies, *Worship of the English Puritans* (Westminster: Dacre Press, 1948), p. 121.

[12] *Prayer Books,* Everyman's Library, p. 427.

[13] *Ibid.,* p. 233.

The Language and Style of the Prayer Book

[1] Brook, *Language,* p. 122.

[2] *Ibid.,* p. 124.

[3] *Ibid.,* p. 128.

[4] *Prayer Books,* Everyman's Library, p. 366.

[5] *Ibid.*

[6] Compare in Brightman, *The English Rite,* pp. 732-3.

[7] See the description of Sunday morning worship, below.

[8] See Hooker, *Laws,* V.35.3, concerning the Lord's Prayer.

[9] *Ibid.,* V.36, especially §3, where Hooker emphasizes the community produced by "sayinge after the minister" as he called it.

[10] Hooker, *Laws,* V.33.1.

[11] Davies, *Worship of the English Puritans*, p. 67.

[12] Brightman, *The English Rite*, p. 148.

[13] See Leo Spitzer, *Classical and Christian Ideas of World Harmony* (Baltimore: Johns Hopkins Press, 1963), for the concepts which rightfully apply to the Prayer Book as well as to other literature of the Elizabethan Age.

[14] See E. S. Duckett, *Alfred the Great* (Chicago: University of Chicago Press, 1956), pp. 145-6, and the Lord Bishop of Bristol, "Alfred as Religious Man and an Educationalist," in Alfred Bowker, ed., *Alfred the Great* (London, 1899), pp. 82-3.

[15] See the Waldgrave edition of *A Booke of the Forme of Common Prayer* in Peter Hall, *Fragmenta Liturgica*, Vol. 1 (Bath: Binns and Goodwin, 1848), 1:31-46 for two post-sermon prayers.

Sunday Morning in a Tudor Parish Church

[1] *Book of Common Prayer, 1559*, p. 270.

[2] William Harrison, *The Description of England*, Georges Edelen, ed., Folger Documents of Tudor and Stuart Civilization, 14 (Ithaca, N.Y.: Cornell University Press, 1968), pp. 33-4.

[3] See John Booty, "Preparation for the Lord's Supper in Elizabethan England," *Anglican Theological Review* XLIX, no. 2 (April 1967), pp. 131-48.

[4] Willis, *Church Life in Kent*, pp. 30-31.

[5] *Ibid.*, p. 18, 19, 30.

[6] See above, p. 176.

[7] Gee and Hardy, *Documents*, pp. 425-6.

[8] *Ibid.*, p. 426.

[9] Brightman, *The English Rite*, pp. 174-177.

[10] See *ibid.*, 694-5.

[11] See John Booty, "The Bishop Confronts the Queen: John Jewel and the Failure of the English Reformation," in *Continuity and Discontinuity in Church History*, F. F. Church and T. George, eds. (Leiden: E. J. Brill, 1979), pp. 215-231, for the importance of this concern for a learned ministry.

[12] That *metanoia*—or repentance—was a paramount concern during the sixteenth century has never been denied. It is the subject of Hooker's Book VI, where he speaks of it as "a pensive and corrosive desire" (VI.3.4). That it was of central importance in any consideration of the reform of society is in large part the subject of this book.

[13] Brightman, *The English Rite*, p. 184.

[14] *Prayer Books*, Everyman's Library, pp. 219-228.

[15] See *Book of Common Prayer, 1559*, p. 370.

[16] *Laws*, V.67.5-6.

[17] *Prayer Books*, Everyman's Library, pp. 212, 377.

[18] *Ibid.*, p. 145-7.

[19] The original meaning of "wealth" was "'happiness' or 'prosperity' or 'well-being' of any kind" (Brook, *Language*, p. 46).

[20] See J. W. Blench, *Preaching in England in the late Fifteenth and Sixteenth Centuries* (New York: Barnes and Noble, 1964), pp. 102-3.

[21] See Hugh Latimer, *Sermons*, 2 vols., G. E. Corrie, ed., Parker Society (Cambridge: At the University Press, 1844).

[22] See Jewel, *Works*, Parker Society, Vol. 2, John Ayre, ed. (Cambridge: At the University Press, 1847), pp. 947-1139.

[23] W. P. M. Kennedy, ed., *Elizabethan Episcopal Administration*, Alcuin Club Collections, 25 (London, 1924), 1:cxxxvi.

[24] *Prayer Books*, Everyman's Library, pp. 381-2, and see Kennedy, above, p. cxxxix, and Hooker, *Laws*, V.79.

[25] See *Book of Common Prayer, 1559*, p. 398.

[26] See the Introduction, p. 20, above, and note.

[27] Harrison, *Description of England*, p. 34.

[28] See J. A. Thurmer, "Matins and Ante-Communion," *Church Quarterly Review*, 160 (Ap.-June 1959), p. 236.

[29] Brightman, *The English Rite*, p. 662.

[30] See the Introduction, p. 20, above.

[31] *Prayer Books*, Everyman's Library, pp. 385-6.

Conclusion

[1] G. W. Bromiley, *Thomas Cranmer Theologian* (London: Lutterworth Press, 1956), p. 19.

[2] Cranmer, *Works* (PS), 2:121.

[3] Hooker, *Laws*, V.22.1.

[4] Latimer, *Sermons* (PS), 1:85-103.

[5] I have in mind here the beginning of the consecration prayer in Holy Communion; *Prayer Books*, p. 389.

[6] See John E. Booty, "George Herbert: *The Temple* and *The Book of Common Prayer*," *Mosaic*, 12:2 (Winter 1979), pp. 75-90.

[7] O what spirit, what fiery whirlwind
Takes my bones and stirs
My deepest thoughts? When I was resting
Near my door not long ago,
And it was evening, did I
Swallow a falling star? And is it
Trying to escape, not knowing how
In this disgraceful lodging to be hidden?
Have I in sipping honey
Consumed the bee, in eating up
The house eaten up the mistress of the house?
Not bee, not star has penetrated me.
Most Holy Writ, it's you who've traveled through
All the dark nooks and hidden pleats
Of the heart, the alleys and the curves
Of flying passion. Ah, how wise and skilled you are
To slip through these paths, windings, knots.
The spirit that has reared the building
Knows it best.

From *The Latin Poetry of George Herbert: A Bilingual Edition*, trans. by Mark McCloskey and Paul R. Murphy (Athens, Ohio: University of Ohio Press, 1965), pp. 84-5.

[8] See Joseph C. McLelland, *The Visible Words of God: An Exposition of the Sacramental Theology of Peter Martyr Vermigli* (Edinburgh and London: Oliver and Boyd, 1957).

[9] John Jewel, *An Apology of the Church of England*, J. E. Booty, ed. (Ithaca, N.Y.: Cornell University Press for the Folger Shakespeare Library, 1963), p. 31.

[10] Charles Hardwick, *A History of the Articles of Religion* (London: George Bell and Sons, 1895), pp. 328-331, espec. 331: "Corpus Christi datur, accipitur, et manducatur in coena, tantum coelesti et spirituali ratione."

[11] Cranmer, *Works* (PS), 1:52.

[12] *Ibid.*, p. 53.

[13] Hooker, *Laws*, V.67.6.

[14] *Ibid.*, V.67.12.

[15] Davies, *Worship and Theology in England*, 1:83. For a different view, see Peter Brooks, *Thomas Cranmer's Doctrine of the Eucharist: An Essay in Historical Development* (New York: Seabury Press, 1965).

[16] George Herbert, *Works*, F. E. Hutchinson, ed. (Oxford: At the Clarendon Press, 1941), p. 200. This is from the Williams MS.

[17] *Ibid.*, p. 52, from *The Temple*, where it is printed with a companion poem.

[18] Latimer, *Sermons* (PS), 1:461, see the entire sermon.

[19] *A Briefe Homily, wherein the most comfortable and right use of the Lords Supper, is very plainly opened and delivered...Made to be used throughout the Diocese of Lincolne, before everie celebration of the Lordes Supper, in all such Churches and Parishes as have not a sufficient hable Preacher* (London: for Ralph Newberie, 1580), sig. A4ᵇ. STC 13682 as bound with Cooper's *Certaine sermons* (1580), which contains a sermon (pp. 148-159), evidently an abbreviation of the homily.

[20] See A. L. Rowse, *The England of Elizabeth* (New York: Macmillan, 1950), p. 433.

Part Four

RELIGIOUS EDUCATION: FOR CITIZENSHIP

Primer and Catechism

David Siegenthaler

—IV—
RELIGIOUS EDUCATION FOR CITIZENSHIP
Primer and Catechism

David Siegenthaler

Primer

To appreciate the role played by the Tudor authorized primers in effecting the reformed religious settlement of the sixteenth century and in supporting the commonwealth ideal, it is necessary first to recognize the important part that vernacular primers and manuals of devotion had played in English religious life during the preceding centuries. The development of these vernacular prayer books of the laity (called *Primer* in England, *Livre d'heures* in France, *Hortulus animae* in Germany) from the occasional devotions of communities of religious is a long and involuted tale which cannot be repeated in detail here,[1] but some observations about the English primers in the period preceding the authorized primer of 1545 are in order. By 1400, the content of English primers had settled down to a conventional pattern consisting in the Hours of the Blessed Virgin, the Seven Penitential Psalms, the Fifteen Gradual Psalms, Litany, Office of the Dead (Placebo and Dirige), the Commendations, and an unspeci-

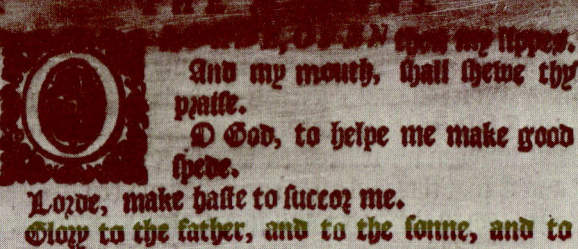

Open thou my lippes, and my mouth, shall shewe thy praise.

O God, to helpe me make good spede.

Lorde, make haste to succor me.

Glory to the father, and to the sonne, and to the holy ghoste.

As it was in the beginnyng, and is now, and euer shalbe, worlde without ende. Amen.

Hayle Mary full of grace, the Lorde is with thee, blessed art thou emonges women, and blessed is the fruite of thy wombe. Amen.

Venite exultemus. Psalm. xciiii.

¶ A song, stirryng to the praise of God.

COme and let vs reioyce vnto the Lorde, let vs ioyfully syng to God our sauior, let vs come before his face with confession & thankes geuyng, and syng we ioyfully vnto hym in Psalmes.

For God is a greate lorde, & a greate kyng ouer al goddes, which doth not forsake his people, in whose power are al the coastes of the yerth, & he beholdeth the toppes of the mountaines.

The sea is his, for he hath made it, & his handes haue fashioned the yerth also: come therefore and let vs worship and fal doune before god, let vs wepe before the lord who hath made vs, for he is our Lord God, and we are his people and the shepe of his pasture.

To daie if ye here his voyce se that ye harden not your hertes as in the bitter murmuryng in the

B   tyme

The Primer (1545).

fied array of ancillary prayers and devotions.[2] Primers appear frequently in wills and legacies as specified bequests, valued more, it would seem, for their use than as objects of intrinsic worth (the English primers seldom achieved the grandeur of their French counterparts). Their use is attested in such rules of devotion as Caxton's *Book of Curtesy*.

> And while that ye be about honestly
> To dress yourself and do on your array
> With your fellow well and tretably
> Our Lady matyns look that ye say;
> And this observance use ye every day
> With pryme and hours.[3]

and in the accounts of eyewitnesses such as the anonymous Italian traveler of the fifteenth century:

> That although Englishmen all attend mass every day, and say many Pater nosters in public, the women carrying long rosaries in their hands, and any who can read taking the Office of our Lady with them, and with some companion reciting it in the church verse by verse in a low voice after the manner of religious; they always hear mass on Sundays in their parish church.[4]

The various English "families" of liturgical use developed primers and manuals of devotion, as they did usages and ceremonial for corporate worship, and Sarum and York primers occur both in English and Latin versions.[5] The distribution of primers greatly increased following the introduction of printing from moveable type. All this suggests that the enormous popularity the primers enjoyed and the prominent part they played in the exercise of private devotion and in the shaping of lay religious life and concepts must not be underestimated. The versatility of these small books was one of their chief attributes and facilitated their widespread use. The offices and devotions of the primers could be used for personal edification and comfort or on behalf of a deceased friend or relative. They could be used at home, in church or countryside; as part of a personally established regimen or casually as time afforded opportunity. An illustration in point is Cavendish's picture of Thomas Cromwell lounging about waiting for Cardinal Wolsey and occupying his time with devotions from his primer:

> Yt chaunced me vppon alhalou day in the mornyng to come there in to the great chamber to geve myn attendaunce where I found master Cromwell leanyng in the great windowe wt a prymer in his hand sayeng of our lady mattens....[6]

As prevalent as primers were in the preceding centuries the sixteenth century saw the demand for books of private devotion markedly increase. This has been attributed to the religious controversy of the times.[7] The gravest struggle in sixteenth-century England was over the issue of jurisdictional authority. Until that issue was resolved, men and women, in some sense, were left to their own devices, and had to assume a new and heavier responsibility for the conduct of their religious life. Primers and similar books of devotion assisted in meeting that responsibility. This devotional literature was not limited to books appearing in primer form but included books of prayers drawn from various sources. Among the more influential examples, many of whose prayers were used in the later authorized primers of 1545 and 1553, were *Prayers of the Bible,* 1534; *Precationes Erasmi,* 1537; and *Preces et meditationes generales,* 1539, of Juan Luis Vives, the Spanish humanist whom Catherine of Aragon brought to England to be her tutor.

Familiar and prevalent, primers quickly came to be seen as ready vehicles for the dissemination of religious ideas even as they fulfilled the purposes of their original intent of encouraging and providing for the practice of personal piety and spirituality. Controversalists on both sides of the great religious issues of the beginning of the sixteenth century made use of primers as a means of propounding their views. In England and on the continent, English, Latin, and English/Latin primers were published in support of the religious status quo. On the other hand, among those volumes whose authors sought to effect religious change, the series of primers printed by John Bydell for William Marshall (the first appeared in 1534)[8] and *The Manual of Prayers,*

Religious Education for Citizenship   223

1539[9] of John Hilsey, bishop of Rochester, advocated a reformed theology and piety. In the England of the reign of Henry VIII, primers of conflicting viewpoints were very much part of the erupting mix of religious ideas and partisan theology, and contributed to the unsettling effect on the body politic of a quarreling body ecclesiastic. Religious controversy with its disruptive consequences was not to Henry's liking. It was not conducive to his maintenance of peace and tranquility in church and state. It did not contribute to the clear and untrammeled religious education of young people nor provide them or their elders the kind of straightforward religious certitude he sought.

In the 1530's several attempts had been made to overcome controversy by exacting moderation and uniformity. One such attempt at moderation had to do with fiercely partisan preaching: On 7 January, 1536, "a circular in the King's name, backed by a covering letter from the vicegerent (Thomas Cromwell), went to all the bishops, exhorting them to stop extremism on either side, to promote the middle way, and to beware Henry's anger if they neglected their duty and failed to keep the peace."[10] In an attempt at uniformity at the end of the decade, authorization of uniform textbooks for use in schools, an ABC, a primer of prayers in English, and a Latin grammar with an English introduction[11] was an attempt to overcome disruptive variation. The primer was *The Primer in English most necessary for the education of children.*[12] It was based on Hilsey's *Manual* but had rearranged and simplified the contents of the *Manual* and rendered the offices in English and Latin.

Finally to eliminate dissension in practice and teaching and to assure harmony and concord, Henry VIII in 1545 issued his own primer: *The Primer set forth by the King's Majesty and his clergy; to be taught, learned, and read, and none other to be used throughout all his dominions.*[13] Henry's reasoning for authorizing a primer ran even deeper than the two pragmatic considerations of peace and orderly instruction. That the Crown would issue a single, authorized primer was consonant with a long established understanding of royal responsibility for the spiritual as well as the physical well-being of a realm and its people. It was an understanding reinforced by the language of the Act of Supremacy in such phrases as "reform and redress all errors" and "for increase of virtue in Christ's religion within this realm of England."[14] This rationale for authorization was clearly set forth in Henry's preface to his Primer of 1545:

> It is the part of kings (whom the Lord hath constituted and set for pastors of his people,) not only to procure that a quiet and peaceable life may be led of all his universal subjects: but also that the same life may be passed over godly, devoutly, and virtuously in the true worshipping and service of God, to the honor of him, and to the sanctifying of his name, and to the everlasting salvation of their own selves.[15]

The king's supremacy in matters of religion was alike a matter of orderly governance and of spiritual nurture, and this double responsibility was reflected in the Injunction authorizing and establishing use of the *Primer*. The authorized primer was to guard against the confusion engendered by the plethora of competing primers and to be the vehicle for the religious instruction of the young. The authorization of an ABC, primer, and Latin grammar at the end of the preceding decade is evidence of the linkage of education in religion and education in letters seen as necessary to the proper training of citizens in a godly kingdom. An affirmation of this linkage is proclaimed in the king's Injunction printed in the *Primer*:

> Among the manifold business, and most weighty affairs appertaining to our regal authority and office, we much tendering the youth of our realms (whose good education and virtuous bringing up redounds most highly to the honor and praise of Almighty God) for divers good considerations, and specially for that the youth by divers persons are taught the *Pater noster,* the *Ave maria,* Creed, and X Commandments all in Latin and not in English, by means whereof the same are not brought up in the knowledge of their faith, duty and obedience, wherein no Christian person ought to be ignorant....

It was not children alone, however, who were to benefit from the approved content of the *Primer,* according to the Injunction,

Religious Education for Citizenship 225

but it was "also to be used for ordinary prayers of all our people... as well of the elder, as also of the youth...."

In taking up a primer as one means of furthering his program of religious reform and restructuring, Henry had in hand what Helen White has characterized as "...clearly one of the readiest ways to influence the religious thought and feeling of the average literate English layman."[16] It was a perception not lost on Henry, whose primer of 1545 appeared in twelve subsequent editions (English and Latin) during the rest of the year of its first publication and the next. Nor was it a perception lost on Henry's successor. Edward VI reissued Henry's primer in November of his first regnal year (1547), slightly modified in a protestant direction as were his subsequent reissues of *The Primer, 1545*. In 1553 he authorized a new primer of his own: *A Primer or book of private prayer needful to be used of all faithful Christians, Which book is authorized and set forth by the King's Majesty, to be taught, learned, read, and used of all his loving subjects.*[17]

The intention of each of these primers, the Henrician of 1545 and the Edwardian of 1553, was that it would contribute to the fashioning of the godly kingdom, but each differed from the other in its character and in its view of the contribution it would make.

Henry's primer of 1545 stands in direct lineal descent from the primers of the preceding centuries, and its character is derived from them. At its core, it is a manual for personal devotion, containing those elements which had become traditional in such manuals: basic Christian texts, conventional series of Psalms, Offices for the daily hours, for personal recitation, and supplications in behalf of the departed, employed of the charity of the user. It is often bright where its predecessors were often lugubrious. (It contains what "is probably the most triumphant and cheerful Dirige on record."[18]) It is open-ended, to a certain extent, with a minimum of directing rubrics or confining structure. It can be picked up and put down at will, adjusted to an individual life pattern, fitted to suit the time and space of one's daily life and inclination. It does not allow, of course, for heterodoxy, but, within the commodious bounds of received Christian teach ing, allows a good deal of room for personal reflection and appears to expect, as did earlier primers, such contemplation. Primers were designed to foster meditation as well as provide stated prayers and at times included discourses on spiritual discipline in their prefatory pages:

> When you have arrayed you, say in your chamber or lodging, Matyns, Prime, and Hours if ye may. Then go to the church... and abide in the church the space of a low mass, while there ye shall think and thank God of his benefits.... Think a while on the goodness of God, on his divine might and virtue...what grace he hath done to you...."[19]

Henry's primer was very much in keeping with this design, and provided resources for the kind of reflection evidenced here.

Something of the same character can be perceived in Edward's primer of 1553. It is a book for private, as over against corporate, use, for the person alone at home rather than joined with the congregation at church. It is a private book, but in contrast to its predecessor, it is not as personal a book. Certainly, those making use of it are encouraged to reflection on their lives:

> At the beginning of the morning and evening private prayer, thou shalt daily read, meditate, weigh and deeply consider one of these sentences of holy scripture that follow. And then from the bottom of thine heart add the confession of thy sins and the prayer following.[20]

There is, also, a discourse by Thomas Cottesforde, "A Preparative unto Prayer," which calls for self-examination. On the whole, however, Edward's primer leaves little to chance. It provides orders for morning and evening prayer, Sunday through Saturday, but the structure and content of these orders is the structure and content of Morning and Evening Prayer in the 1552 *Book of Common Prayer,* with the rubrical pronouns changed to the first or second person. The Psalms and Lessons appropriate to each Office are given in full, in place, and constitute a readily available selection of important biblical passages. In this regard, Edward's primer serves as a handbook and guide to saying conveniently the morning and evening Prayer Book offices by oneself and ties private devotion directly to public worship. Its conformation to the *Book of Common Prayer* was its undisguised intention from the outset: in granting *privilegio ad imprimendum solum* to William Seres, the grant was for printing primers

> set forth agreeable and according to the book of common prayers by us established in our high court of Parliament. (An Extract of the King's Majesty's Privilege)

Differences in character notwithstanding, both Henry's primer of 1545 and Edward's of 1553 were intended for the task of shaping the religious consciousness of the people of a godly kingdom and were thereby fulfilling an educational task long associated with primers. Emerging as they had out of the Psalters and occasional devotions of religious communities, primers originally had been intended as prayer books, not text books. The secondary function of primers, of providing basic Christian texts for instruction and reinforcement in the faith, became virtually inseparable from their primary function, of providing for personal devotion. The description by Chaucer's prioress of

> This litel child, his litel book lernynge,
> As he sat in the scole at his prymer

is reflective of the venerability of this function, and inclusion of Our Father, Hail Mary, Creed, and Ten Commandments together with graces and other prayers allowed primers to fulfill this educational function. In addition, primers intended for children often included an ABC among their instructional matter. *The Primer in english for children after the use of Sarum*[21] published in 1537 is an example of this, combining in one volume fundamental religious and educational material.

The primer authorized by Henry VIII and the primer authorized by Edward VI, as were the unauthorized primers published earlier in the sixteenth century, were intended, following in this tradition, to fulfill an instructional function as well as a devotional one. The instructional intent of the 1545 and 1553 primers was not easily missed. Authorization itself was part of the educative thrust in its clear pronouncement that these two primers were to be regarded as without peer or competitor. To authorize, as had been done in each case, only one primer for use throughout the entire kingdom, its licensed printers restricted, was an unmistakable message that the content of the primer had been determined and shaped on the highest authority and was possessed of that authority's exclusive approbation. Whatever fugitive primers might still be lurking about the remote recesses of England — and all others had been proscribed by royal proclamation[22] — there was now only one official, licit book of private devotion.

Henry, by his authorization of *The Primer, 1545*, exercised the warrant of the Act of Supremacy and its designation of the Crown as supreme head on earth of *Ecclesia anglicana*. The *Primer* was to be received perforce with a respect and attention commensurate with the respect and attention owed the king's majesty itself. In comparison with earlier primers, Henry's primer of 1545 is remarkably non-didactic. There are no ringing expositions of the royal supremacy (although that was the chief issue of the day) nor are there any homiletical explications of the finer (or rougher) points of reformed theology. Such were scarcely necessary in a book so explicitly representing, by its authorization and Injunction, the intention of the king to compel a single, authorized book of prayers, in order to neutralize the disruptive effect of the welter of competing books provided by many and lesser sources. Although not didactic in the sense of overtly instructional, Henry's primer, nevertheless, was very much part of his program of religious reform and reformation. The *Primer* was a book intended to serve a double usefulness. It was, first of all and importantly, a primer, which to the king's mind was desirable in itself, and useful as a means for the encouragement of the people's private devotions. It was useful also as a means of defining a standard of a moderate, approved theological attitude (if not formulation) in those acts of devotion themselves. The *Primer's* message was its medium. Helen White in speaking of the *Primer* as an instrument of religious settlement speaks of the process which produced it as a process of salvage and modification.[23] People deafened by a chorus of conflicting cries, for retrenchment on the one hand and for radical change on the other, heard in the *Primer* a voice that asserted that some of the past is to be retained and some of it adapted. (Some of the material customarily found in primers of preceding centuries, to be sure, was not retained in Henry's primer of 1545, as is seen in the excision of numbers of saints from the calendar and from the invocations.) The *Primer's* treatment of Hail Mary ("The Salutation of the Angel to the Blessed Virgin Mary") is an example of the process of salvage at work: it is placed with other basic texts at the start of the book, and it is to be found still in its accustomed place at the beginning of Matins.

It may be observed, parenthetically, that this salvage of Hail Mary in the *Primer* came too late to save this venerable Christian devotion from, in the long run, losing its time-honored stature. The standing of Hail Mary with other basic devotional texts had been undermined by the Injunctions of 1536 and 1538, where it was not included with Our Father, Commandments, and Creed as matters required to be taught by parsons to their gathered congregations and by parents and masters to their households.[24]

The treatment of the Dirige is an example of the process of modification: its form is familiar, although shortened, but as an intercessory supplication it now could be used as well for the living as for the dead. In keeping with the January 1536 circular against extremism of preaching (see above page 223), Henry's primer endeavored to travel a middle way between the old and the new. In light of Henry's perception of the distressed state of the realm, this middle way was itself a contribution to public well-being and a schooling in responsible citizenship.

The social concern evidenced in Henry's primer is propounded primarily by inference and by assumption. Loyal subjects of a godly kingdom obey their sovereign and, therefore, eschew all primers save his. God prospers a people devoted to him, and this devotion is a personal duty of each faithful person: how fortunate, then, that his pastor, our king, has provided in this primer a means for our devotion. More explicitly, the Litany and Suffrages included in the *Primer,* which had been composed by Archbishop Cranmer in the preceding year, articulated a concern for the whole English nation: for the royal family, the lords of the council, and all magistrates, for all people in their varying needs, and for defense against sedition and privy conspiracy. This litany is the one corporate act of worship included in the *Primer,* and it was included to prepare people for participation in its public and corporate use:

> As these holy prayers and suffrages following, are set forth of most godly zeal for edifying, and stirring of devotion of all true faithful Christian hearts, so is it thought convenient in this common prayer of procession, to have it set forth, and used in the vulgar tongue for stirring the people to more devotion; and it shall be every christian man's part, reverently to use the same to the honour and glory of almighty God, and the profit of their own souls. And such among the people as have books and can read, may read them quietly and softly to themselves; and such as cannot read, let them quietly and attentively give audience in time of the said prayers, having their minds erect to almighty God and devoutly praying in their hearts the same petitions which do enter at their ears; so that with one sound of the heart and one accord, God may be glorified in his church.[25]

The educational function which Henry's primer of 1545 attempted implicitly and inferentially, Edward's primer of 1553 attempted explicitly and manifestly. Edward's primer is, to use Isaiah Berlin's metaphor,[26] a hedgehog of a book (appropriately, according to its colophon, "to be solde, at the weste ende of Paules toward Ludgate, at the sygne of the Hedgehogge"), that is, all its parts related to a single, central vision. That vision can be indicated by the pairing: Commonwealth — Common Prayer. Henry had used his authorization to clear the devotional air of strident competitiveness. Edward used his authorization to shape and mold a universal commonality of devotion. The commonwealth ideal which had fostered the *Book of Common Prayer* — one encompassing national liturgy in the people's tongue and in the people's hands — would foster a primer which would unite people at their private devotions as the Prayer Book united them at their public worship. *A Primer, 1553* is based on the daily offices of the *Book of Common Prayer, 1552*, and this basing itself implies two assertions about the dependent relationship of private devotion upon the corporate devotion of the whole church: that private prayer derives from corporate prayer and that the forms and concerns of private prayer are the forms and concerns of public prayer. The final section of Edward's primer, "Sundry Godly Prayers for Divers Purposes," is a manifest of the book's central vision of commonality. Of the sixty-one prayers included there, twenty-three are concerned with positions in society, Judges, Lawyers, Masters, Servants, Householders, and the like, the prayers being either in behalf of or a petition of the person in the position designated. Not surprisingly, the prayers are for good conduct and godly faithfulness, but they often reflect an assumption that each person has "his alloted place and his function in society, with which he should be content and from which he should not expect to move."[27] The following examples are illustrative:

For Gentle men.

Albeit whatsoever is born of flesh is flesh, and all that we receive of our natural parents is earth, dust, ashes and corruption, so that no child of Adam hath any cause to boast himself of his birth and blood, seeing we have all one flesh and one blood, begotten in sin, conceived in uncleanness, and born by nature the children of wrath; yet forasmuch as some for their wisdom, godliness, virtue, valiantness, strength, eloquence, learning and policy, be advanced above the common sort of people unto dignities and temporal promotions, as men worthy to have superiority in a christian commonwealth, and by this means have obtained among the people a more noble and worthy name: We most entirely beseech thee, from whom alone cometh the true nobility to so many as are born of thee and made thy sons through faith, whether they be rich or poor, noble or unnoble, to give a good spirit to our superiors, that as they be called gentle men in name, so they may show themselves in all their doings gentle, courteous, loving, pitiful and liberal unto their inferiors; living among them as natural fathers among their children, not polling, pilling, and oppressing them, but favouring, helping, and cherishing them: not destroyers, but fathers of the commonalty; not enemies to the poor, but aiders, helpers, and comforters of them; that when thou shalt call them from this vale of wretchedness, they afore shewing gentleness to the common people, may receive gentleness again at thy merciful hand, even everlasting life, through Jesus Christ our Lord. Amen.[28]

For Labourers and men of occupations.

As the bird is born to fly, so is man born to labour: for thou, O Lord, hast commanded by thy holy word, that man shall eat his bread in the labour of his hands and in the sweat of his face: yea, thou hast given commandment that if any man will not labour, the same should not eat. Thou requirest of us also, that we withdraw ourselves from every brother that walketh inordinately, and giveth not his mind unto labour; so that thy godly pleasure is, that no man be idle, but every man labour according to his vocation and calling: we most humbly beseech thee, to grave in the hearts of all labourers and workmen a willing disposition to travail for their living according to thy word, and to bless the labourer's pains, and travails of all such as either till the earth, or exercise any other handicraft; that they studying to be quiet and to meddle with their own business, and to work with their own hand, and through thy blessing enjoying the fruits of their labours, may knowledge thee, the giver of all good things, and glorify thy holy name. Amen.[29]

The prayer of a true subject.

As it is thy godly appointment, O Lord God, that some should bear rule in this world, to see thy glory set forth, and the common peace kept: so it is thy pleasure again, that some should be subjects and inferiors to other in their vocation, although before thee there is no respect of persons. And forasmuch it is thy godly will and pleasure to appoint and set me in the number of subjects, I beseech thee to give me a faithful and obedient heart unto the high powers, that there may be found in me no disobedience, no unfaithfulness, no treason, no falsehood, no dissimulation, no insurrection, no commotion, no conspiracy, nor any kind of rebellion, in word or in deed, against the civil magistrates, but all faithfulness, obedience, quietness, subjection, humility, and whatsoever else becometh a subject; that I, living here in all lowness of mind, may at the last day, through thy favour, be lifted up into everlasting glory, where thou, most merciful Father, with thy Son and the Holy Ghost livest and reignest very God for ever and ever. Amen.[30]

For poor people.

As riches, so likewise poverty is thy gift, O Lord. And as thou hast made some rich to despise the worldly goods, so hast thou appointed some to be poor, that they may receive thy benefits at the rich men's hands. And as the godly rich are well beloved of thee, so in like manner are the poor, if they bear the cross of poverty patiently, and thankfully; for good and evil, life and death, poverty and riches, are of thee, O Lord: we therefore most humbly pray thee, to give a good spirit to all such as it hath pleased thee to burthen with the yoke of poverty, that they may with a patient and thankful heart walk in their state, like to that poor Lazar of whom we read in the gospel of thy well beloved Son, which chosed rather patiently and godly to die, than unjustly or by force to get any man's goods; and by no means envy, murmur, or grudge against such as it hath pleased thee to endue with more abundance of worldly goods: but knowing their state, although never so humble and base, to be of thee their Lord God, and that thou wilt not forsake them in this their great need, but send them things necessary for their poor life, may continually praise thee, and hope for better things in the world to come, through thy Son Jesus Christ our Lord. Amen.[31]

Closely linked with the sense of place and function, in these prayers, is a cognizance that each position in society has its attendant responsibility to the welfare of the whole. In combining this recognition with prayer for appropriate behavior, the Sundry Godly prayers serve present-day readers as windows through which may be glimpsed the socio-economic turmoil of the sixteenth century. The grinding imbalance in a shifting agrarian society is one example:

For Landlords.

The earth is thine, (O Lord,) and all that is contained therein; notwithstanding thou hast given the possession thereof unto the children of men, to pass over the time of their short pilgrimage in this vale of misery: We heartily pray thee, to send thy holy Spirit into the hearts of them that possess the grounds, pastures, and dwelling places of the earth, that they, remembering themselves to be thy tenants, may not rack and stretch out the rents of their houses and lands, nor yet take unreasonable fines and incomes after the manner of covetous worldlings, but so let them out to other, that the inhabitants thereof may both be able to pay the rents, and also honestly to live, to nourish their families, and to relieve the poor: give them grace also to consider, that they are but strangers and pilgrims in this world, having here no dwelling place, but seeking one to come; that they, remembering the short continuance of their life, may be content with that that is sufficient, and not join house to house, nor couple land to land, to the impoverishment of other, but so behave themselves in letting out their tenements, lands, and pastures, that after this life they may be received into everlasting dwelling places: through Jesus Christ our Lord. Amen.[32]

The nascent internationalism of an expanding mercantile society is another:

For Merchants.

Almighty God, maker and disposer of all things, which hast placed thy creatures necessary for the use of men in divers lands and sundry countries, yea, and that unto this end, that all kinds of men should be knit together in unity and love, seeing we have all need one of another's help, one country of another country's commodity, one realm of another realm's gifts and fruits: We beseech thee to preserve and keep all such as travel either by land or sea, for the getting of things that be necessary for the wealth of the realms or countries where they dwell, and not to bring in vain trifles and unprofitable merchandise to the enticing and impoverishing the commonwealth. Give them (gracious Lord) safe passage both in their going and coming, that they having prosperous journeys may shew themselves thankful to thee, and beneficial to their neighbours, and so occupy their merchandise without fraud, guile, or deceit, that the commonwealth may prosper and flourish with the abundance of worldly things through their godly and righteous travails, unto the glory of thy name. Amen.[33]

None of this is meant to suggest that Edward's primer is concerned only to promote prayers in behalf of abstract categories of the commonwealth's populace. In the section of "Sundry Godly Prayers" and in a brief collection earlier in the book are prayers of pronounced personal concern: "For the true knowledge of ourselves," "For a pure and clean heart," "For humility," "For health of the body," to give a few examples. Nor ought one to conclude that the commonwealth's strong sense of vocation and assigned place, evidenced in the prayers given above, allowed an individual to indulge in complacent callousness or indifference. The conclusion of Thomas Cottesforde's "Preparative unto Prayer":

> And that thy prayer may be more effectuous, let it be joined always with temperate fasting and charitable alms to thy needy neighbour according to the godly counsel of the good man Tobias: Prayer is good with fasting and alms.[34]

To summarize the educational intent of the primers of 1545 and 1553 in support of the godly kingdom: Henry's primer of 1545 says that the function of a primer is to provide devotional material rooted in the rich heritage of the past and yet adapted to the changed religious temper of the present, in order to promote godly faithfulness and devotion throughout the realm. Edward's primer of 1553 says that the function of a primer is to provide devotional material that will explicate the interdependence and commonality of the realm and its use unite the people in prayerful concern at home as at church, for the peace and well-being of the whole in all its parts.

The Tudor monarchs successive to Edward VI (Mary I and Elizabeth I) also issued vernacular primers. Upon her accession to the throne in 1553, Mary reissued Edward's primer, with *Edward* changed to *Mary* and *king* changed to *queen* (exept on the title-page), and the Dirige, Seven Penitential Psalms, and the Commendations, as they had appeared in Henry's primer of 1545, restored.[35] In all other points, Mary's primer of 1553 corresponds to Edward's, even including, as had Edward's, the catechism from the 1549 *Book of Common Prayer*. This last, anomalous as it may appear to be, is indicative of that clemency which characterized the beginning of Mary's reign and which is so overshadowed by later events.[36] Subsequent to Mary's marriage with Philip of Spain, a second primer was authorized:

Confirmacion.

what doest thou chiefly learne by these commaundementes?

Aunswer.

I learne two thynges. My duetie towardes God, and my duetie towardes my neighbour.

Question.

what is thy duetie towardes God?

Aunswere.

My duetie towardes God is, to beleue in hym, to feare hym, and to loue hym with all my hearte, with all my mynde, with al my soule, and with all my strength. To worship him. To geue hym thankes. To put my whole trust in him. To call vpon hym. To honoure hys holye name and hys woorde, and to serue hym truely all the dayes of my lyfe.

Question.

what is thy duetie towardes thy neyghboure?

Aunswere.

My duetie towardes my neighboure is, to loue hym as my self. And to doe to al men as I would they should doe vnto me. To loue, honour and succoure my father & mother. To honoure and obeye the kyng and hys ministers. To submit my self to al my gouernours, teachers, spirituall Pastours and maisters. To ordre my self lowly and reuerently to all my betters. To hurt no body by worde nor dede. To be true and iuste in all my dealynge. To beare no malice nor hatred in my heart. To kepe my handes from pickyng and stealyng, and my tongue fro euil speaking, lying and slaunderyng. To kepe my body in temperaunce, sobernes, and chastitie. Not to couet nor desyre other mens goodes. But learne and labour truly to geat myne owne liuing, and to doe my duetie in that state of lyfe, vnto whiche it shall please God to call me.

Question.

My good childe knowe this, that thou art notable to doe these thynges of thy selfe, nor to walke in the commaundementes

Book of Common Prayer (1549) "My Duty Towards My Neighbor" question from the Catechism.

An uniform and catholic primer in Latin and English, with many godly and devout prayers, newly set forth by certain of the clergy with the assent of the most reverend father in God Lord Cardinal Pole his grace: to be only used (all other set apart) of all the king and queen's majesties loving subjects throughout all their realms and dominions, according to the queen's highness letters patent in that behalf given.[37]

This primer of 1555 belongs to the Sarum/York use category of primers and as such is very much like Henry's authorized primer of 1545.

Elizabeth's first authorized primer of 1559[38] also followed the pattern of her father's authorized primer of 1545, but her second authorized primer of 1560[39] is the same as her brother's *A Primer, 1553*, with the Seven Penitential Psalms included and three additional prayers (Prayer for a woman to say travailing a child, A woman with child's prayer, and Prayer for a woman to say when she is delivered).

It is difficult to ascertain Mary and Elizabeth's motives in authorizing primers. They each made use of both preceding primers and perhaps intended what the original authorizers intended. Surely other evidence about Mary and Elizabeth indicates that they would see it as their duty to encourage personal devotion among their people, and perhaps speculation about their motivation must be left at that.

Catechism

The task of educating for citizenship in a godly kingdom to which Henry VIII and Edward VI in part set their authorized primers was part, also, of the educational agenda of the catechisms of the Church of England, reformed. Catechesis is for instruction in the faith and as such has a long and honored history in the Christian Church.[1] The composition of catechisms to facilitate that instruction, however, is a rather recent development. In general terms, it can be said that catechisms (systematic, question and answer expositions) are of sixteenth-century invention and emerge from that century's reformation movement, catholic and protestant, beginning with Martin Luther's *Shorter Catechism* of 1529. The process which led eventually to the composition of catechisms included treatises intended for sacramental preparation (especially confession), for edification, and for devotion: *Opus tripartitum de praeceptis decalogi, de confessione et de arte moriendi* of Jean Gerson (1363-1429) and *Discipulus de eruditione Chritifidelium* of John of Herolt, O.P. (d. 1468) being two examples. Such writings were designed for use by pastors and teachers in instructing children under their care. Clerical responsibility for instruction had been asserted from time to time by synodal decree: at Béziers in 1246 and at Albi in 1254, for examples.[2] This, also, was the designation of Henry's Injunctions of 1536 and 1538 in which the customary catechetical technique — learning by rote in dialogue — was the method enjoined upon the parson:

> Item, That ye shall every Sunday and holy-day through the year, openly and plainly recite to your parishioners, twice or thrice together, or oftener, if need require, one particle or sentence of the *Pater Noster,* or Creed, in English, to the intent that they may learn the same by heart; and so from day to day, to give them one like lesson or sentence of the same, till they have learned the whole *Pater Noster* and Creed in English, by rote.... And that done, ye shall declare unto them the Ten Commandments, one by one, every Sunday and holy-day, till they be likewise perfect in the same.[3]

Although the Injunctions required that an exposition accompany the rote learning, the matter of the Injunctions was catechetical but not a catechism *per se.*

Of longer standing than clerical responsibility for the religious instruction of children was parental responsibility. Parents and godparents were to see to the instruction of their children as were masters and mistresses to that of their households. The parental responsibility was a clear obligation:

> They were to teach their children the creed and the Our Father, and in the late Middle Ages care was taken to include the Hail Mary and the ten commandments. Works of edification such as

Religious Education for Citizenship 239

the *Himmelsstrasse (The Way to Heaven)* of the Vienna provost, Stephen of Landskron (d. 1477), and the *Christenspiegel (The Mirror for Christians)* of Dietrich Kolde (1435-1515), urged parents to carry out this duty. The *Seelenführer (Director of Souls)* charges the mother: "You must bless your child, teach him the faith, and bring him early to confession, instructing him in all he needs to know in order to confess properly."[4]

The householder's role was argued with equal force in such books of instruction as *A Work for Householders* (London, 1530) by Richard Whitford of the Brigittine Convent of Syon:

> How be it we thynke it be not sufficient nor ynough for you to lyve well your selfe/ but that all other christians also lyve the better for you and by your example/ and specyally those that you have in charge and governaunce/ that is to say/ your childer and servauntes. And me semeth it shuld also be a good pastyme and moche merytoryous/ for you that can rede/ to gader your neyghbours aboute you on the holy day/ specyally the yonge sorte/ and rede to them this poor lesson. For therin ben suche thynges as they ben bounde to knowe/ or can saye/ that is/ the Pater noster/ the Ave maria/ and the Crede/ with suche other thynges as done folowe.
> I wolde therfore you shulde begyn with them bytyme in youthe as soone as they can speke. For it is an olde sayenge. The pot or vessel shall ever savour or smell of that thynge wherwith it is fyrst seasoned. And your englyssh proverbe sayth/ that the yonge cocke croweth as he dothe here and lerne of the olde. You may in youthe teche them what ye wyll/ and that shall they longest kepe and remembre.[5]

The author continues with a lengthy exposition of Our Father, Ave Maria, Creed, Ten Commandments, and the Seven Deadly Sins, offering it as a model for instruction.

Both these agencies, the parental and the magisterial, were obligated in the religious education of their children and households. That obligation appears in rubrics of the Tudor Books of Common Prayer:

> And all fathers, mothers, maisters, and dames, shall cause theyr children, servantes, and prentices (whiche are not yet confirmed),

to come to the churche at the dai appoynted, and obediently heare and be ordered by the curate, until suche time as they have learned all that is here appointed for them to learn.⁶

The actual instruction, as specified in the rubric, was to be done by the parson. The assertion of the parental and magisterial involvement can be seen not alone as continuation of past practice. It can be seen as well as consonant with the principle of shared societal and ecclesial responsibility in the godly kingdom. The implication is clear that among the duties falling to parents and householders was participation in the process of religious instruction. This was an involvement clearly enunciated in prayers in Edward's *Primer* of 1553:

For Fathers and Mothers.

The fruit of the womb and the multitude of children is thy gift and blessing, O Lord God, given to this end, that they may live to thy glory, and the commodity of their neighbour. Forasmuch therefore, as thou of thy goodness hast given me children, I beseech thee give me also grace to train them up even from their cradles in thy nurture and doctrine, in thy holy laws and blessed ordinances, that from their very young age they may know thee, believe in thee, fear, love, and obey thee, and diligently walk in thy commandments all the days of their life, unto the praise of thy glorious name: through Jesus Christ our Lord. Amen.⁷

Of Householders.

To have children and servants is thy blessing, O Lord, but not to order them according to thy word deserveth thy dreadful curse: Grant therefore, that as thou hast blessed me with an household, so I may diligently watch, that nothing be committed of the same that might offend thy fatherly goodness, and be an occasion of turning thy blessing into cursing; but that so many as thou hast committed to my charge, may eschew all vice, embrace all virtue, live in thy fear, call upon thy holy name, learn thy blessed commandments, hear thy holy word, and avoiding idleness, diligently exercise themselves every one in his office, according to their vocation and calling, unto the glory of thy most honourable name. Amen.⁸

The Tudor church was not to leave this important matter of

education to the unstructured informality of preceding centuries. The precursors of catechisms, such as the manuals of preparation and edification cited above, had been prompted by the realization that instruction by indirection — by images in glass, wood, stone, by plays, by the drama of the Mass itself, by parental and magisterial admonition and example — was not of itself sufficient. This realization led in time to the conviction that systematic, official, and comprehensive manuals of instruction were required. Catechisms were just such manuals.

The first of the official Reformation catechisms in Tudor England was the catechism of the *Book of Common Prayer, 1549*, which appeared virtually unchanged in the Prayer Books of 1552 and 1559 and Edward's 1553 primer.[9] The Prayer Book Catechism is an instruction in the faith: a succinct exposition of Creed, Ten Commandments, and Lord's Prayer. The Prayer Book Catechism is spare and direct; two other catechisms of the sixteenth-century Church of England are considerably more elaborate: John Ponet, *A Short Catechisme* (1553),[10] a translation of his *Catechismus brevis* (1552) and Alexander Nowell, *A Catechisme or first instruction and learning of Christian religion* (1570),[11] a translation by Thomas Norton of Nowell's *Catechismus, siue prima Institutio, Disciplinaque Pietatis Christianae* (1570). Ponet was bishop of Winchester when his catechism was published, and Nowell was Dean of St. Paul's, London, when his appeared. The official character of Ponet's and Nowell's catechisms in respect to ecclesiastical approbation is not easily determined from the muddled historical data, but each catechism was published under royal privilege and, therefore, has the official character that that implies. The setting in which these two catechisms were intended for use was markedly different from that of the Prayer Book Catechism and the primers, and the difference is indicative of their differing character, as well:

> It (Ponet's) is, indeed, a typical piece of Renaissance-Reformation writing in its purpose as well as in its execution, with its dual purpose of serving education as well as religion. The scene is no

longer the home, with the child learning the Lord's Prayer from a primer before the fire, nor the church, with children and "young people" being catechized during the service, but the grammar school, with lessons to be learned and a master to be reckoned with; for the Catechism was deliberately intended as a schoolbook, a Latin reader. It is, therefore, not only written in careful classical Latin but the author takes pains to vary his words and phrases so as to give as wide a vocabulary and syntax as he can.[12]

According to the translator's preface, the same schoolbook intention was part of Nowell's rationale, too:

> ...in which Catechism there hath also great labor and diligence been bestowed about the purity of the Latin tongue, that such as were studious of that language...might at once with one labor learn the truth of religion and the pureness of the Latin tongue together.[13]

The structure of Ponet's catechism is based on the Prayer Book Catechism, consisting in expositions of Ten Commandments, Creed, and Lord's Prayer, with a section on sacraments following. Nowell's, in turn, is based on Ponet's although its commentary is considerably expanded.

Each of these catechisms, in addition to sharing a common, basic structure, share, also, a view of the world and of proper conduct in it. In the process of expounding doctrine, they indicate approved social attitude and behavior. In the Prayer Book Catechism, for example, the response to the question "What is thy duty toward thy neighbor?" is an answer which includes a manifest commitment to a hierarchical idea of society in which place and dependent relationship are assumed:

> To honor and obey the king and his ministers. To submit myself to all my governors, teachers, spritual pastors and masters. To order myself lowly and reverently to all my betters.

Like their predecessor in the *Book of Common Prayer*, the catechisms of John Ponet and Alexander Nowell also assume and affirm a hierarchical society which is very clear about relationships within it. Nowell takes the occasion of expounding the commandment "Honor thy father and thy mother" to expound this societal reality:

> *Master.* Doth the law extend only to parents by nature?
> *Scholar.* Although the very words seem to express no more; yet we must understand that all those to whom any authority is given, as magistrates, ministers of the church, schoolmasters; finally, all they that have any ornament, either of reverent age, or of wit, wisdom, or learning, worship, or wealthy state, or otherwise be our superiors, are contained under the name of fathers; because the authority both of them and of fathers come out of one fountain.
> *M.* Out of what fountain?
> *S.* The holy decree of the laws of God... Because by these it has pleased God to rule and govern the world.
> *M.* What is meant by this, that he calleth magistrates, and other superiors, by the name of parents?
> *S.* To teach us that they are given us of God, both for our own and public benefit.... For by the name of parents, we are charged not only to yield and obey to magistrates, but also to honor and love them. And likewise, on the other part, superiors are taught so to govern their inferiors, as a just parent useth to rule over good children.[14]

In further elaboration of this theme, Nowell's catechism turns its attention to the nature of loyalty to country and crown:

> *Master.* But it is much more heinous for a man to offend or kill the parent of his country than his own parent.
> *Scholar.* Yea, surely. For if it be for every private man a heinous offence to offend his private parents, and parricide to kill them; what shall we say of them that have conspired and borne wicked armor against the commonweal, against their country, the most ancient, sacred, and common mother of us all, which ought to be dearer unto us than ourselves.... So outrageous a thing can in no wise be expressed with fit name.[15]

Responsible citizenship in the godly kingdom is predicated upon faithful ascription to the Christian religion, and the summation of that religion is

> In two points; that is to say, true faith in God... and in charity, which belongeth both to God and to our neighbor.[16]

The understanding of that as determinative for communal life in that godly kingdom is both direct, in the words of the Commandments themselves, and subtle, in the perceived consequences of the Commandments. The commandment "Thou shalt not steal" is understood not only in the Prayer Book's catechetical injunction "To keep my hands from picking and stealing" but also in an understanding of fundamental plain-dealing with others:

> ...to beguile no man...to think nothing profitable, that either is not just, or differeth from right and honesty....[17]
>
> By which commandment are condemned...all frauds and deceivings. For they that break faith labor to overthrow the common succor of all men. We are...commanded that we deceive no man; that we undermine no man; that we suffer not ourselves to be allured with advantage or gain of buying or selling, to do any wrong; that we...seek not wealth unjustly, nor make our profit by untrue and uneven measures and weights, nor increase our riches with sale of slight and deceitful ware.[18]

What emerges over and over again in the social pronouncements attendant upon the catechisms' theological exposition is the consciousness that an individual's failure to keep the commandments and teachings of the church affects the public weal. What is at stake in personal morality in the godly kingdom is the well-being of the kingdom itself. This conviction is borne out as well in the Prayer Book's insistence that general, corporate confession of sin is normative in the Church of England, reformed; that private sin has public consequences and, hence, requires public acknowledgement.

The end of these instructions is the stability and health of the godly kingdom, the commonwealth, the whole nation. One consequence of this encompassing view is the swallowing up of individual godliness in an aggregate godliness. In forbidding covetuousness and greed, for example, the Prayer Book's catechism demands not just restraint but responsible independency of providing for oneself and does so within the framework of the common good:

Not to covet nor desire other men's goods. But learn and labor truly to get mine own living, and to do my duty in that state of life, unto which it shall please God to call me.

In catechism, as in primer, education for citizenship was not alone a matter of inhibiting and nay-saying. Citizens of the godly commonwealth hear not only prohibitions against wrong action but exhortations to right action, as well. Such exhortations are notes struck with equal clarity in catechism and in primer and are points of coalescence of the social teaching found in both. Implicitly and explicitly, catechism and primer teach a broad understanding of citizenship that identifies personal godliness with corporate godliness and that invokes rejoicing in the well-being of neighbor as well as in the well-being of self:

> A praier agaynst envye
>
> LORD, the inventour and maker of al thinges, and the disposer of thy giftes, which thou bestowest of thy bounteous liberalitie, gevying to each man more then he deserveth, unto each man sufficiently, so that we have no cause of grudge or envye, sith thou gevest unto al men of thine owne, and unto such as deserve it not, and to eache man sufficiently toward the hevenly blessednes: graunt us that we be not envious but quietly content with thy judgement, and the disposyng of thy giftes and benefites. Graunt us to be thankful for that we receive, and not to murmur secretli with our selves agaynst thy judgement and blessed wil in bestowyng thy fre benefites, but rather that we love and praise thi bouteous liberalitie aswel in others as in our selfe, and always magnifie the o lord, the wel of al giftes and goodnes. To the be glory for ever. Amen.[19]

NOTES

Religious Education for Citizenship: Primer and Catechism

Primer

[1] See Helen C. White, *Tudor Books of Private Devotion* (Madison: University of Wisconsin, 1951), especially chapters 1-5, for a general historical treatment of the development. For hand lists of primers and detailed analyses of individual primers, see Edgar Hoskins, *Horae Beatae Mariae Virginis or Sarum and York Primers with kindred books and primers of the reformed Roman use* (London: Longmans, Green, 1901).

[2] Henry Littlehales, *The Prymer or Prayer-book of the Lay People in the Middle Ages in English dating about 1400 A.D.* (London: Longmans, Green, 1891).

[3] Quoted in Hoskins, *op. cit.*, p. xv.

[4] *A Relation, or rather a True Account, of the Island of England.* Camden Society, No. 37, p. 23.

[5] Hoskins, *op. cit.*, pp. 105ff.

[6] George Cavendish, *The Life and Death of Cardinal Wolsey,* edited by Richard S. Sylvester, Early English Text Society, No. 243 (London: Oxford University Press, 1959), p. 104.

[7] White, *op. cit.*, pp. 149f., 174, *inter alia,* and Horton Davies, *Worship and Theology in England* (Princeton: University Press, 1970), vol. 1, p. 407f.

[8] The sixteenth century primers, including the authorized primer of 1545, are discussed at length in Charles C. Butterworth, *The English Primers (1529-1545), their publication and connection with the English Bible and the Reformation in England* (Philadelphia: University of Pennsylvania Press, 1953).

[9] Hoskins, *op. cit.*, No. 143.

[10] G. R. Elton, *Reform and Reformation England, 1509-1558* (Cambridge, Mass.: Harvard University Press, 1977), p. 256.

[11] Joan Simon, *Education and Society in Tudor England* (Cambridge

Religious Education for Citizenship

University Press, 1966) p. 191.

[12] Hoskins, *op. cit.*, No. 144.

[13] *Ibid.*, No. 174 and *The Primer set furth by the Kinges maiestie & his clergie* (1545) (New York: Scholars' Facsimiles & Reprints, 1974).

[14] C. H. Williams, ed., *English Historical Documents 1485-1558* (New York: Oxford University Press, 1967), p. 745f.

[15] David Wilkins, *Concilia magnae britanniae et hiberniae* (London: Gosling, 1737), vol. 3, p. 873.

[16] White, *op. cit.*, p. 101.

[17] Joseph Ketley, ed., *The Two Liturgies, A.D. 1549 and A.D. 1552*, Parker Society (Cambridge: Printed at the University Press, 1844).

[18] White, *op. cit.*, p. 109.

[19] Hoskins, *op. cit.*, No. 92: Sarum Primer, Latin, Antwerp, 1530.

[20] Ketley, *op. cit.*, p. 382.

[21] Hoskins, *op. cit.*, No. 131.

[22] Paul L. Hughes and James F. Larkin, eds., *Tudor Royal Proclamations*, vol. 1: The Early Tudors (1485-1553), No. 248. This proclamation is identical to the Injunction printed in *The Primer* itself.

[23] White, *op. cit.*, p. 108.

[24] C. H. Williams, ed., *op. cit.*, pp. 805ff. and pp. 811ff.

[25] Hoskins, *op. cit.*, No. 174.

[26] Isaiah Berlin, *The Hedgehog and the Fox: an essay on Tolstoy's view of history* (New York: Simon and Schuster, 1966).

[27] C. H. Williams, ed., *op. cit.*, p. 229.

[28] Ketley, *op. cit.*, p. 457.

[29] *Ibid.*, p. 459.

[30] *Ibid.*, p. 461.

[31] *Ibid.*

[32] *Ibid.*, p. 458.

[33] *Ibid.*

[34] *Ibid.*, p. 377.

[35] Hoskins, *op. cit.*, No. 201.

[36] cf. Mary's first Proclamation on religion, 1553 *in* C. H. Williams, ed., *op. cit.*, pp. 858ff.

[37] Hoskins, *op. cit.*, No. 207.

[38] *Ibid.*, p. 239.

[39] *Ibid.*, p. 243.

Catechism

[1] Two articles which offer historical reviews of the development of catechisms and catechetical instruction are: "Catéchése — Catéchisme — Catéchuméne" *in* F. Cabrol and H. Leclerq, *Dictionnaire d'Archéologie chrétienne et de liturgie* (Paris: Librarie Letouzey et Ané, 1925) and "Catechisms" *in* James Hastings, *Encyclopedia of Religion and Ethics* (New York: Scribner, 1911).

[2] Hubert Jedin and John Dolan, eds., *Handbook of Church History* (New York: Herder and Herder, 1970), IV, 578.

[3] C. H. Williams, ed., *op. cit.*, p. 811.

[4] Jedin and Dolan, *op. cit.*, IV, 578.

[5] Richard Whytford, *A Werke for Householders*, edited by James Hogg (Salzburg: Universität Salzburg, Institut fur Anglistik und Amerikanstik, 1979), p. 11f.

[6] *Book of Common Prayer, 1549:* second part of the first rubric at the end of Confirmacion. The wording varies only slightly in the Books of Common Prayer of 1552 and 1559.

[7] Ketley, *op. cit.*, p. 462.

[8] *Ibid.*, p. 465.

[9] For the development of the catechism in the Church of England, see: F. Procter and W. H. Frere, *A New History of the Book of Common Prayer* (London: Macmillan, 1920), pp. 597-602, and "Catechism, The Church" *in* G. Harford and M. Stevenson, eds., *The Prayer Book Dictionary* (London: Pitman and Sons, 1912).

[10] John Ponet, *A Short Catechisme*, edited by T. H. L. Parker *in English Reformers*, Library of Christian Classics, vol. 26 (Philadelphia: Westminster Press, 1966).

[11] Alexander Nowell, *A Catechism*, edited by G. D. Corrie, Parker Society (Cambridge: University Press, 1853).

[12] Ponet, *op. cit.*, pp. 150f.

[13] Nowell, *op. cit.*, p. 107.

[14] *Ibid.*, p. 130-131.

[15] *Ibid.*, p. 132-133.

[16] Ponet, *op. cit.*, p. 156.

[17] *Ibid.*, p. 157f.

[18] Nowell, *op. cit.*, p. 134.

[19] *The Primer set furth...*, *op. cit.*, sig. T.

Afterword

In the foregoing chapters of this book we have been reminded that at the heart of the English Reformation there were certain Great Books which were instrumental in the reforming of the sixteenth-century Church of England. We have also been reminded that these books were composed at a particular time of economic and social — as well as religious — distress. They were, quite naturally, influenced by the crises of the age, but they were designed to affect the outcome of such crises and thus to aid in the growth of the Godly Kingdom of Tudor England — the *Respublica* or *Societas Christiana*. The Great Books were not only the products of reformers, they were also instruments of the state, a particular state which still considered itself Christian and therefore accepted responsibility for the souls of its citizens as well as for their bodies and minds. More narrowly considered, these books were vital instruments during the reign of Edward VI for the advancement of a social policy, and social reform, intended to protect the poor against the destructive avarice of the rich. Beyond that, the policy the books supported was a policy intended to promote *communio*, or that mutuality of concern and love which is variously expressed by Commonwealth Men and by the Great Books.

The authors of these chapters have stressed various influences working in those responsible for the Great Books. The humanist vision of the Christian society achieved through active charity has been indicated as central to the message and meaning of both the *Paraphrases* and the first *Book of Homilies*. The Prayer Book has been analysed as an instrument for the creation and maintenance of the Christian commonwealth. Primarily the work of Cranmer, it yields evidence of the influence of the piety of the Middle Ages, but most importantly there is acknowledged the influence of Protestant humanism, that rich complex of religious affirmations to which Cranmer and others came in time, an understanding of the universe and of human existence akin to that of Melanchthon, Bucer, and Calvin. In basic ways the Great Books were influenced by those who rejected the secular humanism of some and adopted the Christian humanism of Erasmus and others, modifying it with the Reformation doctrine of justification and much that logically accompanied that doctrine. The study of the *Primer* and the Catechism has revealed the strong interrelationships between personal morality and the well-being of the commonwealth. Through the use of *Primer* and Catechism the citizenry was educated, warned against morally wrong actions and exhorted to do that which is right. The chapter strongly argues the identification of personal godliness with corporate godliness in Tudor England.

Now, at the end of these perusals of the Great Books, we may reach certain conclusions and set them in the midst of some further historical reflections. Scripture, studied and preached in the context of Prayer Book worship by persons raised and nurtured in biblical, humane Christianity, affects all of life, the life of the individual and the life of society. Of this, the leaders and defenders of the English Reformation were certain. Furthermore, they were convinced that individual and societal health and well-being were dependent upon the sincere and orderly participation of persons and societies in the worship of God. At the head of the "Causes of a ruinous Commonweale," Elizabeth I was reminded as she processed to her Coronation in 1559, was "Want of the feare of God," and the first of the "Causes of a florishing Commonweale" was "Feare of God."[1] It is true that persons such as Cranmer, Latimer, Jewel and others were genuinely concerned for those who suffered on account of the greed of landlords and merchants, but on the deepest level their concern was motivated by biblical and theological principles concerning the relationship of persons and societies towards the God "who hath put down the mighty from their seat: and hath exalted the humble and meek."[2] Thus they fashioned instruments, the Great Books, to lead their people in the right way, to create in England a godly kingdom such as would please God and bring prosperity to the commonwealth.

Afterword

Tudor Christians believed that calamities, personal and societal, were loving visitations of a righteous God. The birth of a child with a ruff of flesh in Surrey in 1561 was for some a sign of God's displeasure with those who dressed extravagantly.[3] The birth of a monster in Sussex in 1562 was a demonstration of "The great abuse and vyce/ That here in England now doeth raygne." Such events condemn sin and call for repentance: "Repent, amende both hygh and lowe/ The woorde of God embrace/ To lyve therto, as we should doe/ God gyve us all the grace."[4] In the prayers added to the end of the Litany in the 1552 Prayer Book, it is acknowledged that foul weather, dearth and famine, war, and plague and sickness are the just punishments of God visited upon a sinful people.[5] In a ballad printed by John Awdely at the accession of Elizabeth I, the point is forcefully made that because of the sin of the English, God took young King Edward to himself and let loose the agents of antichrist, the papists. Persecution, idolatry, hunger, war, the loss of Calais, economic ruin, and a general darkness plagued the land. But there were those who repented and patiently endured tribulation. God beheld the faithful and cried out:

> Oh England, England sore doest thou stray,
> My martirs bloud shed out this day,
>   In wofull plyght.
> The infantes young that fatherles be,
> With wydowes poore cryinge to me
>   Wythdrawes my spyte.

With that the skies grew bright and Elizabeth was summoned to guide the realm: "My wyll in thee doo not thou hyde,/ And Vermine darke let not abyde,/ In thys thy Land."[6] Put simply, when the people no longer feared God they suffered: when they feared God once more they prospered.

The most prevalent arousal of the fear of God was that to which Shakespeare referred in Jacques' recitation of the seven ages of personal experience: the decay and death awaiting everyone. That "mere oblivion,/ Sans teeth, sans eyes, sans taste, sans everything" is the certain fate of everyone who strides upon the world's stage.[7] More dreadful than "mere oblivion" was that to which "An Exhortation against the Fear of Death" in the first *Book of Homilies* referred: the deprivation of worldly "honors, riches and possessions," the "pangs and pains" that accompany dying, and most importantly "perpetual damnation in time to come." This is "the second *death*...that is that death which indeed ought to be dreaded, for it is the everlasting loss, without remedy, of the cause and favour of God, and of everlasting pleasure and felicity." Even more, "it is the condemnation of both body and soul, without either appellation or hope of redemption, unto everlasting pains in hell."[8]

Dr. John Faustus sold his soul to Lucifer in order that he might command the spirits to do whatsoever he willed.

> I'll have them fly to India for gold,
> Ransack the ocean for the orient pearl,
> And search all corners of the new-found-world
> For pleasant fruits and princely delicates.
> I'll have them read me strange philosophy,
> And tell the secrets of all foreign kings.
> I'll have them wall all Germany with brass,
> And make swift Rhine, circle fair Wittenberg...[9]

Such was his immodest and selfish ambition. In the last hour of life Faustus contemplated the torments of hell awaiting him, gravely described by the Bad Angel, and spoke to himself:

> Oh Faustus
> Now hast thou but one bare hour to live,
> And then thou must be damned perpetually.
> Stand still, you ever-moving spheres of heaven,
> That time may cease, and midnight never come.
> Fair nature's eye, rise, rise again and make
> Perpetual day; or let this hour be but
> A year, a month, a week, a natural day
> That Faustus may repent and save his soul.
> *O lente, lente currite noctis equi!*
> The stars move still, time runs, the clock will strike,
> The devil will come, and Faustus must be damned.

Afterword

> O I'll leap up to my God! Who pulls me down.
> See, see where Christ's blood streams in the firmament!
> One drop would save my soul, half a drop. Ah my Christ—
> Rend not my heart for naming of my Christ;
> Yet will I call on him: O spare me Lucifer....[10]

Marlowe's play reflects Reformation doctrine, the message of the Scriptures as the reformers understood it. It also reflects the preaching of the time, the piety of the Prayer Book, and the popular convictions of most people. Like the Great Books, the play was designed to arouse in theater-goers that wholesome fear of God that leads to repentance and salvation.

In the Sixth Book of his *Lawes of Ecclesiastical Polity*, Richard Hooker points out the necessity of fear to the working of repentance. "The first thing that wrought the Ninevites' repentance, was fear of destruction within forty days." Yet Hooker also points out that such beneficial fear proceeds from faith, for if we are to repent we must be able to conceive of the possibility of avoiding evil henceforth. And so Hooker wrote: "fear worketh no man's inclination to repentance, till somewhat else have wrought in us love also. Our love and desire of union with God ariseth from the strong conceit which we have of his admirable goodness. The goodness of God which particularly moveth unto repentance, is his mercy towards mankind, notwithstanding sin: for let it once sink deeply into the mind of man, that howsoever we have injured God, his very nature is averse from revenge, except unto sin we add obstinacy," then repentance is worked and a soul saved.[11] Consequently, such fear as we have been considering is not ultimately aroused by vivid portrayals of the loss of worldly honors and possessions, the pangs and pains of death, or the horrors of eternal damnation. The instruments for the creation of the Godly Kingdom are remarkably restrained when dealing with such threatening imagery. Rather, the Great Books aim at leading people to repentance and newness of life by instilling faith, arousing awe and wonder at the greatness of God's merciful love. They are themselves conduits of divine grace, presenting God as one who justifies sinners, beginning thereby that mutual participation from which all good proceeds.

It is love that underlies the fear John Donne experienced as he lay ill, listening to the funeral bell toll. Fear is time and again expressed in Donne's *Devotions*, as when he asks, "Lord, dost thou not accuse me, dost thou not reproach me my former sins, when thou layest me upon this bed?" But the faith and love, without which fear is destructive, are also in evidence, as when he prays:

> O most mighty and most merciful God, who art so the God of health and strength, as that without thee all health is but the fuel, and all strength but the bellows of sins...Life itself is with thee...for thou art life; and all kinds of health, wrought upon us here by thine instruments... *Thou wouldest have healed Babylon, but she is not healed* (Jer. 1:9). Take from me, O Lord, her perverseness, her wilfulness, her refractoriness, and hear thy Spirit saying in my soul: Heal me, O Lord, for I would be healed.[12]

His sickness was in some way understood as recompense for sin. But Donne believed, he repented his sin, and prayed to the merciful God knowing that his prayer would be heard and his plea granted.

Sickness understood from the perspective of God's mercy, like other forms of tribulation, was viewed by the sixteenth-century Christian as an act of divine love. Epaphroditus in Becon's *The Sick Man's Salve* doubts that his sickness is "God's loving visitation." Philemon assures him that it is, "For so are we taught by the Word of God. God himself saith, 'As many as I love I rebuke and chastise.'" The sick man protests that he was good enough before he became ill. To this Philemon sharply retorts: "This is the judgment of the flesh, which ever lusteth against the Spirit. Against such careless fleshly livers hear what our Saviour Christ saith, 'Wo be unto you that are rich! for you have your consolation...'" Christopher adds; "Brother Epaphroditus, the way to enter into glory is the cross. For by that way did our elder brother Christ enter into the kingdom of his Father. And the blessed apostle saith: 'By way of tribulations must we enter into the Kingdom of God.'"[13] It was necessary, then, to bear such tribulation as sickness with patience, repenting of the sins which

Afterword

gave rise to it, resolving to lead a new life, turning one's back upon the things of this world, claiming citizenship in the heavenly kingdom whereby the earthly kingdom of England shall become godly, be in truth the *societas Christiana*.

The Great Books both reflected the popular reformed views of individual and corporate life in sixteenth-century England and helped to mold them. An impressive example is found in the Prayer Book service of the Visitation of the Sick. The exhortation to be made to the sick persons begins, "Dearly beloved know this, that Almighty God is the lord of life and death, and over all things to them pertaining, as youth, strength, health, age, weakness, and sickness. Wherefore, whatsoever your sickness is, know you certainly, that it is God's visitation." The exhortation then explains that sickness is sent to try your patience and to correct and amend in you whatever offends. If you repent your sin and patiently bear your sickness, trusting in God's mercy and submitting yourself altogether to God's will, your sickness will be turned to your benefit and help to forward you "in the right way that leads to eternal life." The 1552 Prayer Book then directs that if the sickness of the person be great, the exhortation may be terminated at this point. For those able to hear and respond, the minister goes on, grounding what he says in Hebrews 12:6-10, saying that "whom the Lord loveth, he chastiseth." Following the example of a father's relationship to his children, he says that if the chastisement is endured God offers himself to the sick person as unto one of his own children. God chastises "us for our profit, to the intent he may make us partakers of his holiness. These words...are God's words, and written in Holy Scripture for our comfort and instruction...." Furthermore, by chastisement God makes us "like unto Christ" in our adversities and sicknesses, suffering as he did. The doorway to eternal life "is gladly to die with Christ, that we may rise again from death, and dwell with him in everlasting life." The exhortation ends with the statement that since, after this life,

> there is account to be given unto the righteous judge, of whom all must be judged without respect of persons: I require you to ex-

amine your self and your state, both toward God and man, so that accusing and condemning yourself for your own faults, you may find mercy at our heavenly Father's hand for Christ's sake, and not be accused and condemned in that fearful judgment. Therefore I shall shortly rehearse the articles of our faith, that ye may know whether you believe, as a Christian man should, or no.

The creed is then recited in interrogative form, as found in Baptism, thus placing emphasis on the absolute necessity of faith prior to repentance.[14] This done, the rubric directs the minister to examine the sick person

whether he be in charity with all the world, exhorting him to forgive from the bottom of his heart all persons that have offended him, and if he have offended other, to ask them forgiveness. And where he hath done injury or wrong to any man, that he make amends ot the uttermost of his power.

After this, and after directions concerning the making of a will, the sick person is invited to "make a special confession, if he feel his conscience troubled with any weighty matter." The priest then pronounces the absolution.[15]

This sequence, from the exhortation through confession and absolution, is based upon the *Ordo ad visitandum infirmum* of the medieval service books.[16] It preserves with remarkable fidelity the essential marks of the historic Sacrament of Penance. Yet viewed within the wider framework of the *Book of Common Prayer,* and in terms of the reformers' understanding of the Word read and preached, the Visitation of the Sick provides another opportunity for engendering repentance and renewal of life such as prepares a person for eternal life *and* for citizenship in the godly commonwealth. For emphasis is placed on love of God and love of neighbor, on forgiveness and restitution, such as restores and enlivens the community of persons, from the poor and powerless to the rich and influential.

The Great Books were thus designed not only for personal salvation but also for social well-being, the one being intimately and sometimes causally related with the other. The books, like the preachments and actions of the Commonwealth Men, were

Afterword

conservative, seeking to preserve that common concern and respect for all persons, regardless of their wealth or position, which was inherited from the Middle Ages and promoted the commonwealth ideal. Looking back, we may discern that the effort to preserve the past was futile, that the commonwealth ideals were impracticable, that the future lay with the adventurous entrepreneur, the gradually developing industrial revolution and laissez-faire capitalism. The reformers, however, were not at liberty to adjust their goals to meet new realities. They were not pragmatic politicians (or ecclesiastics) valuing success above truth. Their humanist educations directed them toward the realization of communal caring and love and their Christian faith bound them to the commandment of love of God and love of neighbor. Thus they preached against the sin of avarice, the satisfaction of selfish appetite at the expense of the poor and other defenseless members of the community. And they brought the people, high and low, rich and poor, into community formed, sustained, and dominated by worship of God, inculcating the virtues of mutual participation with God and with one another in their particular community. Living under the influence of the rhythm of contrition and praise, Tudor Christians learned to live together in a mutually supportive community. When they came together for Holy Communion, they came together as reconciled sinners, reconciled with God as they were reconciled with those citizens whom they offended or who offended them. It was expected that the landlord would care for his or her tenants, not turning them off the land in order to gain greater profit by enclosing the land for the raising of sheep. It was expected that the yeoman farmer would serve the landlord well, not cheating him or her and not undermining just authority in any way.

When they gathered to hear the Word of God read and preached, when they met to partake of the Visible Words in the Holy Communion, their faith was cultivated, their sins condemned, grace was given for repentance and satisfaction, and the *societas Christiana* was nourished and increased. And when they became ill, when they were approached by the great "sumner" death, and the priest came visiting, the Christian knew that what the

Church of England was doing was not crudely and superstitiously coercive, but rather utterly gracious, for the sinner was being guarded by the church's ministration and the nation was being cared for — that the land may be saved from the just wrath of the righteous God in whose hand all of "life doth lie."[17]

That Tudor England did not become the Kingdom of God is neither surprising nor a refutation of the ideals of the reformers. John Foxe may have believed that "God's Englishmen" were a chosen people, a people of destiny, but they were also a human lot whose human nature was flawed with selfishness. The ideals of the reformers concerned the basic truth of human nature, beneath all its flaws. God's people were created to live together in mutual love. The Reformation was concerned to restore humanity to its original and true nature by means of repentance, renewal, and growth in the perfection of the Christian life, both individual and corporate.

John Jewel, bishop of Salisbury (1559-1571), preaching on Romans 12:16-18, spoke of pride as "the mother of all wickedness." Humility he identified as "the mother of all virtue." "Like as pride maketh us like Lucifer, so humility maketh us like unto Christ. Therefore Christ himself, when he first gave his disciples charge to preach, when he first gave them a commandment upon the mount to publish abroad his gospel, *Beati pauperes,* said he. And why so? *Quoniam ipsorum est regnum coelorum:* 'Blessed are the poor, for theirs in the kingdom of God.' And again: *Beati nites.* And why so? *Quoniam ipsi possidebunt terram:* 'Blessed are the meek, for they shall inherit the earth.' So again to his disciples he said: *Discite ex me; quia ego nites sum:* 'Learn ye of me; for I am meek:' I am gentle: learn this of me, said Christ. So Paul: *Hic sensus sit in vobis, qui fuit in Christo:* 'Let the same mind be in you that was in Christ Jesus; which, when he was equal with God, yet nevertheless made himself of no reputation, and humbled himself unto death, even the death of the cross.'"[18]

Jewel preached humility as that foundation on which Christ built the church. Humility "also upholdeth all commonweals." Pride, that which makes us seek to be equal to or to surpass God,

Afterword

to displace others in lawful authority, to satisfy our lusts and fulfil every ambition at whatever cost to others — this pride "overthroweth all good commonweals."[19] In the end he pleads:

> Let us lay aside this pride of our heart, let us not be wise in our own opinions, let us not requite evil with evil, let us, as much as may be, have peace with all men. Alas! it is no great thing that I require of you; I require only your love, I require only your friendship one towards another; I ask no more, but that your hearts be joined in mutual love and unity together. Alas! it is a thing that soon may be granted of such as pray together, of such as have one heavenly Father, of such as are partakers of Christ's holy sacraments, of such as profess Christ, and will be called Christians.
>
> O how can we pray our heavenly Father to forgive us, if we will not forgive our brother wherein he trespasseth against us? How can we with clear conscience come unto the holy communion, and be partakers of Christ's most holy body and blood, if we are not in charity with our own neighbour? Let us therefore lay aside all discord without hypocrisy; let us lay apart all malice without dissimulation; let us join together in brotherly love, let us all be of like affection one towards another: but let us not be high-minded, let us make ourselves equal to them of the lower sort. So shall we make our bodies a quick and lively sacrifice; so shall we make them holy and acceptable to God. . . .[20]

In this essentially radical teaching, Jewel reflects the influence of the Great Books. His preaching is scriptural, presuming a knowledge of the Word on the part of his auditory. His doctrine stands in conformity to that understanding of God's Word as expounded in Erasmus' *Paraphrases* and the first *Book of Homilies*. Peace and unity and love toward God and neighbor are keynotes of the Protestant-humanist ethic and are prominent in Jewel's sermon. Jewel also presumes the cultivation of personal devotion engendered by the *Primer* and instruction in basic Christian beliefs engendered by the Catechism. The Prayer Book, and especially the sacraments, are also prominent in this sermon. He understands the basic teaching of the Prayer Book when he asks, "How can we with clear conscience come unto the holy communion, and be partakers of Christ's holy body and blood, if we are not in charity with our own neighbour?" The worship of the church concerns the mutual participation of Christians in Christ, and thus of persons in society, one with another.

The Great Books of the English Reformation deserve greater attention than is ordinarily afforded them. They were influential not only with bishops such as Jewel and rulers such as Elizabeth I, but with the citizenry in general, in ways which are too complex and numerous to be fully comprehended.[21] At the very least we should now be able to conclude that no matter what their effect may have been they were designed to be instruments for the perfection of the Godly Kingdom of Tudor England.

NOTES

Afterword

[1] *The Quenes Maiesties Passage through the Citie of London to Westminster the Day before her coronation* (STC 7591), J. M. Osborn, ed., The Elizabethan Club Series 1 (New Haven: Yale University Press, 1960), pp. 49, 50.

[2] The Magnificat in Evening Prayer; *Book of Common Prayer 1559*, p. 62.

[3] British Library, Huth 50 (34), a broadsheet.

[4] *Ibid.*, Huth 50 (33).

[5] *First and Second Prayer Books of Edward VI*, pp. 366-367.

[6] *The Wonders of England. 1559* (London: John Awdely, [1559]). Huth 50 (44).

[7] *As You Like It*, ii.7.

[8] *Certain Sermons* (1864), pp. 92, 93, 98.

[9] Christopher Marlowe, *Dr. Faustus*. I.i.

[10] *Ibid.*, V.ii.

[11] Hooker, *Lawes*, VI.iii.3; 7th Keble ed. (1888), 3:8-9.

[12] *Devotions Upon Emergent Occasions* (Ann Arbor, University of

Afterword

Michigan Press, 1959), pp. 19, 27-28.

[13] Thomas Becon, *Prayers and Other Pieces*, Parker Society, J. Ayre, ed. (Cambridge: At the University Press, 1844), pp. 94-95.

[14] *Lawes*, VI.iii.2, v.2; 7th Keble ed. (1888), pp. 7, 56-57.

[15] *Book of Common Prayer 1559*, pp. 301-303; *First and Second Prayer Books of Edward VI*, pp. 260-262, 418-419.

[16] See Maskell, *Monumenta Ritualia*, 1:92-96.

[17] *Certain Sermons* (1864), p. 584, "The Homily of Repentance."

[18] Jewel, *Works*, Parker Society, J. Ayre, ed. (Cambridge: At the University Press, 1847), 2:1093.

[19] *Ibid.*, p. 1094.

[20] *Ibid.*, p. 1097.

[21] In order to proceed further with an estimation of the use and effect of the Great Books in Tudor England a careful investigation of church court records to the death of Elizabeth I would be of great importance. The investigator would be aided by such books as Ralph Houlbrooke's *Church Courts and the People During the English Reformation 1520-1570* (Oxford: Oxford University Press, 1979). Also of use are books recording some of the church court records, such as Arthur J. Willis', *Church Life in Kent, being Church Court Records of the Canterbury Diocese 1559-1565* (London and Chichester: Phillimore, 1975). Another source of information is available in the literature of the age. We need more studies such as Richmond Noble's *Shakespeare's Biblical Knowledge and Use of the Book of Common Prayer* (New York, 1970). The task is immense and daunting but not impossible.

LIST OF ILLUSTRATIONS

Fig. 1 The Great Bible ... ii

Fig. 2 A Devout Treatyse Called the Tree and XII Fruites of the Holy Goost ... 53

Fig. 3 Page from Erasmus' *Paraphrases Upon the New Testament* ... 74

Fig. 4 Page from *Certaine Sermons* ... 86

Fig. 5 Title page of first *Book of Common Prayer* (1549) ... 146

Fig. 6 From *Book of Common Prayer* (1552) ... 178

Fig. 7 From *The Primer* (1545) ... 220

Fig. 8 From *Book of Common Prayer* (1549) ... 236

INDEX

Adiaphora, 64
Adultery, homily on, 121-2
Aelred of Rievaulx, 30
Alfred the Great, 177
Anamnesis, 171, 184-5
Ante-Communion, 192-3
Apostacy, 116
Aquinas, Thomas, 4, 121
Aristotle, 27
Articles and Injunctions, 18-9, 20-1, 47, 68, 85, 87, 101, 127, 150, 181, 183, 224-5, 238
  see Visitations
Articles of Religion
  10 Articles (1536), 147, 148
  13 Articles (1538), 147
  6 Articles (1539), 147
  42 Articles (1552), 12-3
  39 Articles (1571), 9, 16-7; on Holy Communion, 202
Ascham, Roger, 68, 80; *Scholemaster*, 93
Augustine of Hippo, 27, 50
Awdeley, John, *Wonders of England*, 253
Bale, John, 7
Baptism, 166
  see Sacraments
Barnes, Robert, 7
Becon, Thomas, 7, 68, 91, 114
  homily by, 121-2
  Sick Man's Salve, 256
Bible,
  and printing press, 4, 5
  English, 9, 69-73, 126, 127-8
  restored, 14-5
  and Prayer Book, 142, 159, 163-4
  see Scripture
Bidding Prayer, 142
Bilney, Thomas, 36
Bishops Book, 147
Black Rubric, 157, 161

Bonner, Edmund, 47, 91, 92, 127
  homily by, 112-4
Book of Common Prayer, Ch. III; 10, 11, 15-6, 26, 241, 251, 261
  history of, 145-61
  design of, 161-5
  structure of, 166-71
  language, 171-7
  Sunday service, 177-99
  see Prayer Book, *et passim*
Breviary, 149-50, 162
Bucer, Martin, 36, 203, 252
  Censura, 157-8
  de Regno Christi, 29, 52, 159-60
Bullinger, Henry, 156
Burial Office, 170
Bydell, John, 222
Calvin, John, 36, 179, 203, 252
Cambridge University, 68, 70
Catechism, 12, 16, 166-7, 252, 261
  discussed, 237-45
Catherine of Aragon, 13, 222
Cavendish, George, 222
Caxton, William, 6, 221
Charity, active, 52, 58, 65-6, 112-4
Chaucer, Geoffrey, 227
Cheke, Sir John, 9, 68, 80, 157
Christian humanism, ix, x, 11, 28, 31
  see Humanism, Protestant-humanism, Erasmus
Church of England, defined, 20-1
Churching of Women, 169-70
Clerk, parish, 163, 182
Cloud of Unknowing, 162
Commonwealth and Commonweal, 24, 26, 30, 37-8, 66, 92, 94, 111, 118-9, 124-5, 141, 159, 204-6, 230, 244, 251-2, 259-60
Commonwealth and the human body, 113-4, 115-6
Commonwealth Men, 35, 36, 205, 258
Confirmation, 167
Contention, homil on, 122-3
Contrition, 152, 177
  see Repentance
Contrition and Thanksgiving, rhythm of, 144
Convocation, 85, 86, 88 147, 148, 150, 151
Cooper, Thomas, 142, 204-5
Coronation Rite, 31

Cottesforde, Thomas, 226, 235
Council of Trent, 118
Coverdale, Myles, 7, 14, 71-2
Covetousness, avarice, 33-38, 180, 260-1
Cox, Richard, 68, 80, 151, 160
Cranmer, Thomas, ix, 7, 8, 13, 47, 48, 49-50, 63, 68
 and Prayer Book, Ch. III, *passim*
 Preface to Bible, 72, 200
 and *Homilies*, 85, 87-8, 91, 98, 102-11, 127
 and Ket's rebellion, 38-9
 and Devon rebels, 142-5
 liturgical work, 146-60
 and *Paraphrases*, 73, 79
Cromwell, Thomas, 8, 35, 48, 67-8, 79, 129, 222-3
Death, 25; homily on, 117-8
Devout Treatyse Called the Tree, A, 52-4
Discipline, 188-9
Discourse of the Common Weal, 36, 205
Donne, John, 168-256
Dudley, Edmund, *Tree of Commonwealth*, 55, 106
Education, 59, 79-80, 90, 93-4, 101, 167, 223, 224, 227-8, 230, 235, 238-45
Edward VI, 7, 9-13, 37, 47, 48, 49, 201, 230, 235, 237, 253, *et passim*
Elizabeth I, 13-4, 139, 160-1, 237, 252, 253, *et passim*
Elyot, Thomas, 63, 93
Enclosures, 34-5
Erasmus, Desiderius, 48-9, 261
 and printing, 4
 and Bible, 69-70, 71, 73, 75-6
 Enchiridion, 58-9, 63, 67, 70, 91, 109, 122
 philosophy of Christ, 28-9, 52, 73, 91, 92, 93
 on language, 56-7
Eucharistic doctrine, 141, 143-4, 154-5, 159, 202-5
 see Sacraments, Holy Communion, Participation
Ferrar, Robert, 153-4
Fisher, John, 6
Foxe, John, 4-5, 150-260
Frankfort-on-Main, exiles at, 15, 160
Frith, John, 7, 9
Gardiner, Stephen, 47, 87, 127, 150, 156, 202
Gerson, Jean, 238
Goodrich, Thomas, 154, 157
Good Works, 124; homily on, 107-10
Grafton, Richard, 81

Grindal, William, 9, 68, 80
Guest, Edmund, 161
Gutenburg, Johann Gensfleisch, 3
Hales, John, 35-6, 126-7
Harpesfeld, John, 91, 98; homily by, 102-3
Harrison, William, *The Description of England*, 179
Heath, Nicholas, 154
Henry VIII, 13, 79, 154, 223-5, 228, 235, 237, *et passim*
  and royal supremacy, 8, 9
  and *Homilies*, 87, 88
  see Supremacy
Herbert, George
  on Scripture, 201-2, 215
  on Holy Communion, 203-4
Hermann of Cologne, 148
Hermeneutics of Erasmus, 75-9
Holbeach, Henry, 154
Hilsey, John, 223
Holy Communion, 11, 38, 167
  description, 187-99
  and *Homilies*, 111
  see Sacraments, Cranmer, *Book of Common Prayer*, Eucharistic doctrine
Homilies (1547), 10, 15, 113, 126, 191, 194, 261
  discussion of, 85-128
  plan of, 110-111
Hooker, Richard
  on church and commonwealth, 26-7
  on Prayer Book, 139-42
  on Holy Communion, 188, 202-3
  on Scripture, 200-1
  on repentance, 255
Hooper, John
Hortulus Animae, 219
Humanism, 51-62, 205, 251-2
  problem of definition, 48-9, 50
  continuance of, 63-4
  ideal of, 67
  and education, 84
  see Christian humanism, Protestant-humanism, Erasmus
Human laws, 108
Imitation, concept of, 59, 93-4, 126
Jewel, John, 142, 191, 252, 260-2
John of Herolt, 238

Index

John of Salisbury, *Polycraticus*, 30-1
Joye, George, 7
Justification, 103-5, 107, 115, 124
Kairos, 170-1
  see Time
Key Thomas, 81-2
King's Book, 147
Knox, John, 14, 15, 160
Kolde, Dietrich, 239
Lambert, John, 19
Language, rhetoric
  and Erasmus, 56-7
  and *Homilies*, 95-101
  and Prayer Book, 171-7
Latimer, Hugh, 35, 36-8, 50-1, 91, 95, 99, 100-1, 142, 156, 191, 201, 252
  homily by, 122-3
  on Holy Communion, 204
Lever, Thomas, 35
Liber Precum Publicarum, 16
Litany (processions), 161
  of 1535, 147
  of 1544, 148-9
  description of, 183-7
Livre d'heures, 219
Lucas, Master of Requests, 157
Luther, Martin, 5, 6, 36, 70, 72, 118, 203, 238
Malet, Frances, 81
Manual, medieval, 163, 167
Manual of Prayers, 222-3
Marlowe, Christopher, *Dr. Faustus*, 254-5
Marshall, William, 222
Mary, Queen, 13, 80-1, 160, 235, 237
Matrimony, service, 168
May, William, 157
Melanchthon, Philip, 36, 252
Merbecke, John, *Book of Common Prayer Noted*, 163
Metanoia, 186; *see* Repentance
Missal, 162
More, Thomas, *Utopia*, 59-62; 63, 64, 165
Morison, Richard, 63, 68
Morning Prayer, 167
  and Evening Prayer, 176
  description of, 180-3

National sentiment, 144
Northumberland, Duke of, John Dudley, 158
Norton, Thomas, 241
Nowell, Alexander, *Catechism*, 16, 40, 241-4
Oath of Allegiance, 17-8
Oaths, homily on, 114-5
Obedience, 24, 33, 55, 89, 91, 94, 101, 108, 122-3, 141
   homily on, 118-21
Order of Communion, 152-3, 194-5
Ordinal, 22-3, 163; *see* Priest
Ordo ad visitandum infirmum, 258, 259
Ornaments Rubric, 161
Paraphrases, 9-10, 15, 126, 261
   discussion of, 73-85
   see Erasmus
Parliament and Prayer Book, 150-4, 155, 157, 158, 160, 161
Parr, Catherine, 9, 68, 79-80, 133
Participation, 38, 141, 143, 159, 195, 199, 202-3, 205, 259, 262
Penance, Sacrament, 258
Perjury, 115
Peter Martyr Vermigli, 157, 194, 202
Philip, King of Spain, 13, 14
Pia deliberatio of Cologne, 153
Pole, Reginald, 63-7
Ponet, John, *A Short Catechisme*, 241-2
Pontifical, 163
Poverty, 33, 108, 233
Prayer Book, Preface, 163-4; Of Ceremonies, 164-5
Prayers of the Bible, 222
Preaching, 261
   discussion of, 97-9
   description, 190-1
   Latimer on, 36-7
   Hooker on, 140-1
   see Language and Rhetoric
Precationes Erasmi, 222
Preces et meditationes generales, 222
Priest, presbyter, Hooker on, 140
   see Ordinal
Primer, The, 11-2, 16, 147, 240, 252, 261
   discussion of, 219-37
   social concern in, 229-30
Primer, Lay Folks Prayer Book, 161-2
Primer in english for children, 227

Primer in English most necessary for the education of children, 223
Printing, ix-x, 3-8
Privy Council, 7, 23-4, 150-1, 153, 157
Processional, 163; *see* Litany
Prone, medieval, 192-3
Protestant-humanism, 35-6
　see Christian humanism, Humanism
Purgatory, 144-5
Puritans, 26, 139-40, 142, 175, 177, 200
Quinones, Cardinal, 150
Rationale of Ceremonies, 147-8
Rebellions of 1549, 35, 38, 155, 172
Reformatio Legum Ecclesiasticarum, 157
Reformation faith, ix, x, 11, 12, 31; *see* Justification, Sanctification
Repentance
　Cranmer on, 38, 104, 144-5
　homily on, 102-3
　and Prayer Book, 195-7, 258
　Hooker on, 255
　Donne and, 256
　see Contrition
Ridley, Nicholas, 154, 156
Rogers, John, 72
Sacraments
　Hooker on, 141
　Cranmer on, 143-4
　Visible Words, 202
　see Baptism, Holy Communion, Eucharistic doctrine
Sacrifice, 155, 195-6, 197, 198, 199
Sanctification (true and lively faith) 105-7, 108, 115, 124
Sarum Breviary, 148
Sarum Use, 162
Scory, John, 32-4
Scripture
　doctrine of, 10, 22-3, 38
　Word of God, 47-8
　meaning, 84
　homily on, 102
　effect of, 252
　see Bible
Seres, William, 227
Sermons, *see* Preaching
Shakespeare, William, 22, 253-4
Smith, Sir Thomas, 35, 36

Societas Christiana, 29, 159, 251, 257
Somerset, Protector, 35, 68-9, 126, 129, 139
Starkey, Thomas, 35, 49, 68, 92, 93
   Exhortation, 63-4
   Dialogue, 64-7
Stephen of Landskron, 239
Supremacy, royal, 21-22, 228
Syon, Brigittine Convent of, 239
Tavener, Richard, 63
Taylor of Hadleigh, 157
Thirlby, Thomas, 154
Time, sanctification of, 167; *see* Kairos
Tithes, 192
Tracy, Richard, 7
Tunstall, Cuthbert, 71, 87, 154
Turner, William, 7
Tyndale, William, 20, 56, 58, 70-3, 165
Udall, Nicholas, 80-4
Visitation and Communion of Sick, 168-9, 257-8
Visitations, royal, 16-7, 150; *see* Articles and Injunctions
Vives, Juan Luis, 222
Waldvogel, Procopius, 3
Walsh, John, 70
Westminster Disputation, 21, 165
Whitford, Richard, *A work for Householders,* 239
Whittingham, William, 14
Wilson, Thomas, *Arte of Rhetorique,* 57, 99
Windsor Committee, 153-4
Wolsey, Cardinal, 222
World view, 22, 52, 67, 94-5, 118-21
Zwingli, Huldreich, 203